IMAGES
of America

AFRICAN AMERICANS OF JEFFERSON COUNTY

On the Cover: Students from Page-Jackson High School can be seen as they prepare for homecoming in the 1950s. Here they line up for the annual homecoming parade, which would be followed by the football game and then the homecoming dance. The homecoming queen and her court would preside over all festivities.

IMAGES
of America

AFRICAN AMERICANS OF JEFFERSON COUNTY

Jefferson County Black History
Preservation Society, Inc.

ARCADIA
PUBLISHING

ISBN 978-0-7385-6787-7

Published by Arcadia Publishing
Charleston SC, Chicago IL, Portsmouth NH, San Francisco CA

Printed in the United States of America

Library of Congress Control Number: 2009921942

For all general information contact Arcadia Publishing at:
Telephone 843-853-2070
Fax 843-853-0044
E-mail sales@arcadiapublishing.com
For customer service and orders:
Toll-Free 1-888-313-2665

Visit us on the Internet at www.arcadiapublishing.com

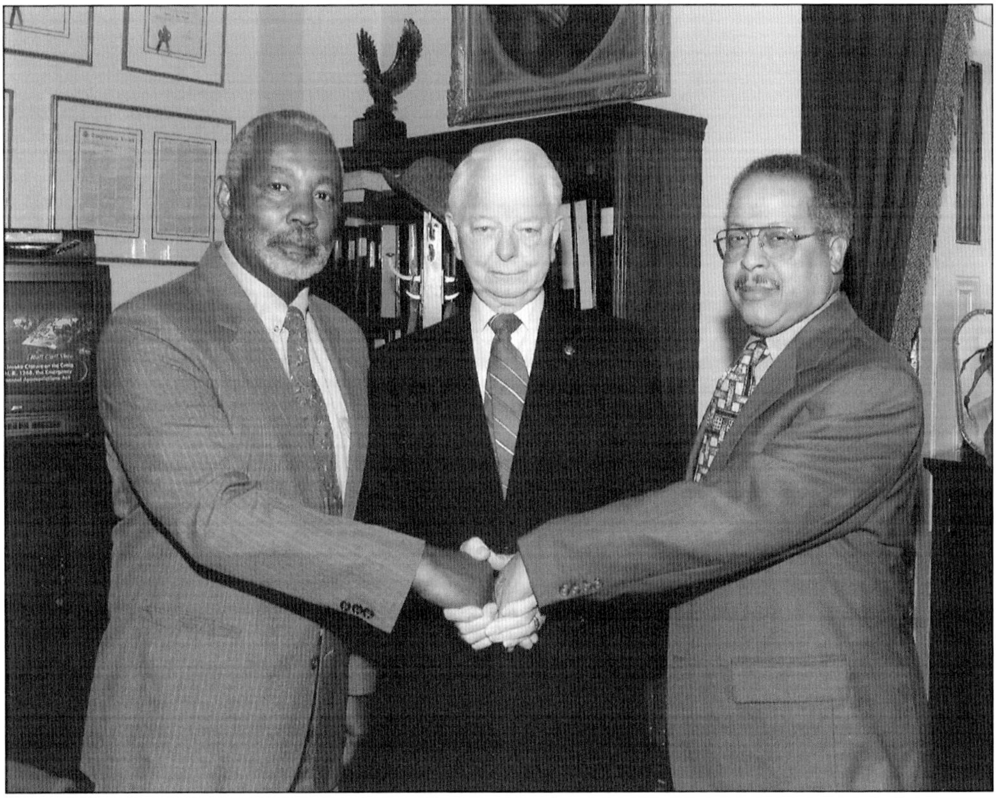

The gentlemen pictured here are, from left to right, George C. Rutherford, Jefferson County NAACP president; U.S. senator Robert C. Byrd of West Virginia; and West Virginia NAACP president James A. Tolbert Sr. Senator Byrd is the longest-serving U.S. senator in history and graciously agreed to write the foreword for this book. The Jefferson County Black History Preservation Society is incredibly grateful.

Contents

Acknowledgments		6
Foreword		7
Introduction		8
1.	John Brown's Raid and Civil Rights	11
2.	Military	21
3.	Notable People	29
4.	Education	39
5.	Events and Entertainment	55
6.	Social and Fraternal Organizations	63
7.	Sports	71
8.	Page-Jackson High School	81
9.	Daily Life	103
10.	Religious Life	119

ACKNOWLEDGMENTS

As with any book about a community, it took many people to make it successful. We recognize that this book on the African Americans of Jefferson County is far from complete. This is simply a pictorial history of the photographs available to us. We attempted to include photographs from the various communities in the county. Where we could not, we apologize.

All photographs are from the archives of the Jefferson County Black History and Preservation Society. We want to give special thanks to the Wainwright Baptist Church, Mount Zion United Methodist Church, and Star Lodge No. 1 F&AM for the use of their facilities as scanning sites for the project. We received and scanned numerous photographs from many people and sources. We are very grateful to the following people and sources that shared their photographs with us: Library of Congress, Harpers Ferry National Historical Park, collection of Jefferson County Black History Preservation Society, the Ohio Historical Society, Jefferson County Museum, Page-Jackson Alumni Association, Bill Theriault, Fannie Hazelton, Linda Downing, Guinevere Roper, Ira J. Pendleton, Velma Twyman, Larry Togans, Claude Stanton, Ora Jean Reeves, Brenda Branson Johnson, Fonda Barron, James L. Taylor, Richard Clark, Gordy Clark, Janet Jeffries, James A. Tolbert, George Rutherford, Madeline McIver, James Surkamp, Sylvia Rideoutt Bishop, Cheryl Roberts, Ruth McDaniel, Rachel Johnson Canady, Charles Ferguson, Larry Good, Edith Clay, Jean Lee Roberts, Johnny Bailey, and the Dorothy Young Taylor Collection. In addition, the *Historical Digest of Jefferson County, West Virginia's African American Congregation 1859–1994*, by Evelyn M. E. Taylor, Thomas J. Scott, and Vivian Jackson Stanton was a very helpful resource.

We want to extend a special thanks to Dolly Nasby, whose assistance in every aspect of this project was invaluable, and without her help this book would not exist. We also extend our profound thanks to Linda Murr for proofing this publication.

We also wish to thank those of you who purchased this book. We hope you enjoy this pictorial history of the African American life in Jefferson County.

We dedicate this work to our parents and teachers for their vision and encouragement during times of segregation and for their unconditional love and their unwavering support.

FOREWORD

African Americans of Jefferson County is an important, much needed book. There has always been a connection between the African American experience in the United States and the history of West Virginia. In fact, it can be argued that the very creation of the state of West Virginia was a result of a division over slavery.

The connection between African American history and West Virginia history is highlighted by the number of renowned African Americans who were West Virginians. These include author and abolitionist Martin Delany, who, with the famous abolitionist Frederick Douglass, edited the *North Star* newspaper; Booker T. Washington, who was a nationally prominent educator and president of Tuskegee Institute, which became one of the leading African American educational institutions in the country; J. R. Clifford, who established the state's first black newspaper and, with his friend W. E. B. DuBois, founded the Niagara Movement in 1905; Rev. Leon Sullivan, a clergyman and civil rights activist who wrote the Sullivan Principles, a code of conduct for U.S. businesses operating in South Africa; and Prof. Henry Louis Gates, a nationally recognized scholar of African American studies.

The role of African Americans in the history of West Virginia is further illustrated by the fact that, until the mechanization of the coal mines in the 1940s, African Americans constituted a significant portion of our state's coal-mining workforce. Many were important leaders in the United Mine Workers of America (UMWA). Anyone who knows West Virginia history knows the importance of coal mining, coal miners, and the UMWA to the history and culture of our state.

So many events important to African American history took place in West Virginia, especially in Jefferson County. Jefferson County was the site of John Brown's raid on Harpers Ferry, considered by some the first battle of the Civil War, the war that led to the abolition of slavery. The county is also the home of Storer College, the famous school for freedmen where former slaves were provided training, skills, education, and other marketable endeavors. And Jefferson County was the site of the second conference of the Niagara Movement, which led to the establishment of the NAACP.

Given the importance of West Virginia to African American history, and the importance of African Americans to the history of West Virginia, we need more publications that recognize and explore this interrelationship.

This book, *African Americans of Jefferson County*, which uses photography to help document the African American experience in Jefferson County, West Virginia, is a welcome contribution to a broader understanding of the synergy between our state and its African American citizens.

—Robert C. Byrd, U.S. Senator

INTRODUCTION

The black populace of Jefferson County had known for years that there had been a lack of information on African Americans and their contributions to the history of the county, state and nation. Therefore, the Jefferson County Black History Preservation Society (JCBHPS) was organized in 2000 by four men who had been collecting black history information going back many years. Our goal is to present this history as it was passed down to us by our parents, grandparents, those in the faith community, and our teachers. Our intention is to present this pictorial history, much of which is unknown to the population, in hopes that it would encourage others to become more aware of the history of African Americans in Jefferson County. Hopefully, this history can be passed down to future generations. The JCBHPS is fortunate that much of the pictorial history collected and saved by others made this book possible. We are grateful for their support and for the use of photographs they provided.

Many people, places, and events make this county rich in African American history, such as John Brown's raid of Harpers Ferry and the five African Americans who came with him. Two were killed; two were captured, tried, and executed in Charles Town; and one escaped. Storer College was the first institution of higher learning for African Americans in the state of West Virginia. The second Niagara Movement Conference was held at Harpers Ferry in 1906. Martin R. Delany was born in Charles Town. His family had to leave because they had broken a Virginia law that forbade slaves or free blacks from learning to read and write. The Jefferson County Colored Horse Show is believed to be the first and only one of its kind in the United States. Freedmen's Bureau presence was in the county after the Civil War with the mission to establish churches and schools for the newly freed slaves. Historic Johnsontown was an all-black town founded by George Johnson. The two treason trials held at the Jefferson County Court House involved African Americans: John Brown's raid and the Miners' Trial. Star Lodge No. 1 was the first Prince Hall Masonic Lodge in the state. "Tent City" at Harpers Ferry was a "contraband" camp for nearly 20,000 slaves who followed the Union army. Many left the area after the war, and some remained, leaving descendants who are living today.

The JCBHPS was the first such organization to ever be formed in Jefferson County. The four founding members were Nathaniel Downing Sr., George C. Rutherford, James L. Taylor, and James A. Tolbert Sr.

Nathaniel Frederick Downing Sr. was born July 14, 1925, in Ranson, West Virginia. When there was discussion regarding the establishment of a black history group, he was one of the first solicited to join the group. He was a founding member and elected vice president of the Jefferson County Black History Preservation Society.

Downing attended the Jefferson County schools. While in high school, he was a member of the Page-Jackson High School Cadet Corps. In 1943, his education was interrupted when he was drafted at age 18 into the U.S. Navy during World War II. He served in the U.S. Navy until 1946 and was honorably discharged. In 1951, Downing earned his general education diploma and later attended Storer College in Harpers Ferry. He was certified as a nursing attendant and worked as a nursing assistant at the Newton D. Baker Veterans Hospital beginning in 1947, retiring in 1981.

He was an avid researcher and major contributor to several books written by the JCBHPS. He was able to document the clergy history of some of the black churches. He was a member of many fraternal, religious, and civic organizations, including a longtime member of the Mount Zion United Methodist Church; 45-year member and past master of Star Lodge No. 1, Free and Accepted Masons; member of the Green-Copeland American Legion Post No. 63; member of the Jefferson County Shalom Organization; and life member of the NAACP and vice president of DASTAR, Ltd. Nathaniel F. Downing Sr. passed in October 2004 and is sorely missed.

George C. Rutherford is a native of Jefferson County and a Page-Jackson High School graduate. He received an A.B. degree in secondary education and a bachelor of arts degree from Shepherd College (now University) in biology. He has a master's degree from Marshall University in biological science.

Rutherford retired from the federal government after 42 years of serving as a Job Corps counselor and teacher, park ranger, finance manager, urban planner, and space utilization specialist. He was a public schoolteacher and was a paratrooper in the U.S. Army Airborne during the Korean War. He was married to the late Barbara Smith Rutherford and is the father of an extended family of seven.

Honors which he has received include the T. J. Nutter Award by the West Virginia State NAACP (highest honor); State of West Virginia Martin Luther King Living the Dream Award; City of Ranson Citizen of the Year Award; Governor's West Virginia Civil Rights Day Award; and Region 3 NAACP President of the Year Award. He is treasurer of the Jefferson County Black History Preservation Society.

James L. Taylor graduated from Page-Jackson High School with the class of 1951. He is a Korean War veteran (U.S. Navy). He graduated from Shepherd College with a B.A. and B.S. degree and from West Virginia University with a master's degree. He was a teacher and coach at Page-Jackson High School for six years. He was also a teacher and coach at Jefferson High School, retiring in 1995, after 35 years in education.

He has authored two books on black history: *Africans-in-American of the Lower Shenandoah Valley: 1700–1900* and *A History of Black Education in Jefferson County, West Virginia, 1865–1966*. He is president of the Jefferson County Black History Preservation Society.

James A. Tolbert Sr. is a native of Charles Town, West Virginia, and serves as the secretary of the Jefferson County Black History Preservation Society. He attended segregated public schools and was graduated from Page-Jackson High School in Charles Town in 1950. A U.S. Air Force veteran, he spent two years of his duty in Japan. Following an honorable discharge, he entered West Virginia State College (now University) and earned a Bachelor of Science degree in zoology in 1958. He was employed by the Department of Veterans Affairs and retired in 1988.

Following college, he immersed himself in civil rights and civic organizations: Charles Town Civic League; Jefferson County NAACP (branch president); West Virginia NAACP president 1986 to 2007; and Harpers Ferry Job Corps Community Relations Committee. He was elected president emeritus of West Virginia NAACP; participated in both the 1963 March on Washington and the Million Man March; helped organize the Charles Town Recreation League in 1964; and was the first black person to serve on the Jefferson Memorial Hospital Board of Directors.

Tolbert has been the recipient of many awards: the West Virginia NAACP's highest honor, the T. G. Nutter Award in 1976; the Living the Dream Award from the West Virginia Martin Luther King, Jr. Holiday Commission for Human and Civil Rights, 1988; and the NAACP's Region III

Dr. Benjamin L. Hooks Award as State Conference President of the Year (two times), in 1991 and 2002. A James A. Tolbert, Sr., Civil Rights Scholarship was even created for West Virginia youth interested in furthering the work of their civil rights movement and the NAACP.

The Jefferson County Black History Preservation Society meets regularly and continues to sponsor projects that record the history and culture of African American in the county. It also maintains a Web site: jeffctywvblackhistory.org.

One

John Brown's Raid and Civil Rights

John Brown and his "army" of 21 men attacked the Federal Arsenal in Harpers Ferry in 1859. Many believe this event marked the beginning of the Civil War. Brown was eventually captured, tried, and found guilty in Charles Town, Virginia (now West Virginia), of treason and then executed by hanging. Brown and his followers were despised by some; by others, Brown and his followers were considered martyrs. In 1906, members of the Niagara Movement (forerunner to the NAACP) held its first meeting on American soil at Storer College to pay tribute to John Brown and his followers.

World War I veterans requested an American Legion charter and then named their unit Green-Copeland Post No. 63. Members of Jefferson County Black Elks Lodge expressed their admiration by chartering the unit "John Brown Elks Lodge." In 1932, NAACP members attending their national convention in Washington made a pilgrimage to Storer College to erect a tablet in memory of John Brown. It was rejected by college officials. However, in 2006, another pilgrimage was made to Storer College by NAACP national convention attendees, and the tablet was finally placed on the campus. Jefferson County civil rights history is extremely unique and has had a major national impact.

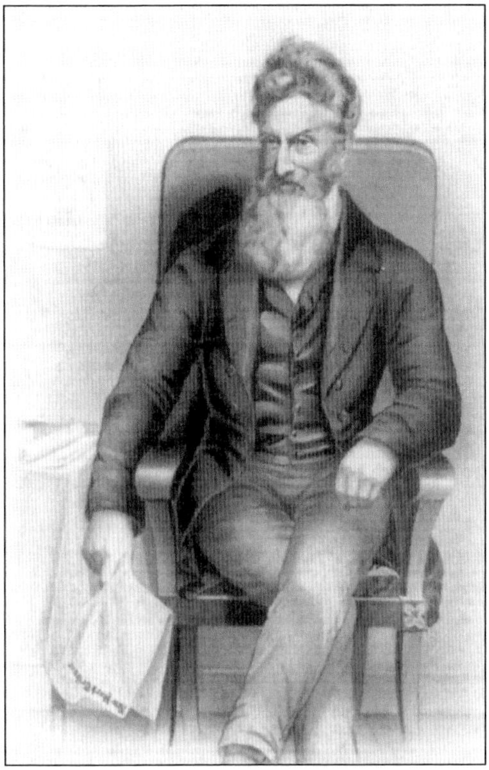

John Brown, an abolitionist, led the ill-fated 1859 raid on the Harpers Ferry Federal Arsenal, an event that would serve as a catalyst for the Civil War. He led 21 loyal followers and holed up on the Kennedy Farm in Maryland to plan their attack. The raid was very violent—of the 22 raiders (including John Brown), 11 were killed, 7 were tried and hanged, and 4 escaped. Five were black.

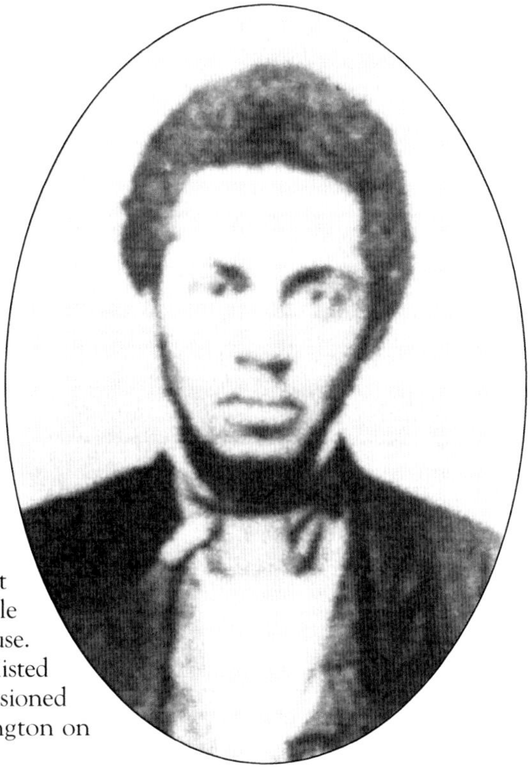

Osborn Perry Anderson was 30 years old at the time of John Brown's raid. He first met John Brown in 1858 in Canada. He and Albert Hazlett (a white raider) held the arsenal while Brown gathered with his men in the engine house. He and Hazlett escaped. In 1864, Anderson enlisted in the army, where he became a noncommissioned officer. He died of consumption in Washington on December 13, 1872.

Lewis Leary was born to a slave mother and an Irish father who freed his mother and all the children she bore him. He grew up in Ohio, where he attended Oberlin College for a time. His wife, Mary Sampson, was the grandmother of poet Langston Hughes. During the raid, Leary was shot and died six hours later.

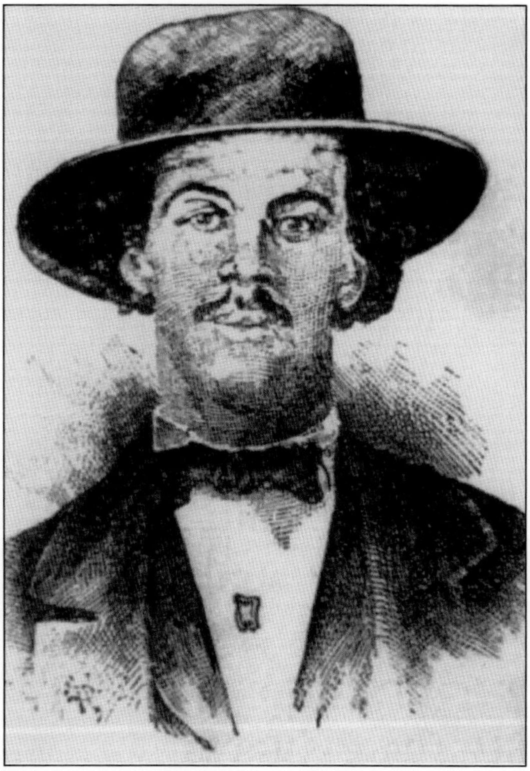

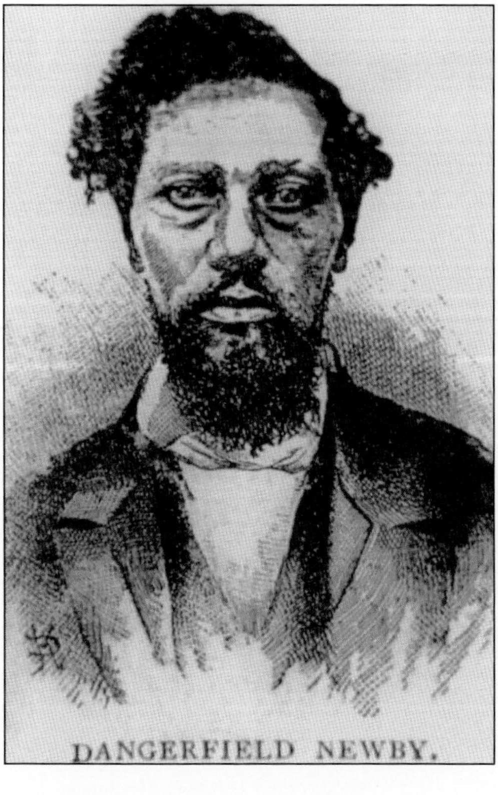

Dangerfield Newby was the first of 11 children who had a white father and a slave mother. Newby was shot by a person who was in a house on the opposite side of the street in Harpers Ferry. He was killed at the arsenal gate. His body was rooted by local hogs. He joined Brown's army to free his wife and children, who were slaves near Warrenton, Virginia.

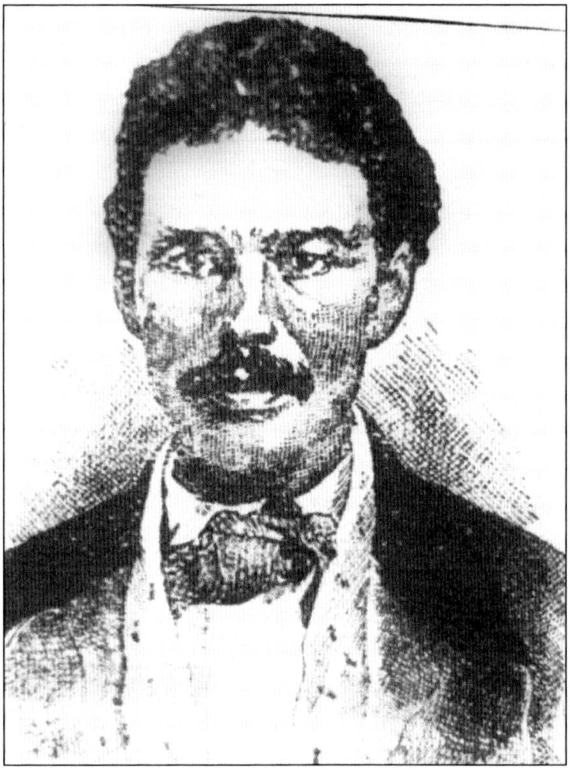

John A. Copeland was born in North Carolina, the son of Delilah Evans Copeland and John Copeland Sr., free blacks who settled in Oberlin, Ohio, where John Jr. studied at Oberlin College. He and Lewis Leary, related by marriage, arrived at the Kennedy Farm on the eve of the raid. He was captured, tried, convicted, and hanged in Charles Town. Medical students moved his corpse to the Medical College in Winchester, Virginia.

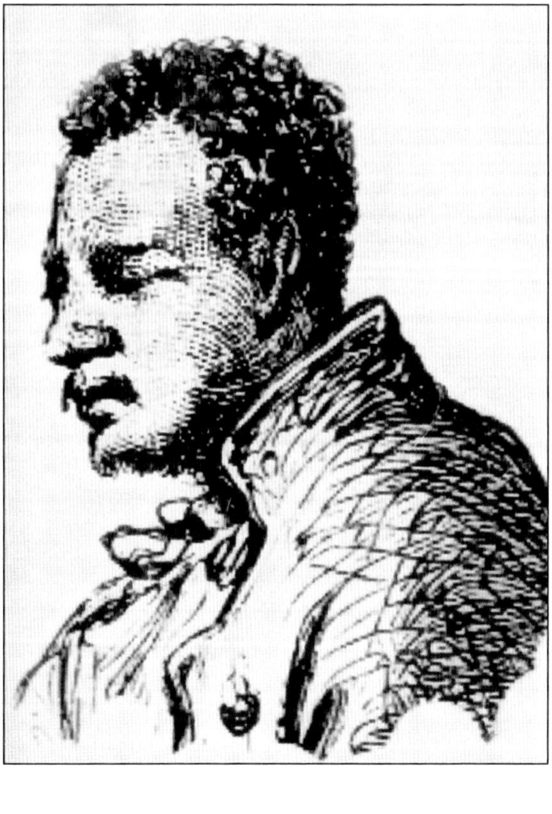

Shields Green, an escaped slave from South Carolina, was a protégé of Frederick Douglass. He escaped to the North after his wife died. He changed his name from Esau Brown to Shields Green in order to escape detection. Green was one of five African Americans—the first recruited—to participate in John Brown's raid in Harpers Ferry. He was captured, tried in Charles Town, and executed on December 16, 1859.

The Right Reverend Ernest Eugene Baltimore was a distinguished clergyman and a great humanitarian. Associated with the King's Apostle Holiness Church of God, he served as senior bishop and general president. For 51 years, he was the pastor of the Baltimore Temple Church. He also served as councilman for Ranson, West Virginia. He was a lifetime member of the Jefferson County branch of the NAACP and served as president.

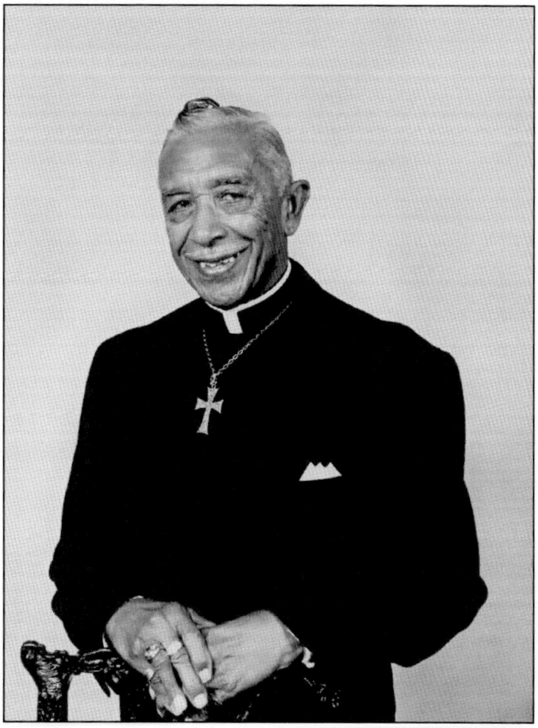

The wagon pictured below carried John Brown to his execution. He was seated on his own coffin as they took him to be hanged in Charles Town. This photograph was taken in the 1920s. The same wagon was used to carry the African American raiders to their executions. Today the wagon is owned by and exhibited in the Jefferson County Museum in Charles Town, West Virginia.

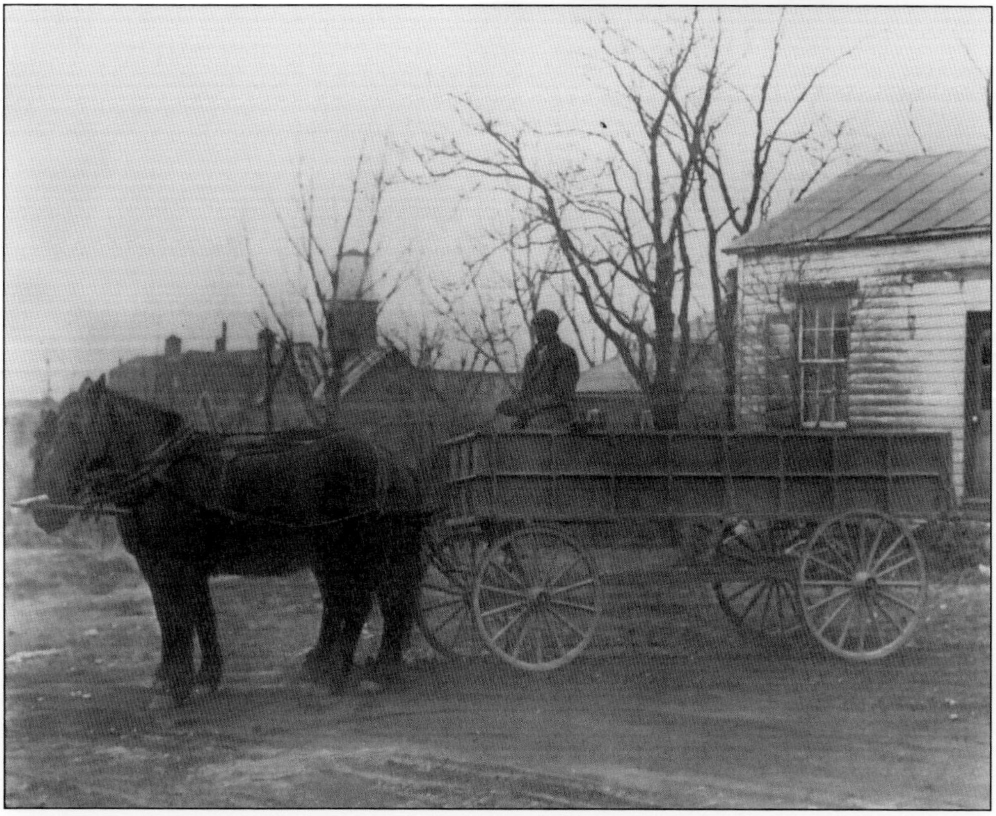

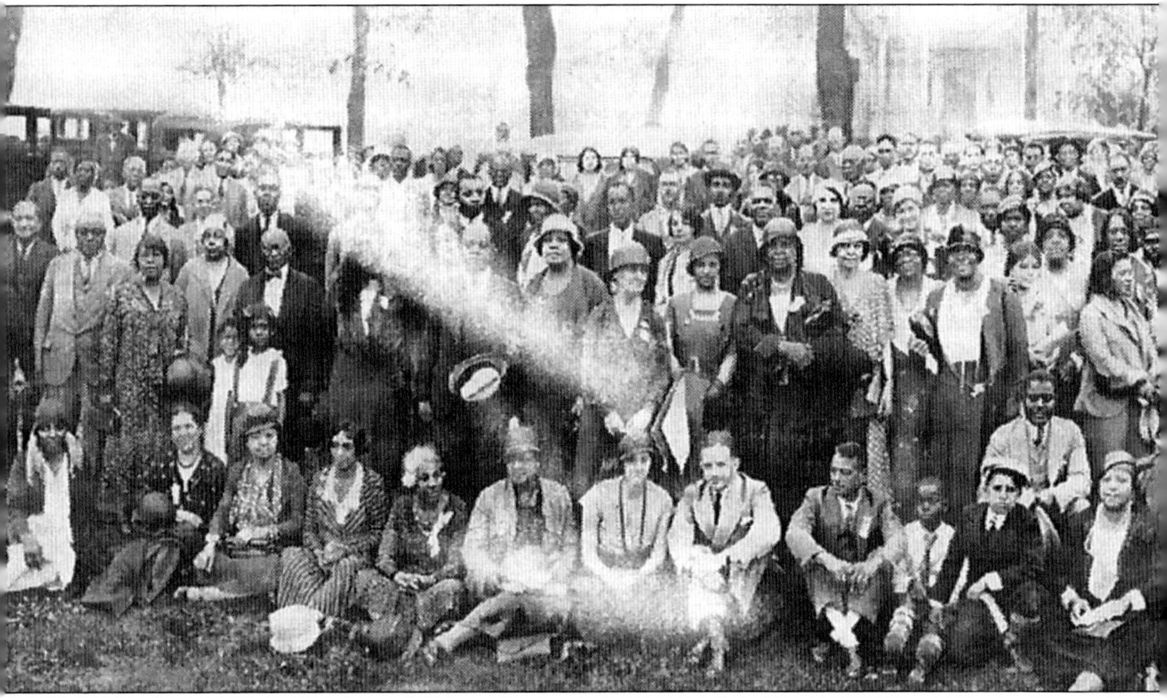

In 1906, the second meeting of the Niagara Movement was held at Storer College in Harpers Ferry. Led by Dr. W. E. B. DuBois, the movement served as the forerunner of the NAACP. Pictured here is the NAACP delegates' pilgrimage to Storer College in 1932, paying tribute to John Brown. The marker was rejected because officials thought it might inflame the public sentiment in those

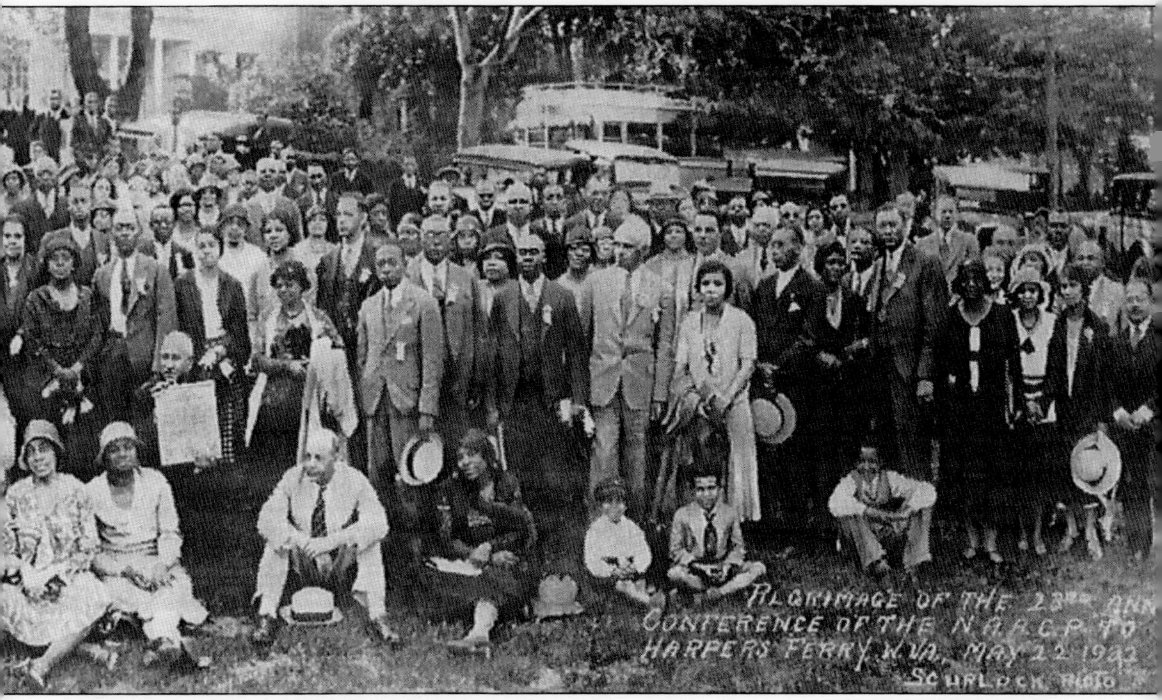

times. In July 2006, NAACP board chair Julian Bond, vice chair Roslyn M. Brock, president/CEO Bruce Gordon, and more than 125 members made a historic pilgrimage to the Storer College campus in Harpers Ferry, paying tribute to John Brown and his army.

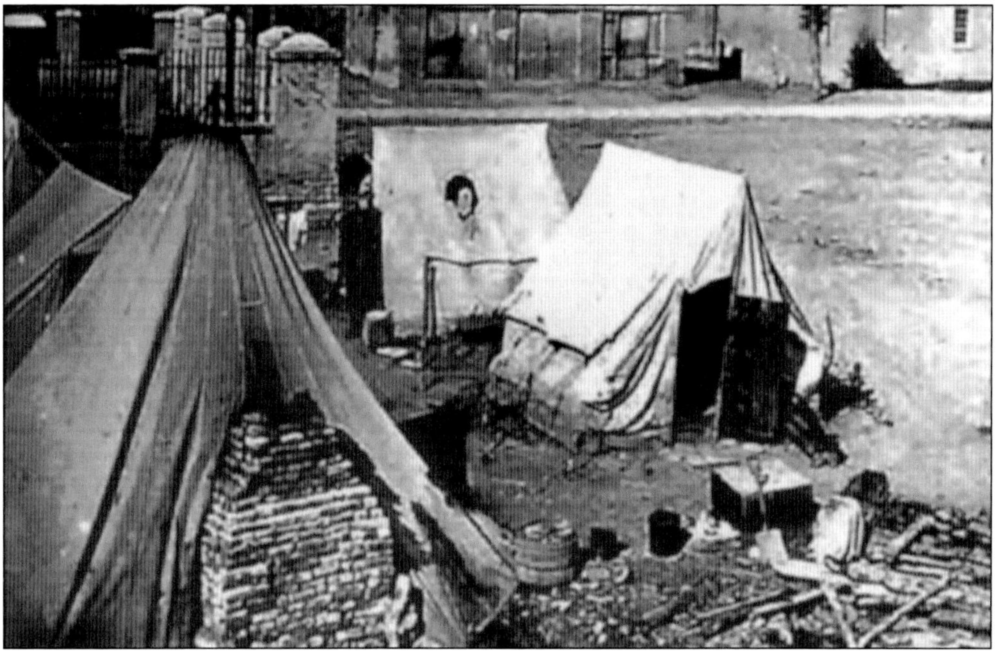

A contraband camp is shown here in Harpers Ferry, inside the former Musket Factory yard and on the armory grounds. Many freed slaves s settled in camps such as this; after the war ended, those freedmen stayed in the area. Some of the African American families can trace their roots back to contraband camps that were established in Harpers Ferry around 1862.

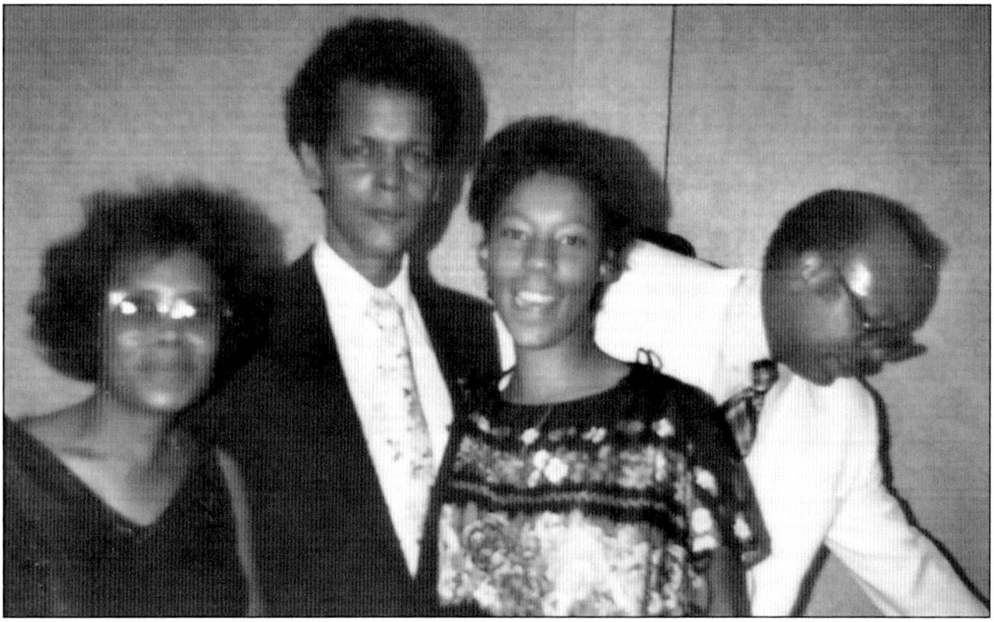

Civil rights activist Julian Bond is second from left, an SNCC member, later an NAACP National Board of Directors chair. The photograph was taken at a West Virginia NAACP banquet in Harpers Ferry. Barbara Smith Rutherford is in front of Bond on his right, and Julie Rutherford is in front of Bond on his left. West Virginia NAACP president Herbert H. Henderson is in the background on the right.

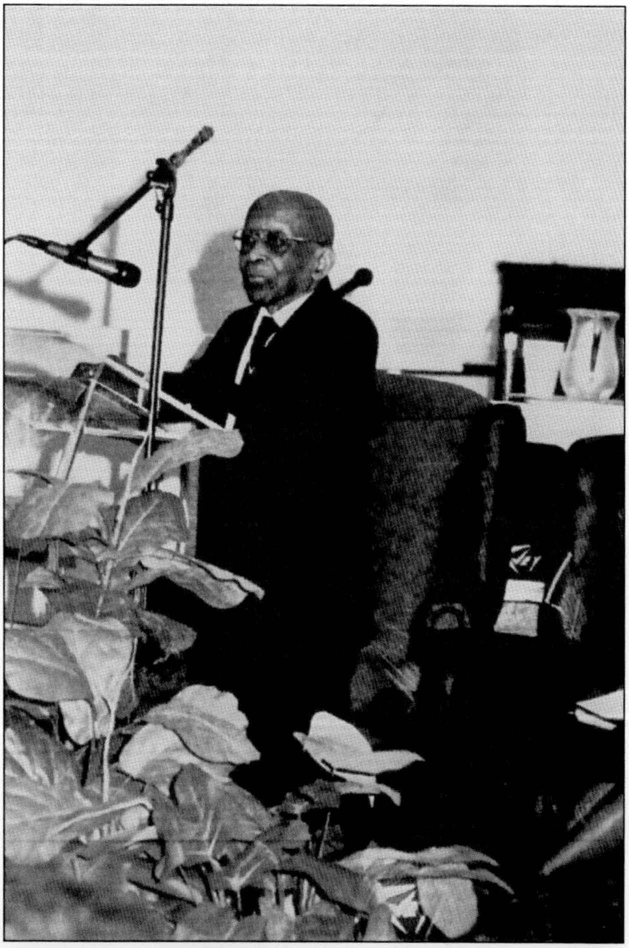

Dewey Fox was from Johnsontown in Jefferson County. Johnsontown was located on Hite Road in Charles Town. Here Fox is shown speaking for the Jefferson County NAACP Black History celebration at Ebenezer/Mount Calvary Church in Summit Point, West Virginia. He taught school and served as principal of schools in Marion and Harrison Counties. He organized the Fairmont NAACP branch.

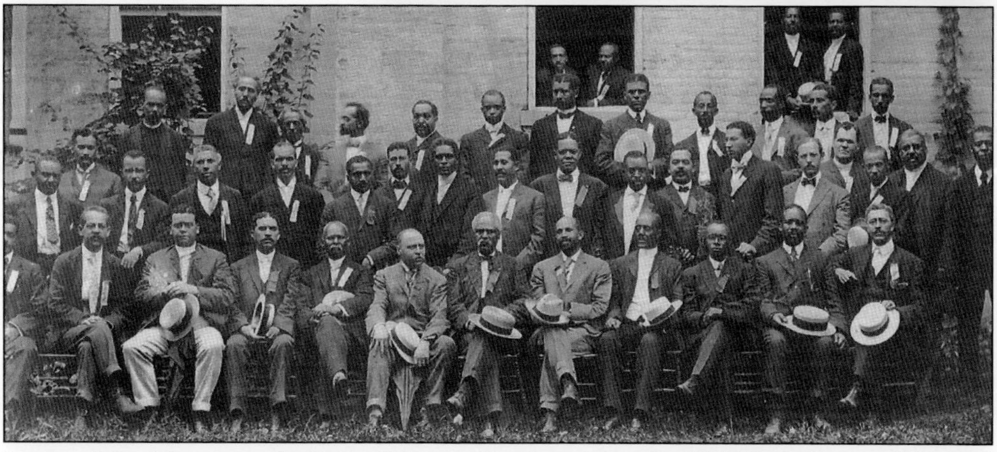

Leader of the delegates to the Second Niagara Conference was Dr. W. E. B. DuBois, and the field secretary was J. R. Clifford. This photograph was taken on August 17, 1906, when the Niagara Conference was held at Harpers Ferry on the Storer College campus in tribute to John Brown. This was its first open and public meeting in the United States. It had met in 1905 in Ontario, Canada, and would become the foundation and forerunner to the NAACP, founded in 1909.

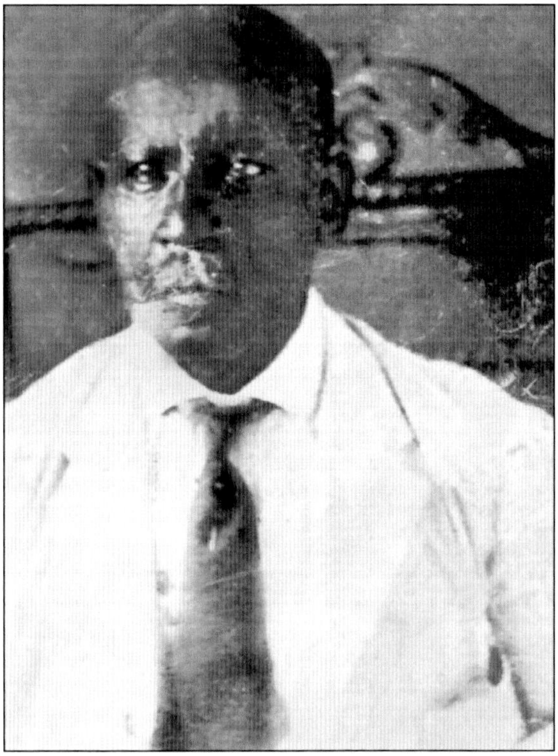

Pictured is John W. Rutherford, a slave until he was nine years old. He was owned by a doctor in Martinsburg, West Virginia. Rutherford was also a town lamplighter and town crier. Rutherford worked at the old Charles Town hospital, which was located on West Congress Street. Currently, the American Public University is housed in that location. He was the great-grandfather of local resident George C. Rutherford of Ranson.

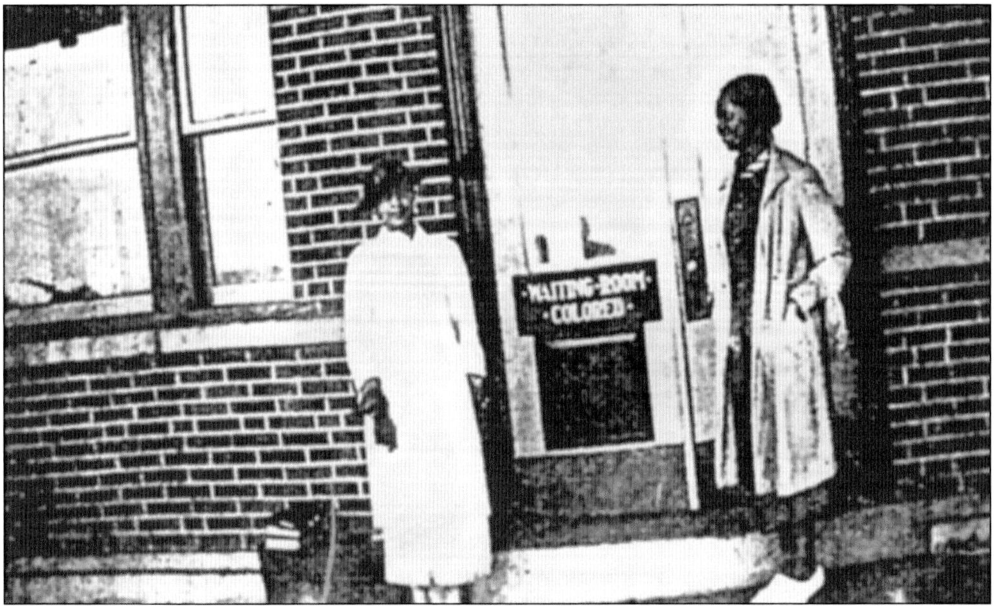

Standing in front of the "colored" waiting room at the Norfolk and Western Train Station, passengers wait in Charles Town. African Americans were not allowed to attend the same schools or use restrooms, water fountains, and a multitude of other facilities that the rest of the population used. School segregation was eventually ruled unconstitutional by the Supreme Court in *Brown v. Board of Education* in 1954. As a result, society was integrated, albeit not without difficulties and violence.

Two

MILITARY

Military service has always served as a means for self-improvement and discipline for black men. During World War II, Edward O. Morgan organized a group of boys at Page-Jackson High School into a "cadet's corps" practicing military procedures complete with uniforms and wooden rifles. Some of these "cadets" entered the military and remained until retirement. More than 100 black men from Jefferson County were drafted for military service in World War I. Both World War I and World War II servicemen served in segregated units. For many, this was their first time beyond the state borders and those of the United States. They had endured segregation in their country but saw and experienced different treatment in foreign countries. After the war, they returned to segregation. Photographs prove that these veterans even remained segregated as they celebrated the war's end. Following World War II, many veterans look advantage of the GI Bill and attended Storer and other colleges. Some became Jefferson County public schoolteachers, while others advanced in other occupations. It must be noted that only one black female from Jefferson County, Madaline Lawson McIver, served in World War II, and she became an inspiration and role model to many young black women.

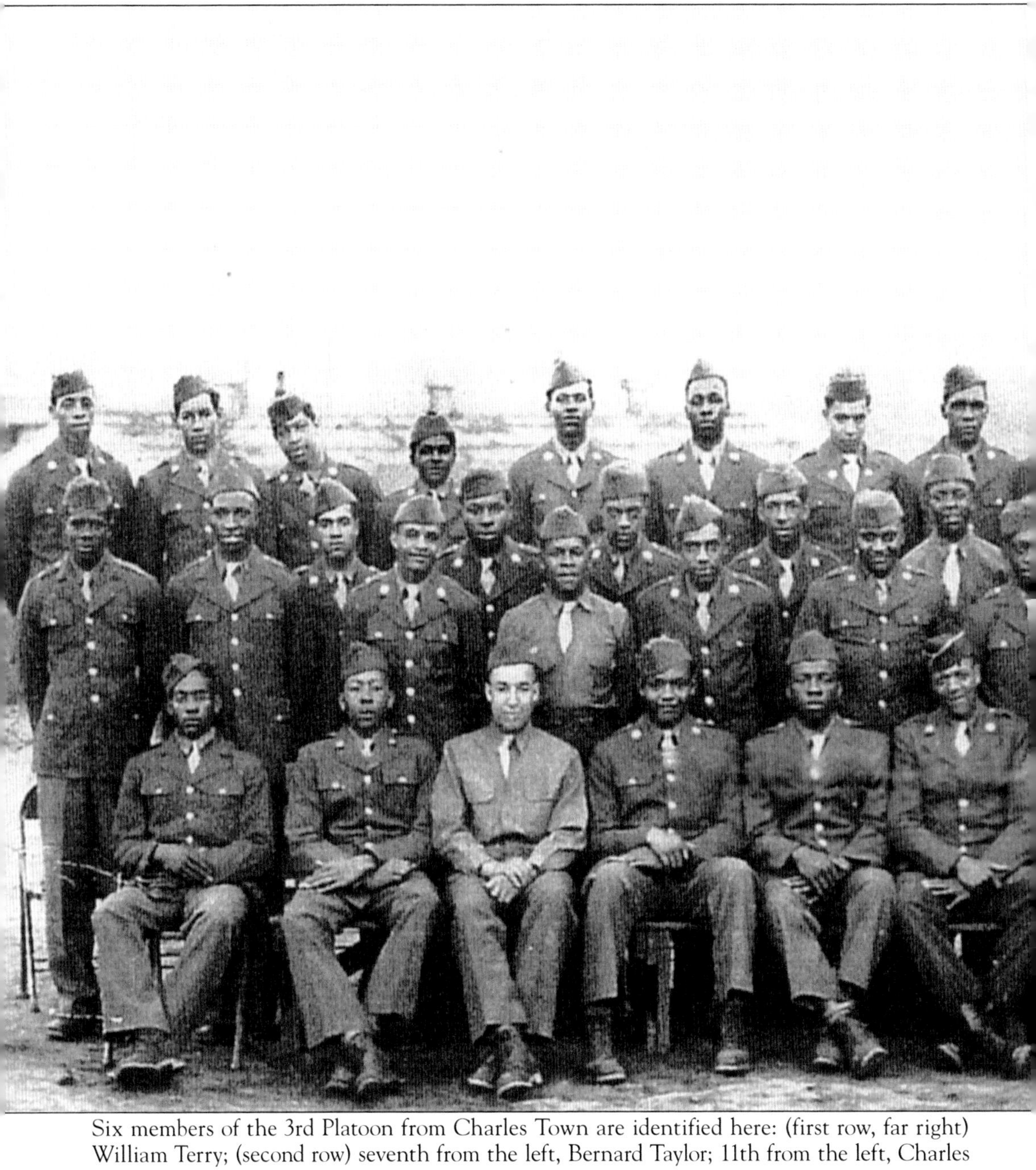

Six members of the 3rd Platoon from Charles Town are identified here: (first row, far right) William Terry; (second row) seventh from the left, Bernard Taylor; 11th from the left, Charles

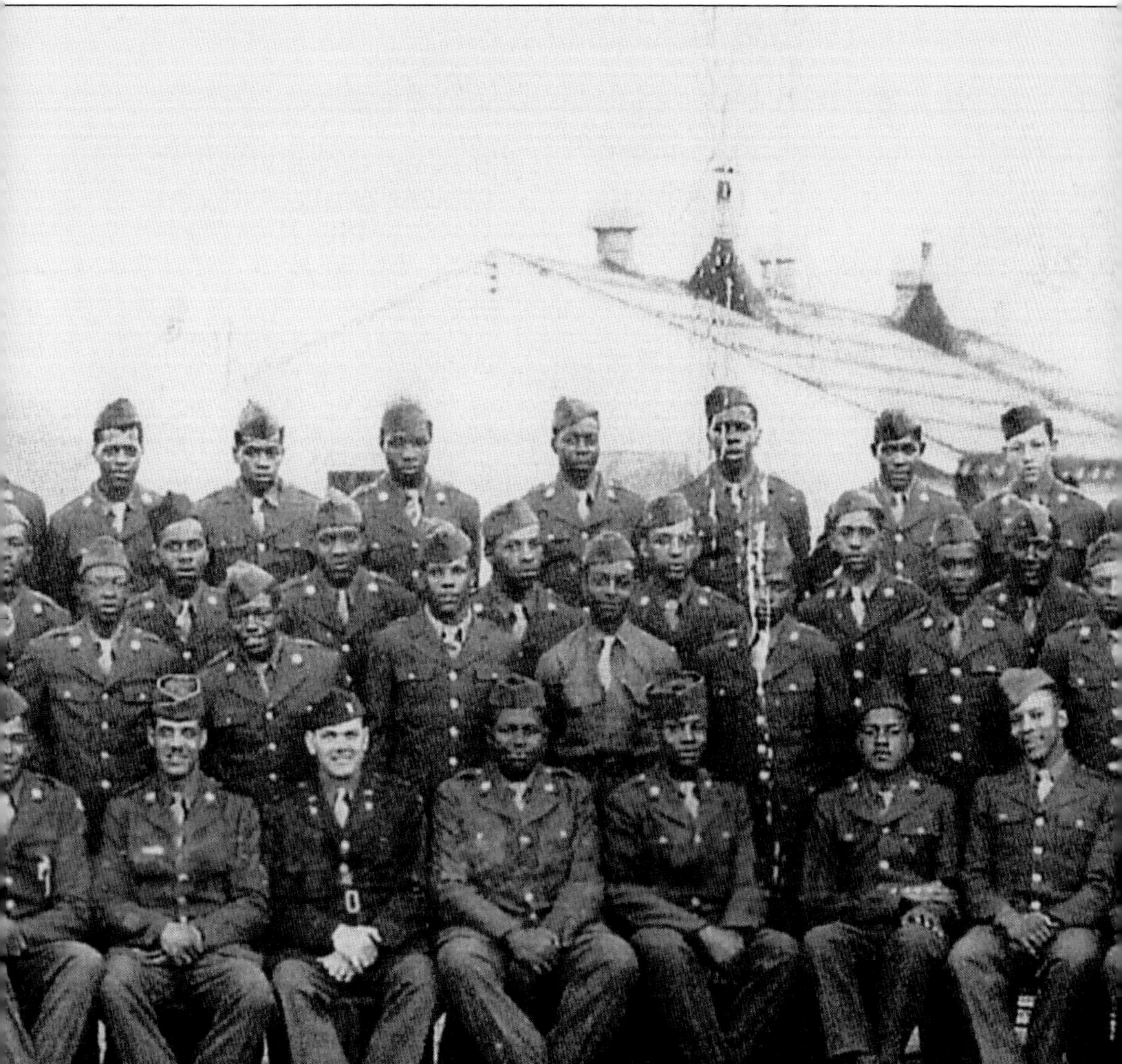

Jackson Sr.; second from right, Douglas Taylor; (third row) third from left, Paul Russ; and eighth from left, Luther Carey.

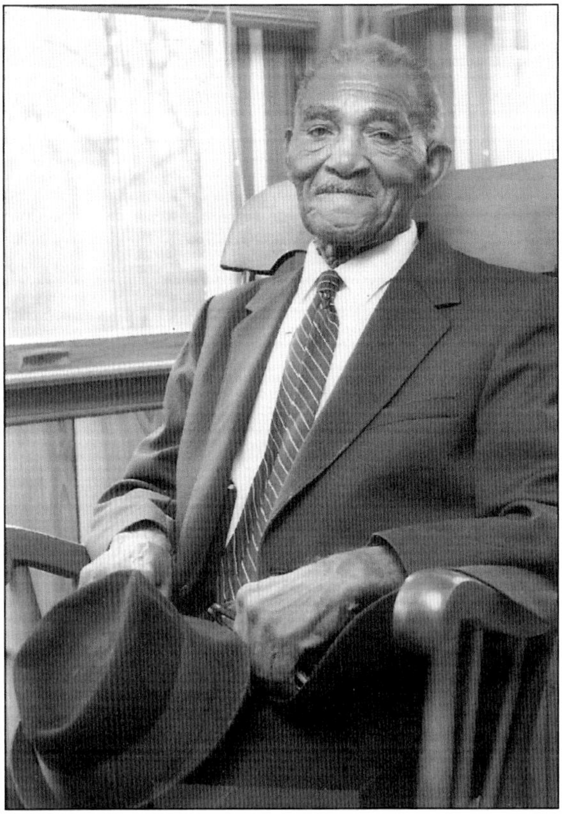

Seated here is World War II veteran John Ferguson. Even though African Americans served in the military service when discrimination and segregation were rampant, they served with distinction and honor. When the war ended, he was a member of the all-black 542nd Engineers of the U.S. Army. A saying that was passed on through many U.S. Army units began "you're in the Army now; you're not behind the plow."

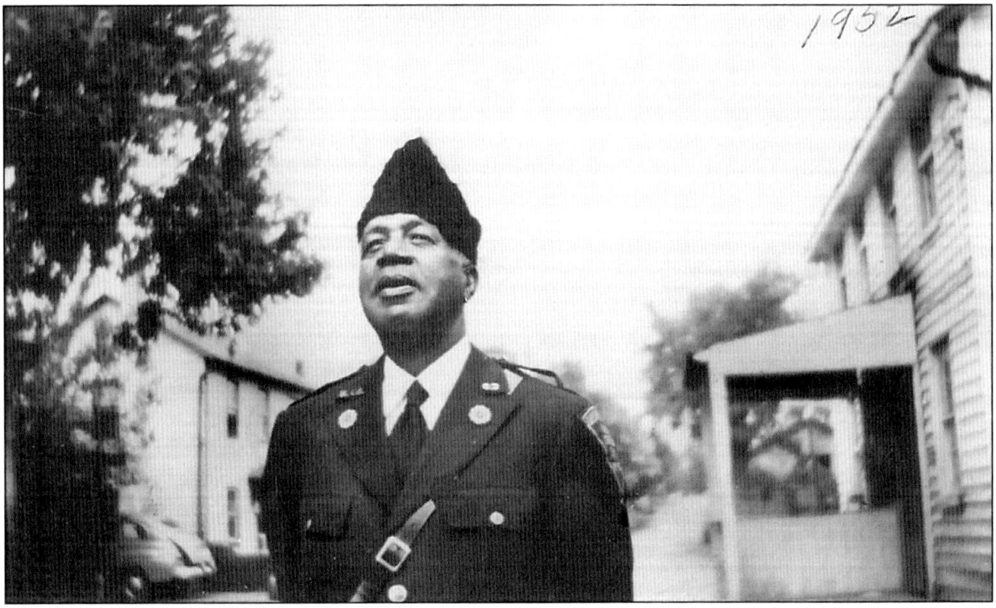

This photograph was taken in the "Dog Town" neighborhood of Charles Town. It shows Matthew Mitchell Sr., a World War I veteran. Mitchell blew Taps each evening in the neighborhood. He was a charter member of American Legion Post No. 63 in Charles Town and a master leatherer at the Hiram Goetz Harness Factory in Ranson, West Virginia.

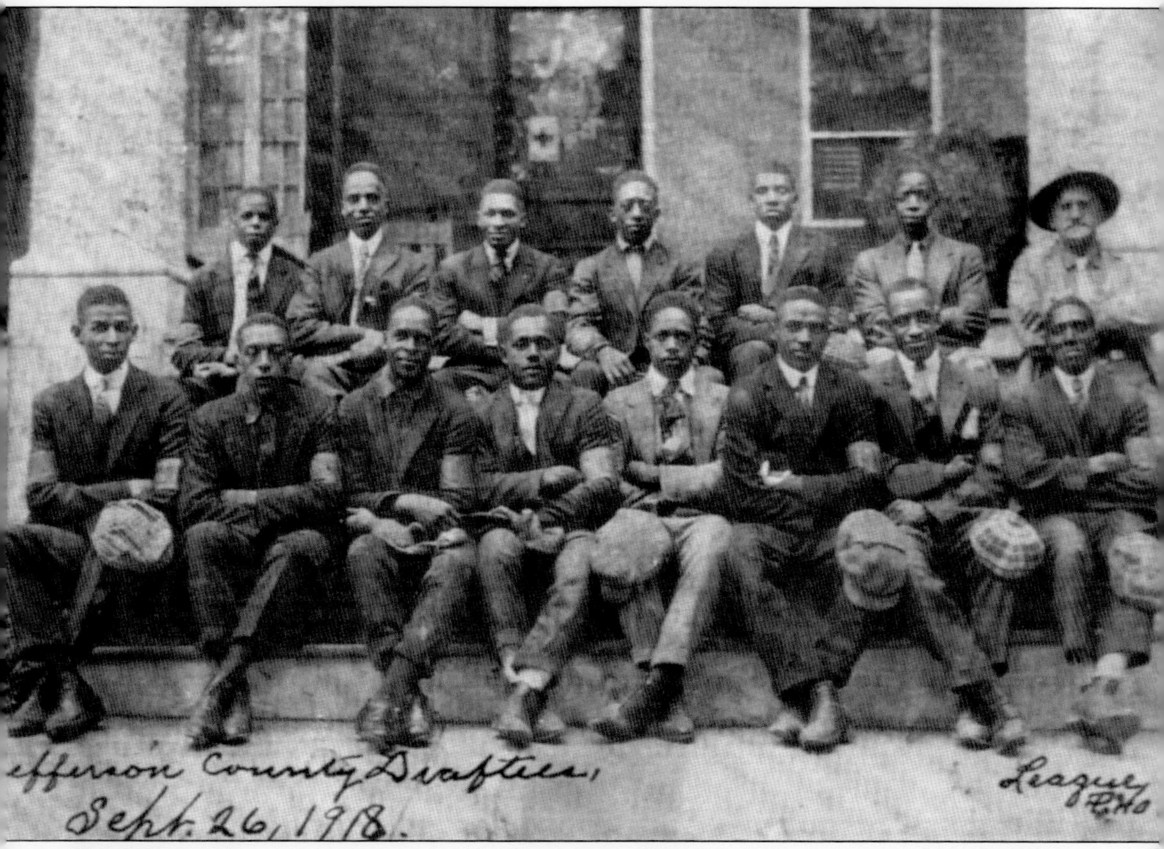

The Selective Service Act was passed by Congress on May 28, 1917, and stated that all males between the ages of 21 and 31 must be registered and could be drafted. There were 247 blacks registered in 1917; there were 314 blacks ages 18–45 a year later. From Jefferson County, a total of 128 African Americans served in the military, of which eight lost their lives. This photograph is of some 1918 draftees.

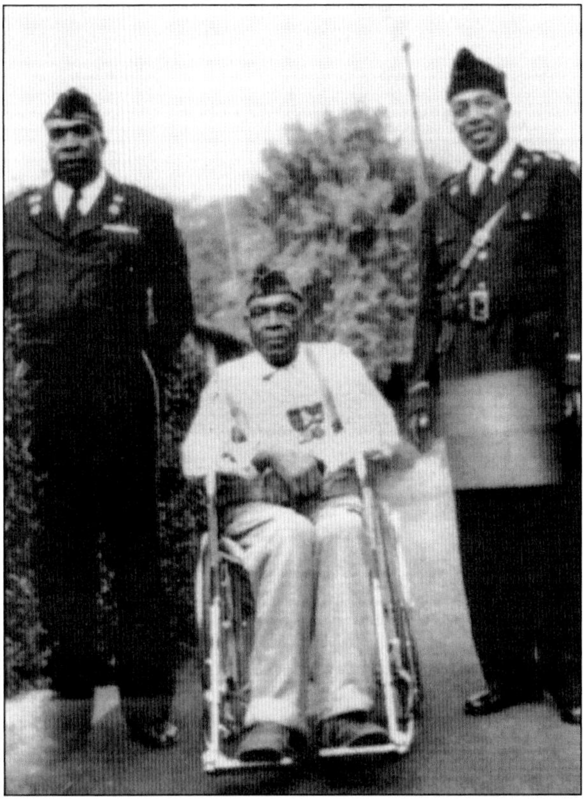

Pictured are World War I veterans who served in our armed forces. From left to right are Edward Morgan, David Carey, and Matthew Mitchell. Corey was also a Spanish-American War veteran Jefferson Country provided 548 men to serve in the armed forces. Of that 548, thirty gave the ultimate sacrifice and did not return home. There were eight African Americans who died in World War I. The sacrifices America's military personnel make can never be forgotten. Here they are proudly wearing their uniforms, as well they should.

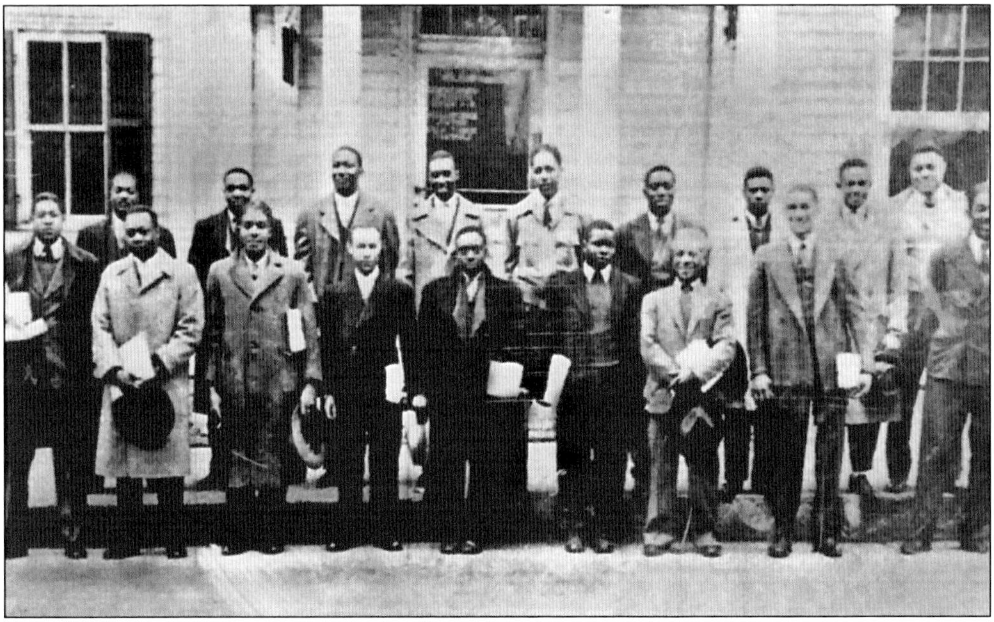

Shown on April 23, 1943, World War II draftees from Jefferson County are shown ready to leave for their pre-induction physicals in Clarksburg, West Virginia. For World War II, a total of 1,447 men (of all races) were drafted from Jefferson County. The troops continued to serve in segregated units throughout World War II.

Pictured is Madeline Lawson McIver—the first and only black female in the enlisted ranks in World War II from Jefferson County. Madeline graduated from Page-Jackson High School in 1943, just in time to get into World War II to serve her country. There were only four females in her graduating class. All of the male classmates had dropped out of high school in order to serve in the military during World War II.

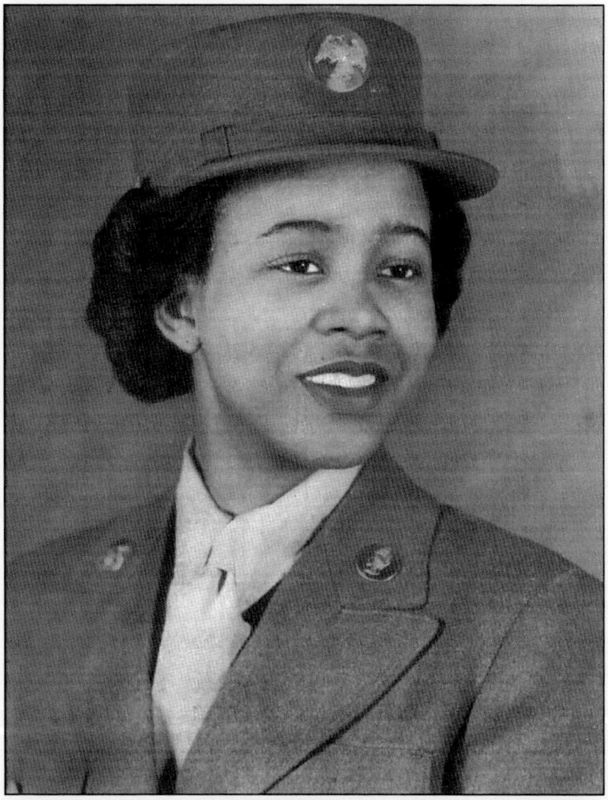

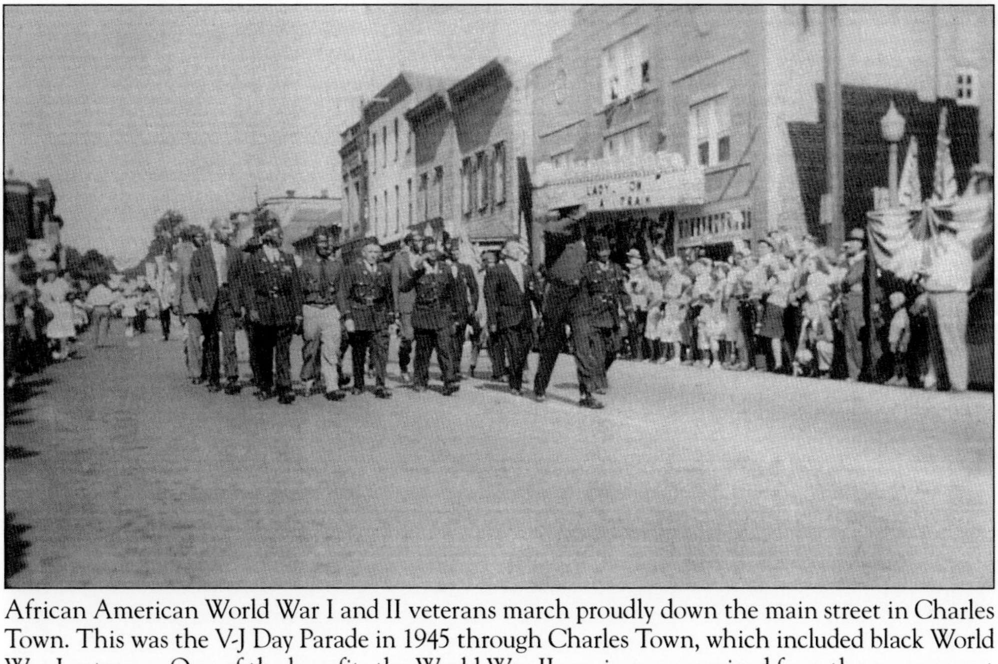

African American World War I and II veterans march proudly down the main street in Charles Town. This was the V-J Day Parade in 1945 through Charles Town, which included black World War I veterans. One of the benefits the World War II servicemen received from the government was the GI Bill. This allowed the veterans the chance to get the education they missed when they were serving their country.

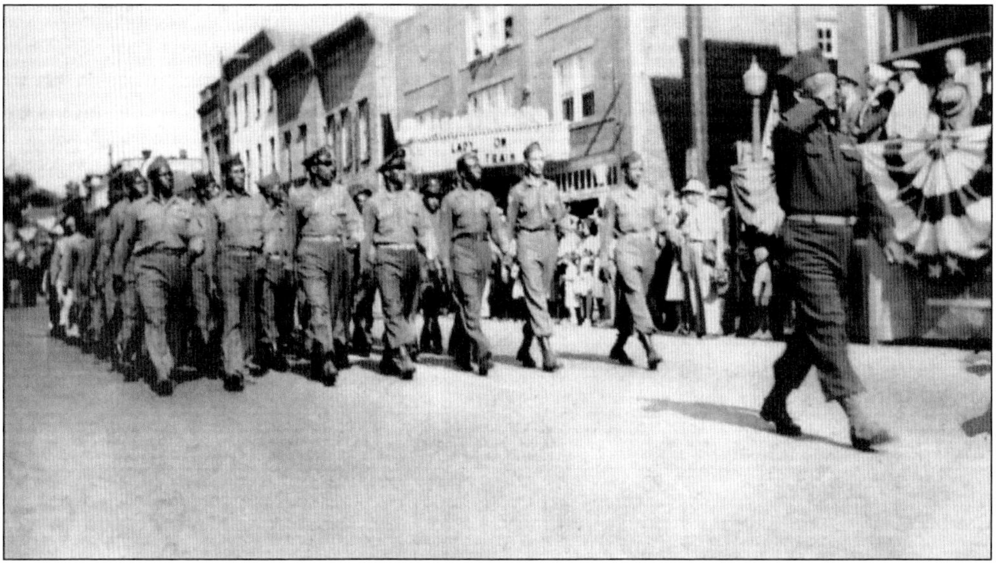

World War II veterans in 1946 march in downtown Charles Town. These African Americans served their country bravely and were welcomed home with open arms. At the time these gentlemen served their country, it was in segregated units. Eventually, all military organizations would be integrated. Even in 1946, the organizations were still not integrated. However, these soldiers served their country bravely.

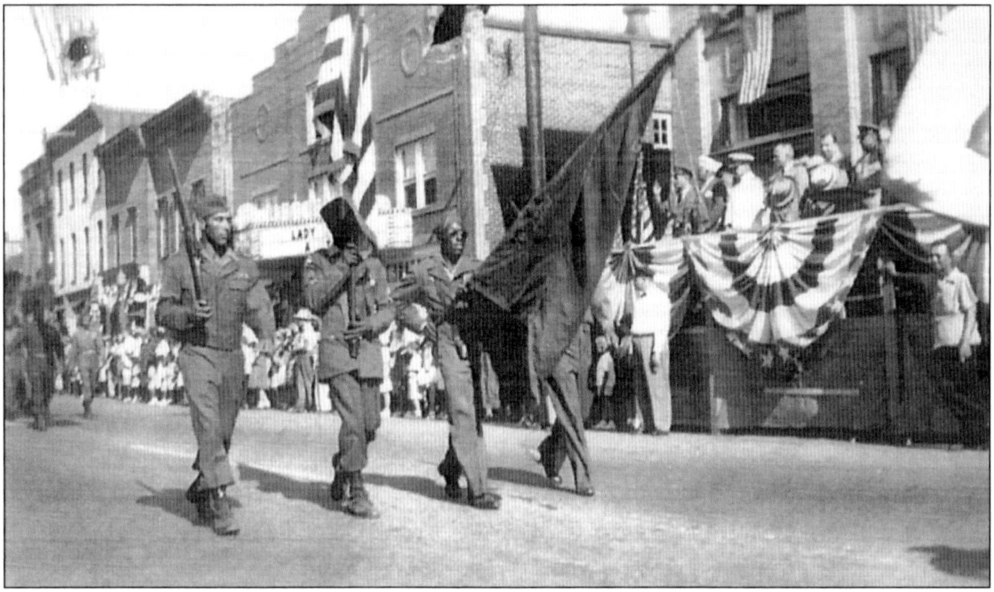

A welcome home parade passes by the reviewing stand. African American veterans proudly display the colors as they march past the reviewing stand. Crowds welcomed them home with thanks for their service. These servicemen served their country with honor even though they were discriminated against throughout their service time. As segregation was phased out throughout the county and the country, so would segregation and discrimination be phased out of the armed services.

Three

Notable People

Some people go through life and make such an impact on others that they are well remembered by many. Jefferson County had many such people, noted locally and/or nationally. This chapter examines a few but nowhere near all.

Martin Robison Delany is foremost and the most notable. Delany was the highest ranking black field officer in the Civil War. He was a doctor, lawyer, author, explorer, and federal official, just to name a few. He is also credited as the first "black nationalist."

The key to success for the black community has always been education, and the holders of that key were the black teachers, who were led by black principals, who the majority of the time had to overcome undue and unforeseen hardship and stress to carry out their responsibilities.

A few blacks sought and achieved political offices. Edward Braxton and Charles Branson were considered the "deans" of those politicians. They served on Charles Town and Shepherdstown City Councils, respectively.

In the area of law enforcement, Robert Carr was unsurpassed. He was the "most feared," the most loved, and the most respected law enforcement officer in the county for many years.

With the horse racing industry in the county, there is a need for someone with skills to care for the horses. The name Theodore Togans stands out. He is considered a legend at the Charles Town Racetrack for his knowledge and skill in the care of horses.

Russell Roper is considered one of the top African American entrepreneurs in the state. He has excelled in many business endeavors and developed and owns the largest subdivision in the state owned by a black person.

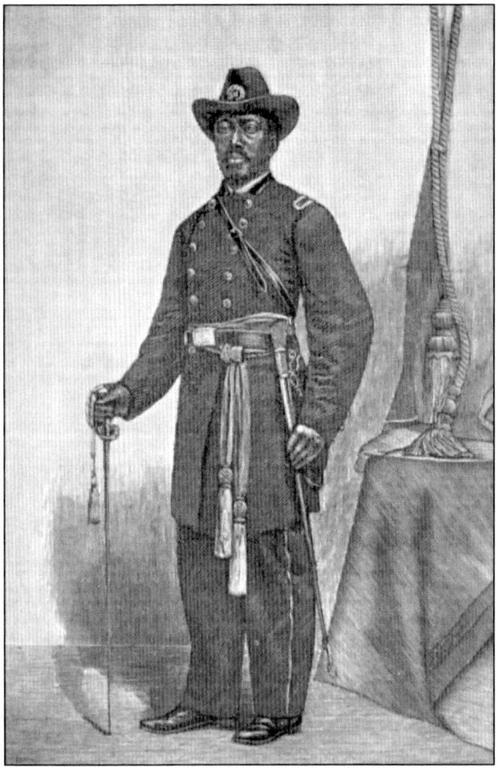

Martin Robison Delany, born in Charles Town, Virginia (now West Virginia), on May 6, 1812, was one of five children. His parents relocated their family because they were persecuted for teaching their children to read and write. Delany would go on to become a physician, scientist, inventor, African explorer, newspaper publisher, and editor. After a meeting with President Lincoln, Delany became one of the highest-ranking black line officers of the Civil War.

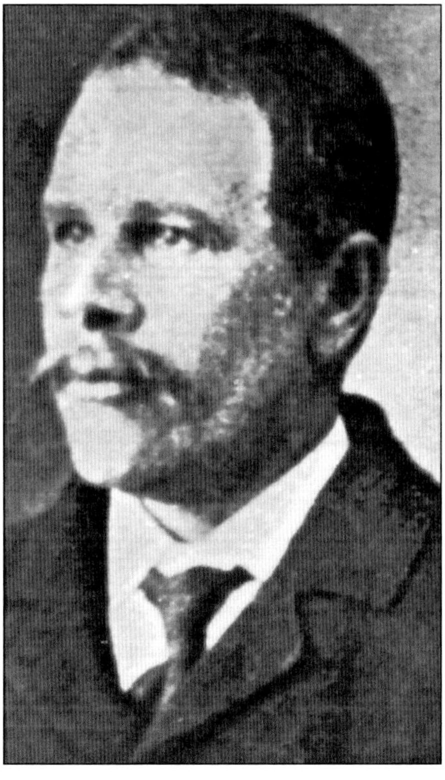

Littleton Lorton Page, an educator in Jefferson County, was on the board of trustees at Storer College. Page-Jackson High School was named after him and Philip Jackson. Page had been born into slavery but escaped to the North, possibly using the Underground Railroad. After the Civil War, he took the name Littleton Lorton Page, after the officer to whom he had served as a page in the Union forces during the war.

Born in Virginia on January 11, 1869, Philip Jackson was a teacher and principal of the Colored School on Harewood Avenue (now Martin Luther King Jr. Avenue) from 1887 until 1937. He graduated from Storer College and began his career in Frederick, Maryland. In 1938, the school board named the first high school for black students Page-Jackson High School after Jackson and fellow educator Littleton Page.

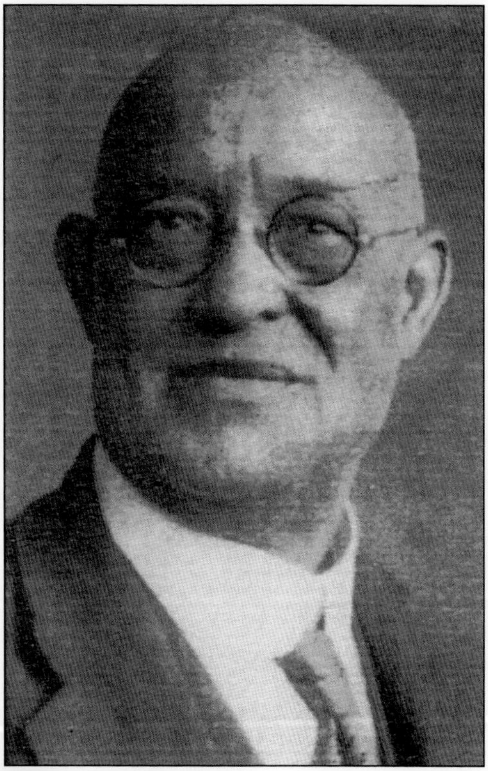

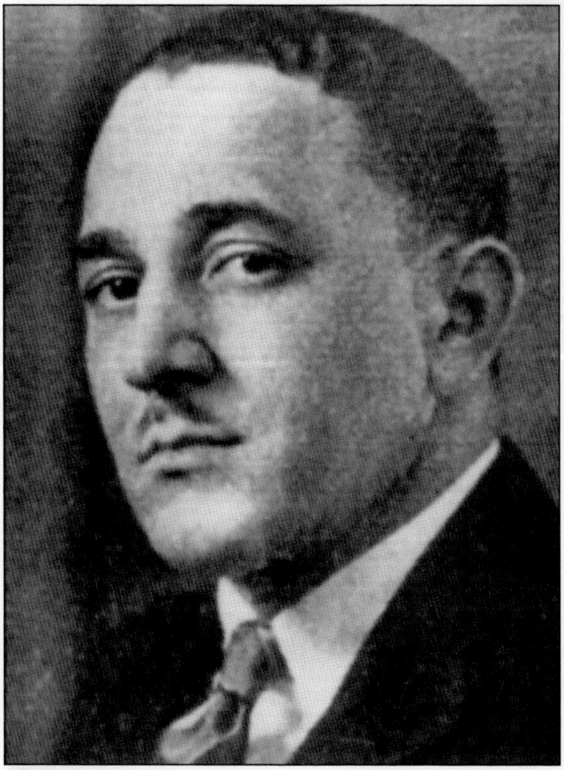

In 1937, Donald C. Wingo became principal at Eagle Avenue School. He made changes and improvements to the school that resulted in a rating as a first-class elementary school. He would later serve as the first principal of Page-Jackson High School. When Page-Jackson High School opened in 1938, there were 30 students enrolled as freshmen. Four years later in 1942, because of World War II, only one-third of those would graduate.

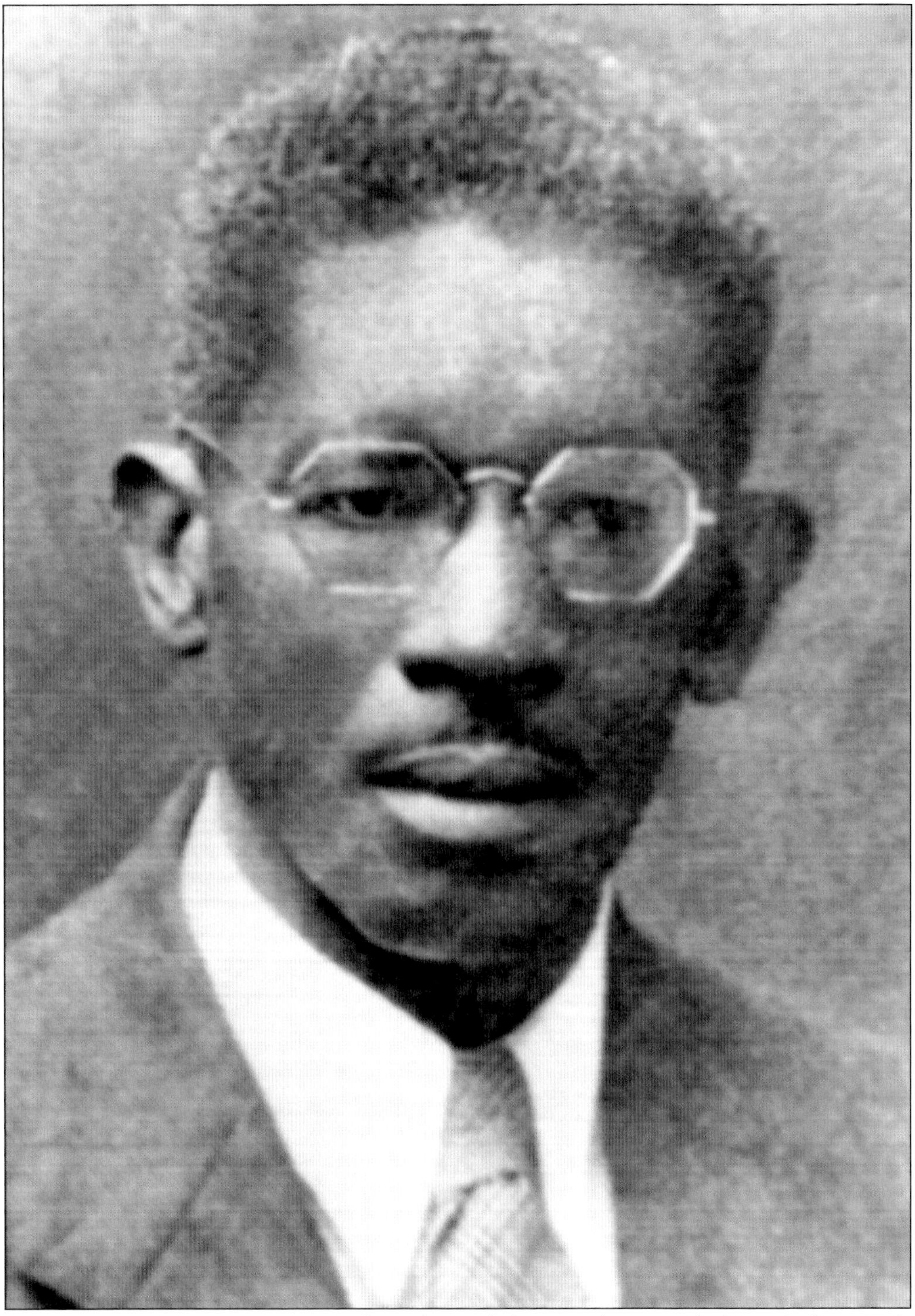

Pictured here is O. M. Stewart, a math teacher and the second principal of Page-Jackson High School. He was principal at Page-Jackson from 1938 until 1949. Two years after he left, Page-Jackson High School (PJHS) would open in a new building on Mordington Avenue. Today that building is used for offices of the Jefferson County Board of Education.

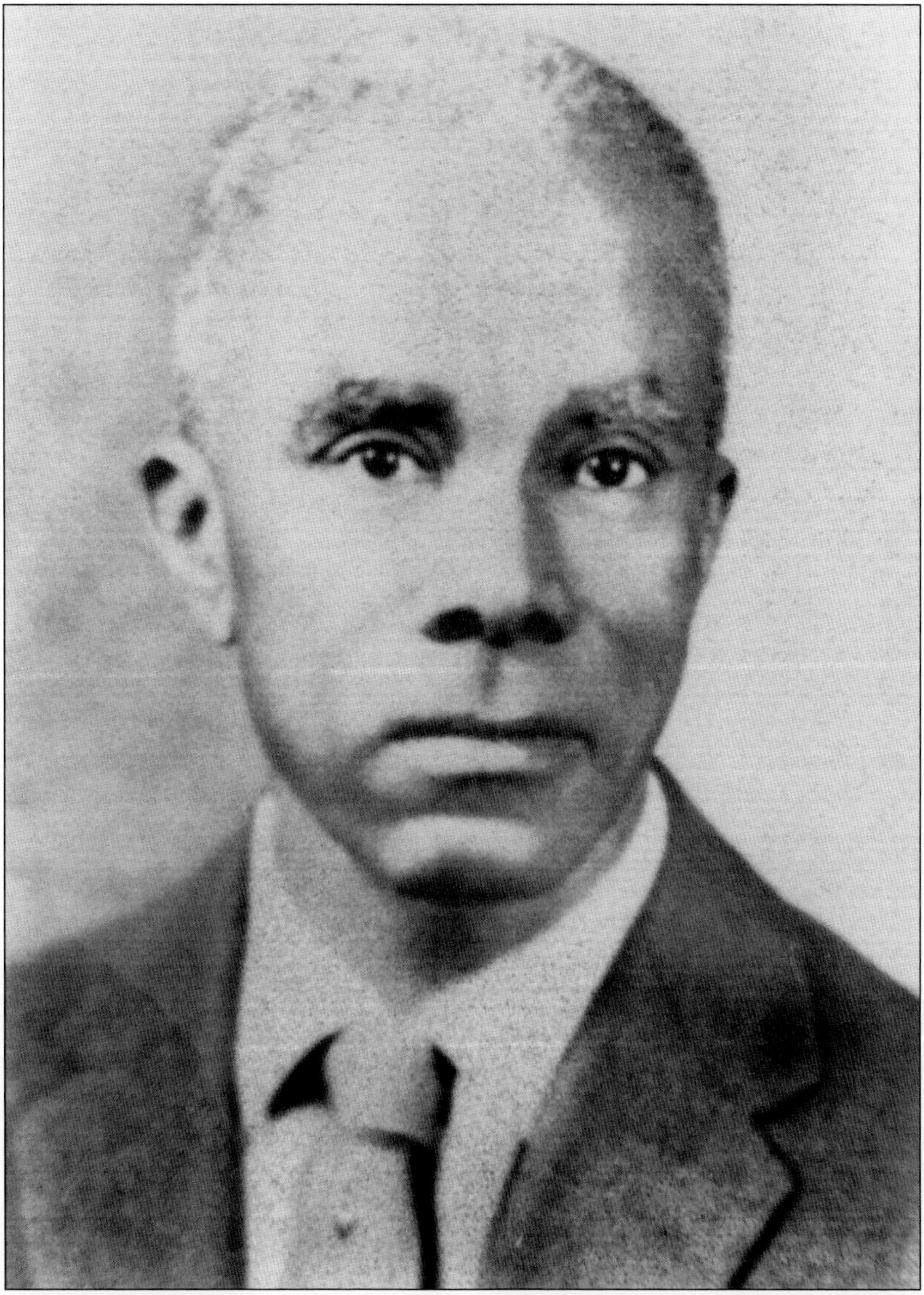

E. M. Dandridge Sr. was a science and math teacher at Page-Jackson. He also was the last principal at PJHS. While there, he served as the first football coach. He was a graduate of Lincoln University. Dandridge was also very civic minded and served as Jefferson County NAACP president as well as being appointed by the State of West Virginia to the West Virginia Human Rights Commission.

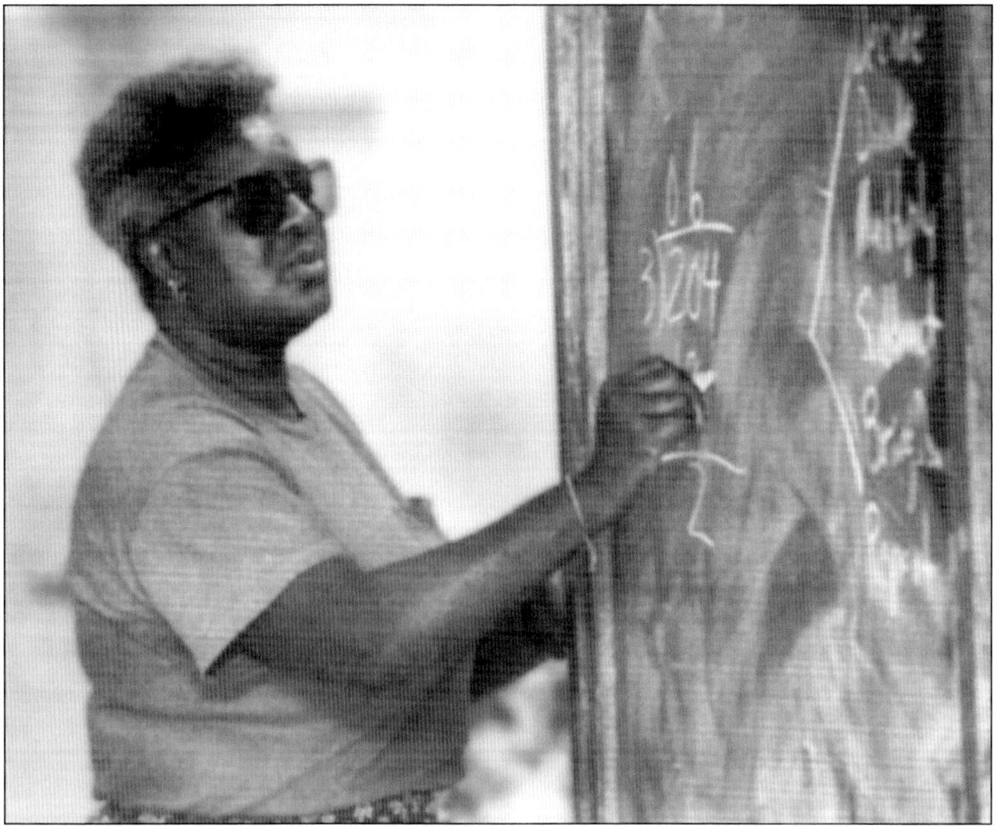

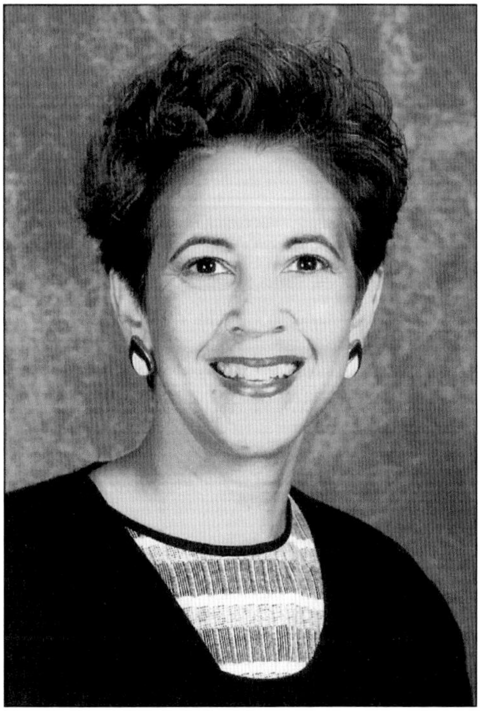

Mary Taylor Doakes solves a problem for her students. A 1953 graduate of Page-Jackson, she attended Storer College and then went on to Shepherd College. She received a master's degree from West Virginia University, was a teacher in Jefferson County at Eagle Avenue Elementary School, and later was promoted to principal at Charles Town Junior High School. In the "Landmarks" section of *The Black Book*, Mary T. Doakes Panther, former principal, is listed in "Groups, Places and Events Named after Africans." In her case, the event was the Mary Taylor Doakes Panther Classic, a basketball tournament.

Deborah Roper Corbett graduated from Fairmont State College. She became the first black principal of the integrated Ranson Elementary School. In 1990, she received the Milliken Award, which recognizes national, state, and county teacher excellence. She wanted all of her students to succeed, and she tried very hard to achieve that goal.

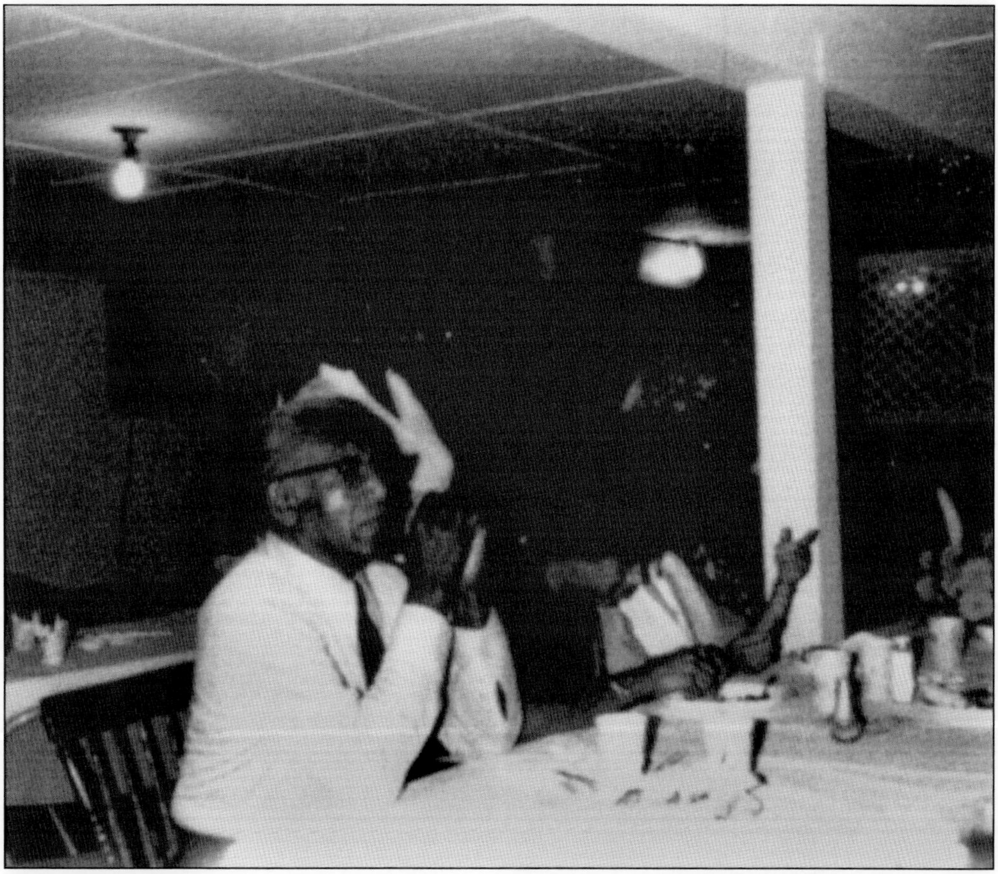

Edward Braxton was the first black member of the Charles Town City Council. He was an auto mechanic and shared ownership of the Braxton Brothers Garage, located in Ranson, West Virginia, for several years. Here he is seated at the Mount Zion United Methodist Church in Charles Town, West Virginia. The photograph was taken in the lower level of the church after Braxton had performed as a soloist on the program.

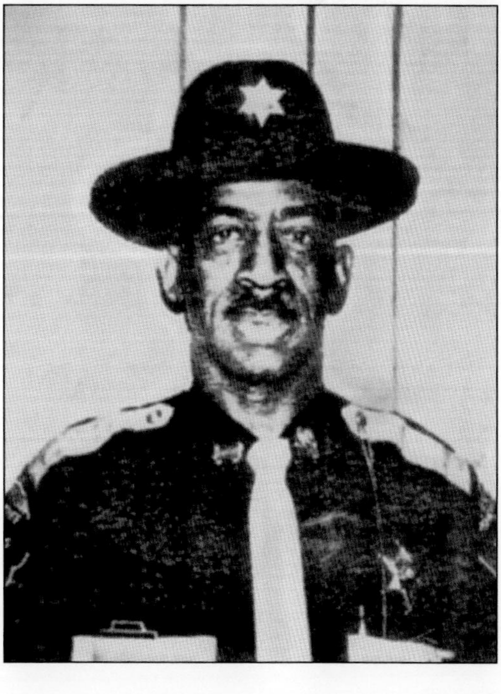

Pictured here is Robert Carr. World War II veteran Carr is renowned for being both in the Charles Town Police Department and a Jefferson County deputy sheriff. He was selected as the first African American law enforcement officer in Jefferson County. He was also the first African American jailer in the county, possibly in West Virginia. In addition, he also became a deputy sheriff. All of his accomplishments were highly commendable and deserve recognition.

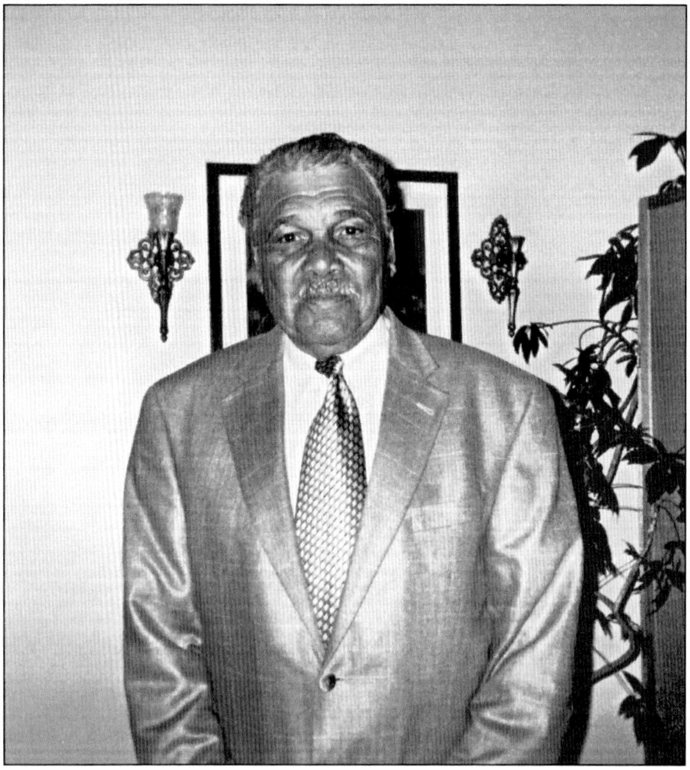

Russell Roper—graduate of Storer College, church leader, entrepreneur, building contractor, community activist, owner and developer of the largest subdivision in the state of West Virginia by a black person—served many years on the Jefferson County Planning Commission. Involved in many civic affairs in the Jefferson County, he was also a World War II veteran who was awarded the Bronze Star and was featured in the PBS airing of a World War II documentary.

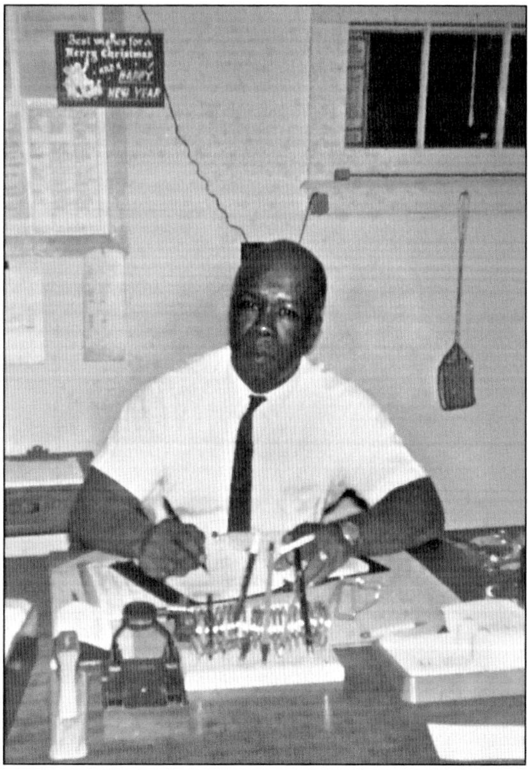

Charles R. Branson—Storer College graduate, teacher, and coach—was the first African American to serve on the Shepherdstown City Council, where he was reelected for 28 years. U.S. Army veteran Branson served in Europe during World War II. A lifelong resident of Shepherdstown, he ensured that the interests of African American neighborhoods were not forgotten and made certain that all members of the community had access to the city's basic services.

Adam Page Craven was the grandson of Littleton Lorton Page, the namesake of Page-Jackson High School. He was also the son of Cerelle Craven, a teacher at Eagle Avenue Elementary School for many years. Adam was a teacher and coach at Page-Jackson until 1959, when he resigned and began teaching and coaching in Virginia and later Maryland. After he retired, he became the first elected black mayor of Harpers Ferry.

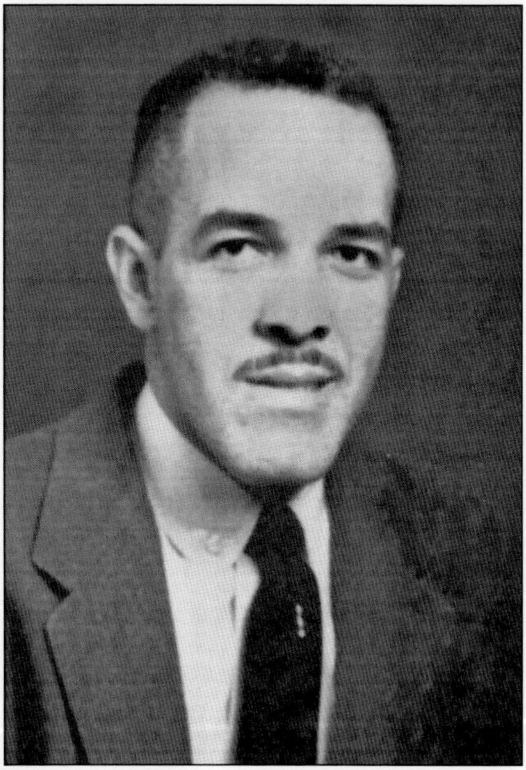

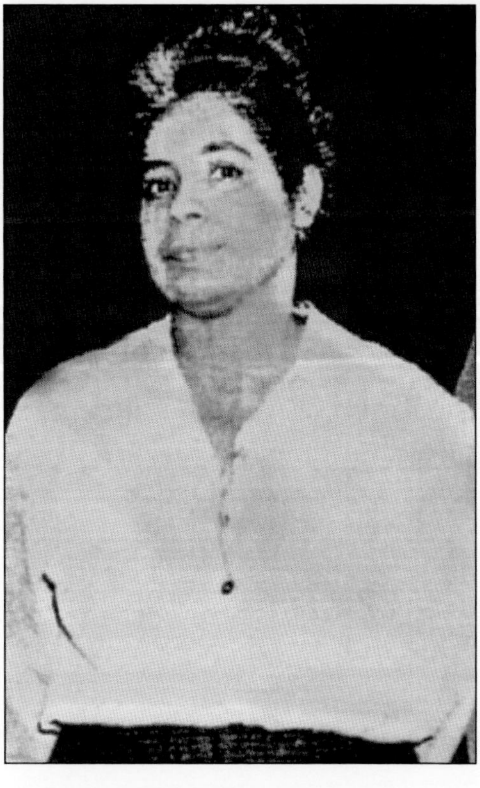

Irma S. Patrick was a teacher at Eagle Avenue Elementary School and later became principal of the same school. She was the only African American female principal of an all-black school in Jefferson County. When Eagle Avenue closed in 1966, Patrick retired. She was the last principal of the last African American school in Jefferson County.

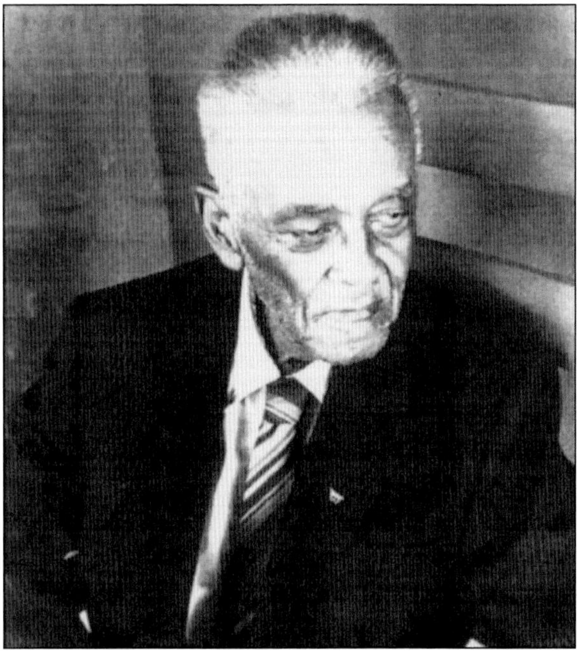

Born and raised in Shepherdstown, Dr. John Wesley Harris graduated from Storer College in 1921. He taught in Maryland, then at Shadyside School, where he served as principal. He remained a principal in the county until his retirement. He was associated with black education for 45 years. He attended West Virginia State College, George Washington University, and LaSalle School of Law and was awarded an honorary doctorate degree from Ohio Christian College.

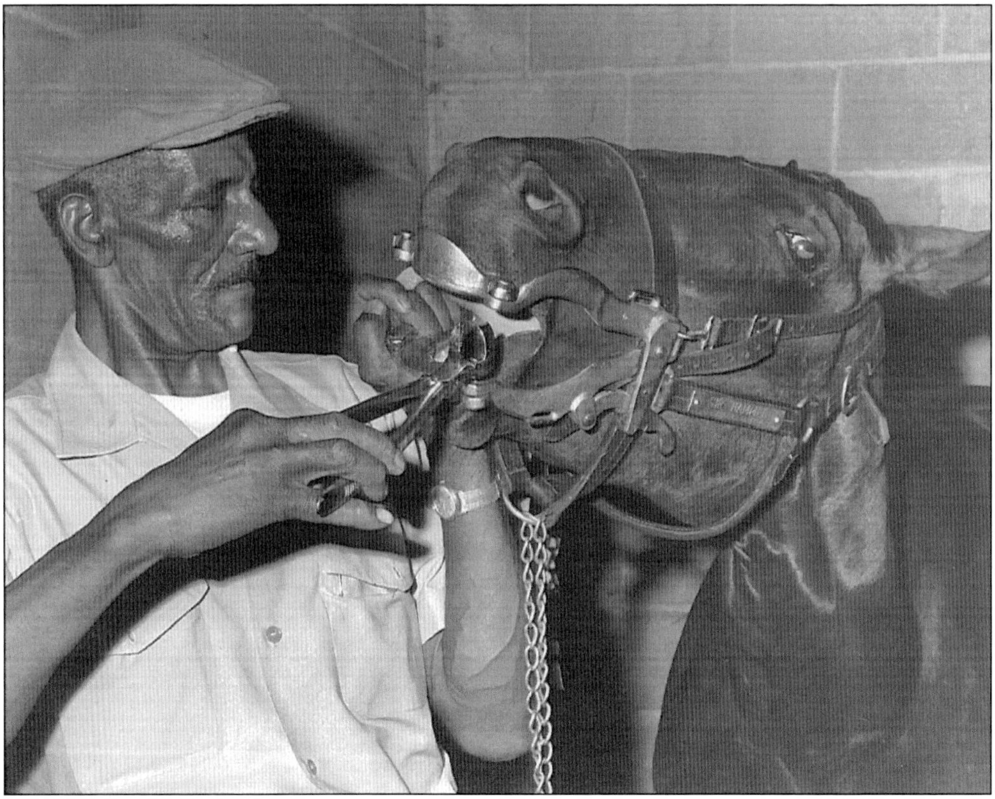

Theodore Togans Sr. is pictured here examining the mouth and teeth of a Thoroughbred racehorse. Togans was a veterinary assistant and worked at the Charles Town Race Track when this photograph was taken.

Four

EDUCATION

On March 3, 1865, Congress passed legislation designed to (1) provide basic and educational services to former slaves and (2) administer abandoned land in the South. The Freedmen's Bureau Act Chapter 90, 13 Stat. 507 [1865], Bureau of Refugees, Freedmen and Abandoned Land (commonly referred to as the Freedmen's Bureau) was established in the War Department. It continued through the Civil War and one year thereafter.

Rev. Nathan C. Brackett was the field agent for the bureau with headquarters at Harpers Ferry. His mission was to establish schools and churches in the Lower Shenandoah Valley for the newly freed slaves.

In September 1865, four women from the Freewill Baptist Home Mission Society in Maine arrived at Harpers Ferry and reported to Reverend Brackett to begin the work of educating blacks in Jefferson and Berkeley Counties.

Anne Dudley and Sabrina Gibbs started teaching at Harpers Ferry, but soon after, Dudley was sent to Charles Town to start a school. Sara Jane Foster and Anna Wright were sent to Martinsburg.

Later these "freemen's schools" were established in Shepherdstown and Smithfield (Middleway). When the Freedmen's Bureau left Jefferson County around 1867, it became the responsibility of the Jefferson County school districts to build schools in their districts. It is estimated that there were at least 20 schools for African Americans throughout the county.

In 1867, Storer College was established in Harpers Ferry and became the first institution of higher learning for African Americans in the state.

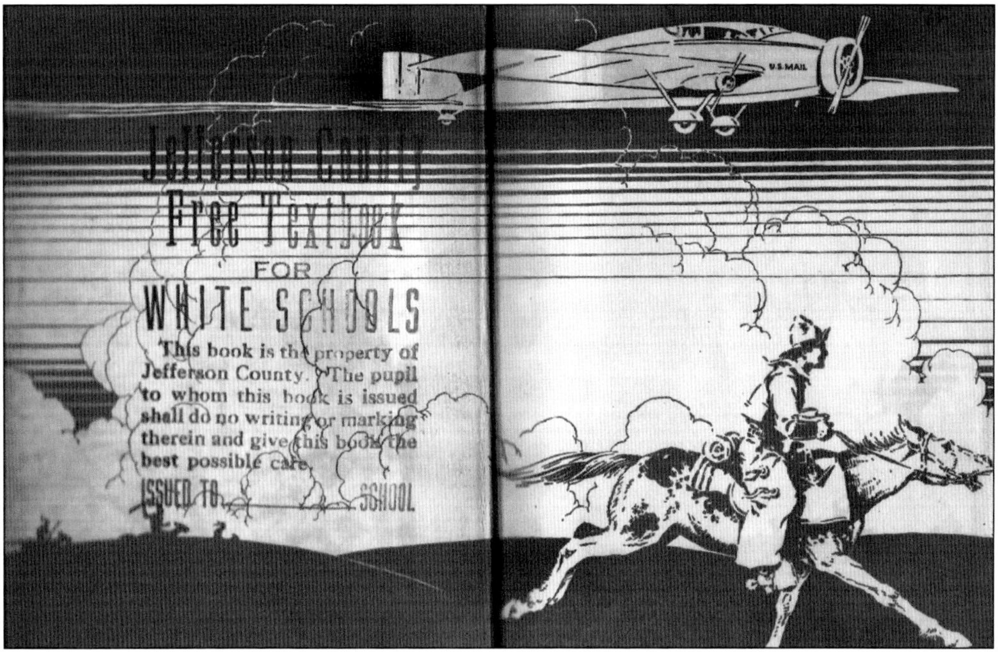

Books that black students used were the hand-me-downs from white schools. This photograph shows the inside front cover of a book. Originally it had been purchased by the board of education for the exclusive use of white students. Inside the cover, it clearly states that the book is identified as "Jefferson County Free Textbook for White Schools."

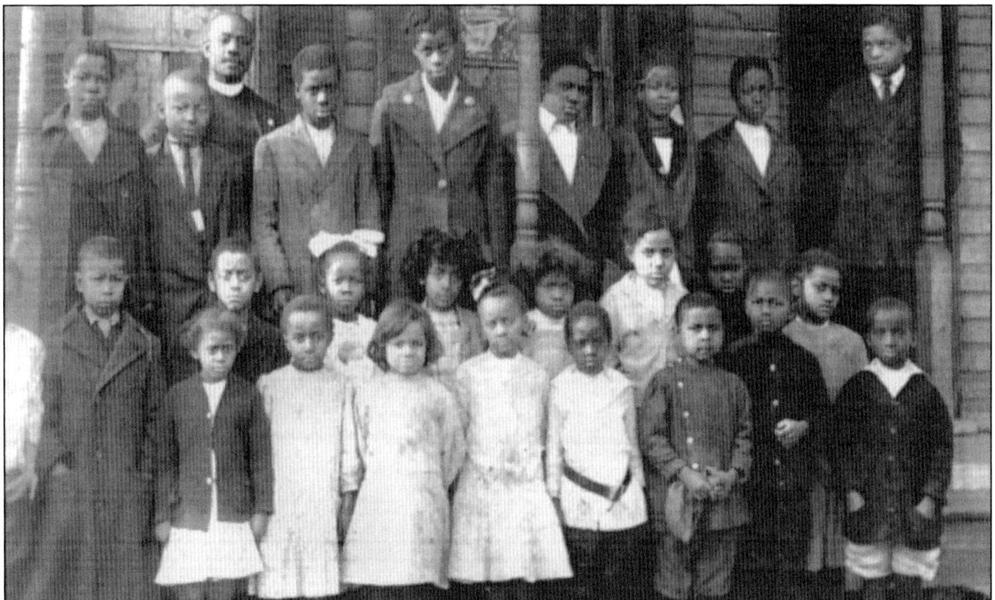

How nicely dressed these students are. In this undated photograph, the Reverend J. N. Yearwood is standing at the back, left. Others pictured, in alphabetical order, are as follows: Helen Burman, Georgia Cook, Margaret Jackson, B. Johnson, Louis King, Gertrude Brown Lawson, Josephine Luckett, Hallie Rutherford, John Rutherford, Julia Rutherford, Norman Saul, Sigesmund Taylor, Ruth Tucker, Elizabeth Williams, and Lem Wise.

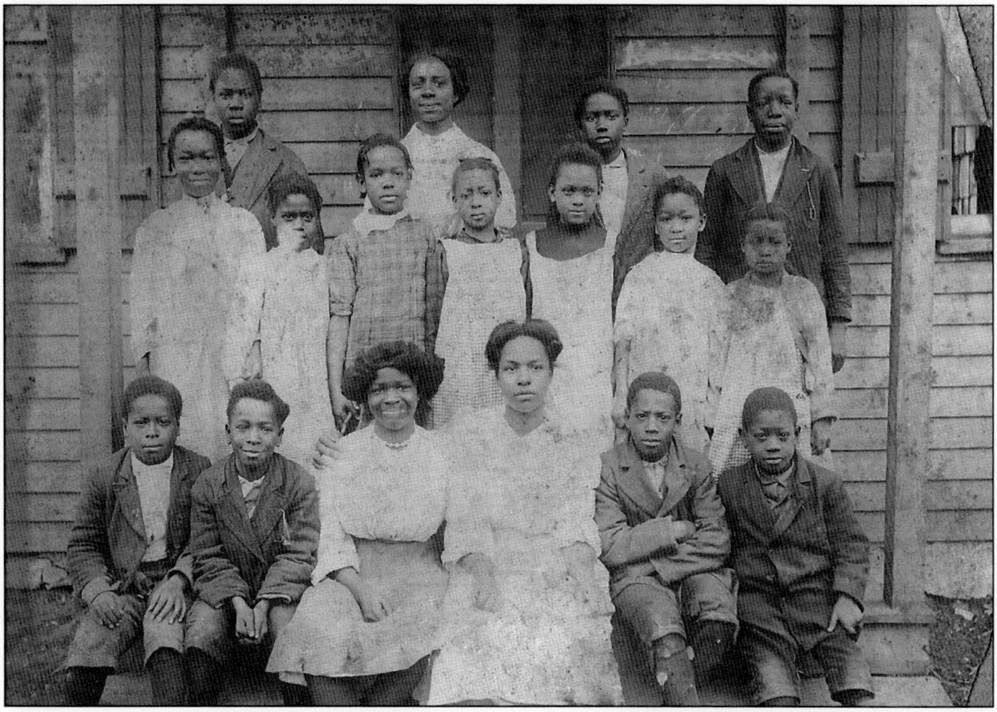

Students pose in front of this unidentified early school. By February 13, 1877, there were 10 "colored" schools. On February 18, 1901, the West Virginia Legislature passed an act that provided primary public schools for African Americans from age 6 to 21. In 1921, when students were ready for high school and none was available in Jefferson County, the board of education paid tuition for seven pupils at Storer College.

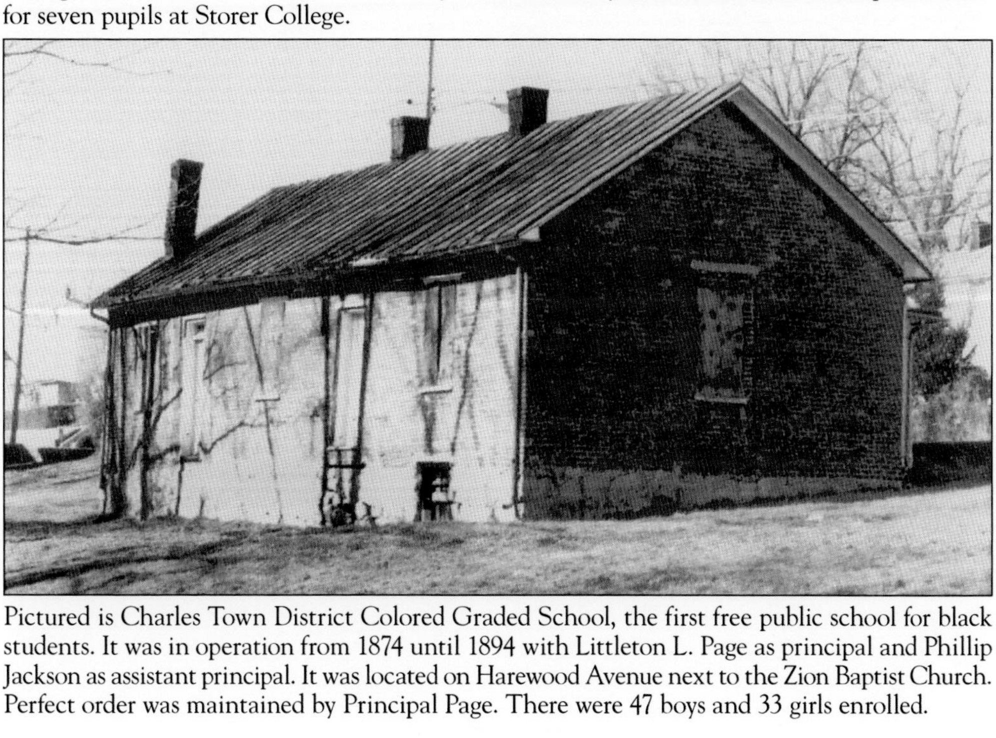

Pictured is Charles Town District Colored Graded School, the first free public school for black students. It was in operation from 1874 until 1894 with Littleton L. Page as principal and Phillip Jackson as assistant principal. It was located on Harewood Avenue next to the Zion Baptist Church. Perfect order was maintained by Principal Page. There were 47 boys and 33 girls enrolled.

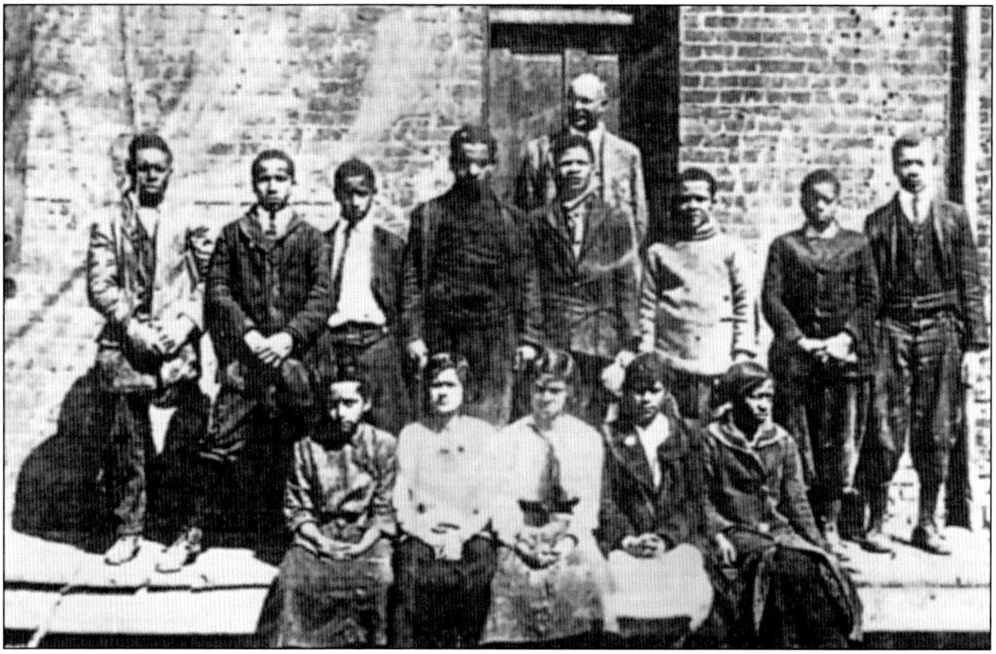

Philip Jackson is shown standing behind his students at the Charles Town District Colored School on Harewood Avenue/Martin Luther King Jr. Avenue. The school started in 1874 and continued to 1897. Philip Jackson was instrumental in the early education of African American children in the county. The exact date of this photograph is unknown.

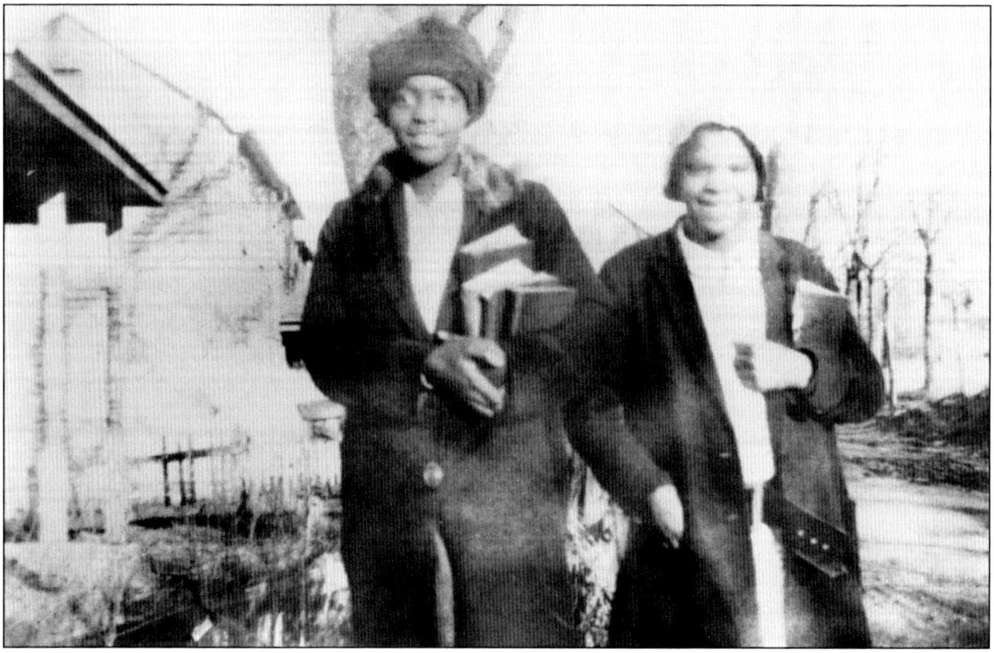

School friends are important in life. Gussie Taylor Baylor (left) and Carrie Roman are pictured walking home from Eagle Avenue Colored School. The school was located on "Potato Hill," and the photograph is probably from the 1920s. By 1937, the school had earned a rating as a first-class elementary school from the state.

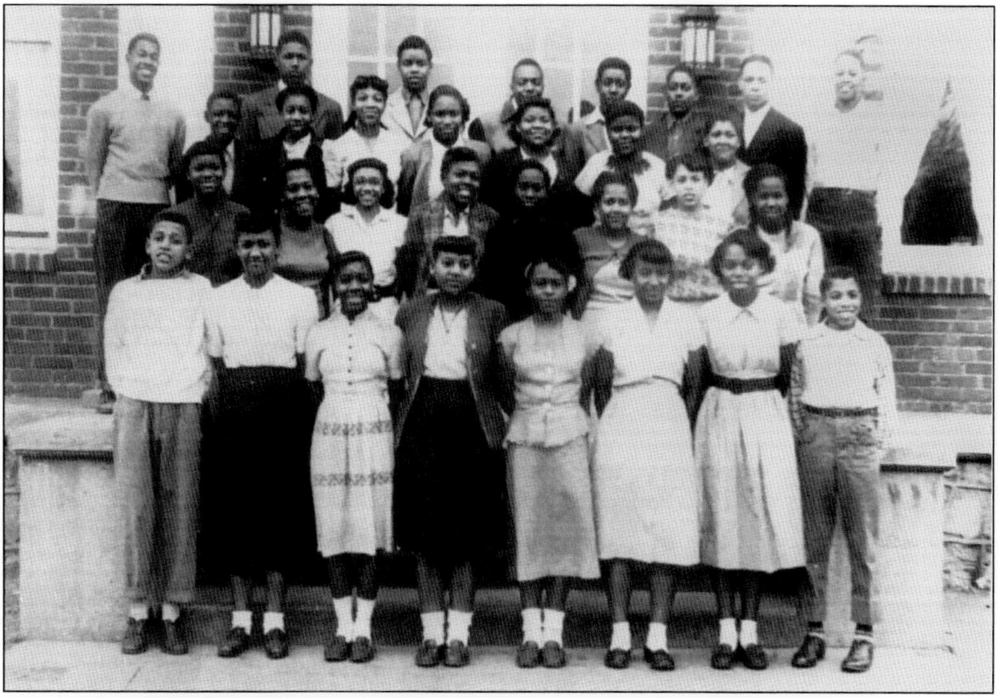

Page-Jackson High School's class of 1952 is shown when they were all students at Eagle Avenue Elementary School in Charles Town. When the class of 1952 finally graduated, these 16 graduates were listed: Johnnie Bailey, Florence Baltimore, JoAnn Berry, Hortense Brown, Robert S. Brown, Dorothy Campbell, Virginia Campbell, Elmer Dyson, Katherine Jackson, Doris Jackson, Carrie A. Kidrick, Nancy Lewis, Lolita Newman, Delorse Stevenson, Ralph Wilson, and Kenneth Young.

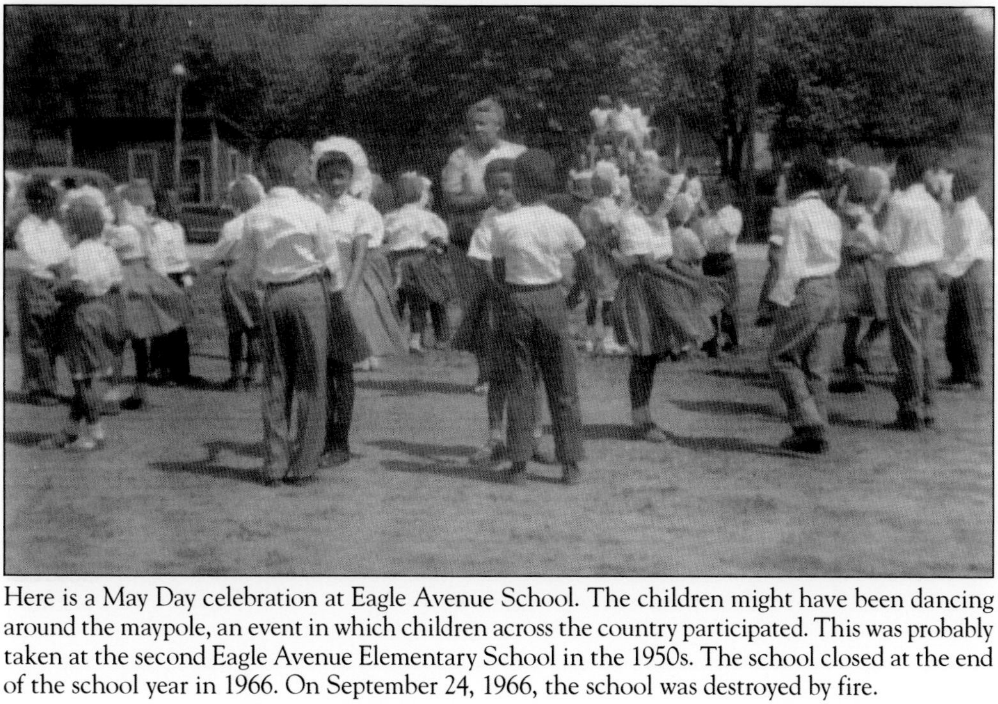

Here is a May Day celebration at Eagle Avenue School. The children might have been dancing around the maypole, an event in which children across the country participated. This was probably taken at the second Eagle Avenue Elementary School in the 1950s. The school closed at the end of the school year in 1966. On September 24, 1966, the school was destroyed by fire.

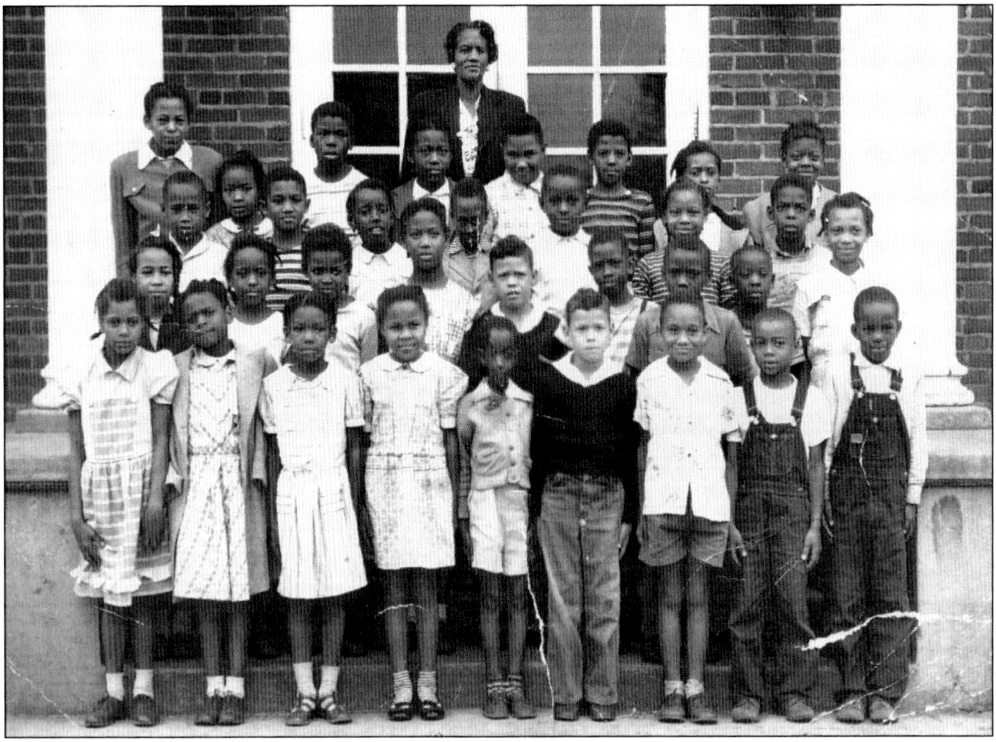

Students at Eagle Avenue Elementary School pose in front of the building. Teacher Lucy Saunders is standing in the back in the center, wearing a dark jacket. Eagle Avenue Elementary School was located on the corner of Eagle Avenue and Harewood Avenue/Martin Luther King Jr. Avenue. Saunders also taught in the Linwood School in Kearneysville Area School. Eventually all of the black schools would close when desegregation was accomplished.

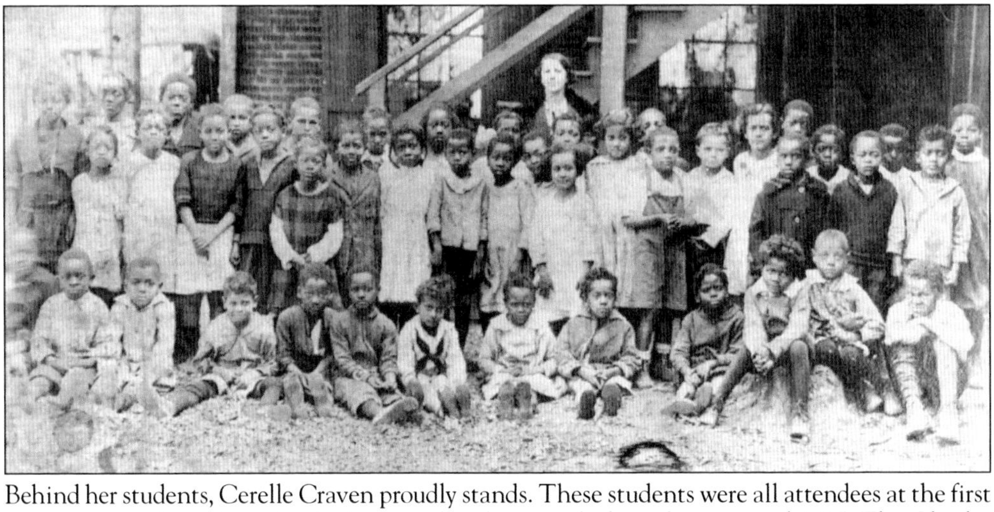

Behind her students, Cerelle Craven proudly stands. These students were all attendees at the first Eagle Avenue School in Charles Town. The photograph dates from around 1925. The Charles Town District Board of Education had purchased a lot on Eagle Avenue from George and Emily Washington for $500 in 1894. It was a four-room building that had two rooms added in 1906. As enrollment increased, additional expansion was necessary. This building was in use until 1929, when a new building was erected on Harewood Avenue.

Students learn life's lessons both in and out of the classroom. Here are students at Eagle Avenue School. These students helped during the Masonic Grand Lodge Session held here in the 1950s, thereby teaching them that civic responsibility and responsible citizenship are required in an educational curriculum. Eagle Avenue School was located in Charles Town on Eagle Avenue. The building burned in 1966.

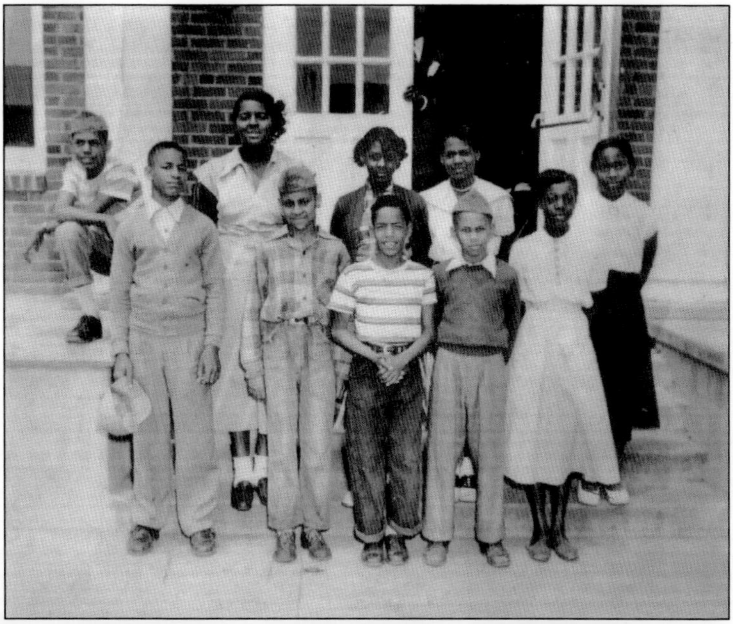

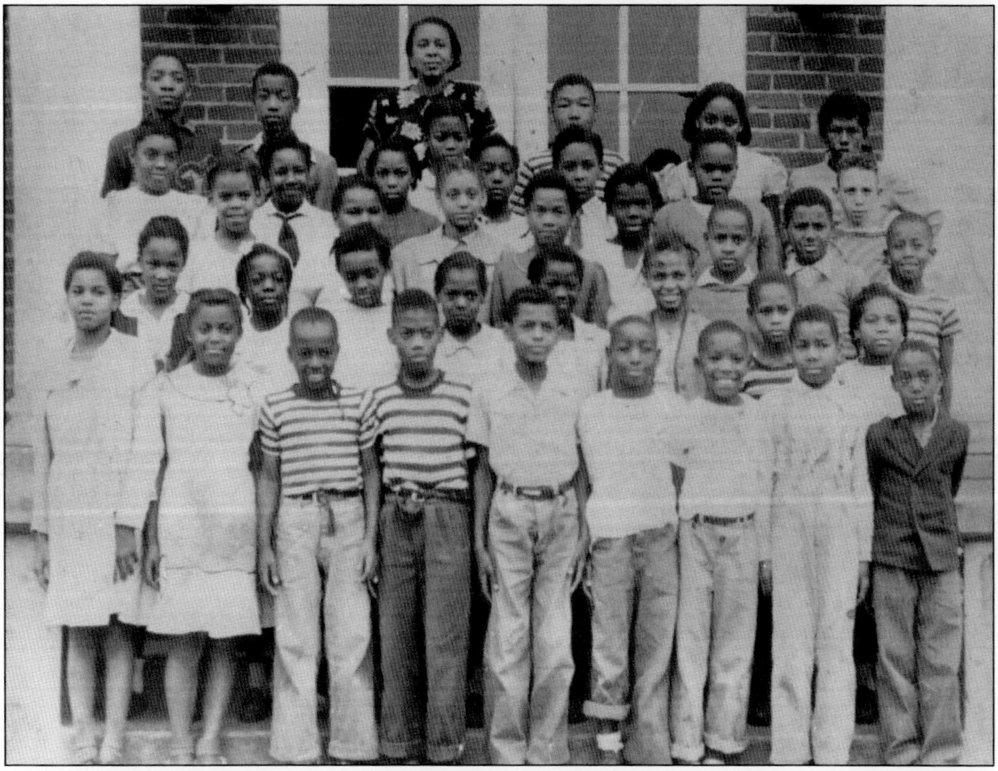

Students pose in front of Eagle Avenue Elementary School. In the back is teacher Elsie Braxton Clinton. She also taught in Skeetersville Colored School (Duffields School) in the Shenandoah Junction area schools. The exact date the school opened is not known, but an article in *The Spirit of Jefferson* on March 17, 1882, stated that "the governor approved an act establishing the independent school district Duffields."

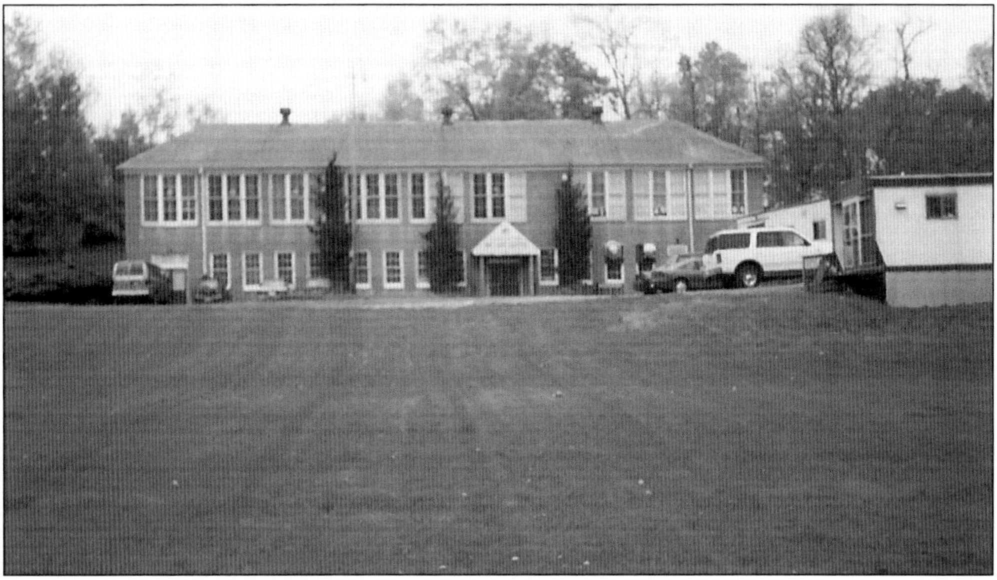

Eastside School for black students was opened in 1948 in Shepherdstown. The school taught elementary grades first through seventh. It would be consolidated with Linwood School in Kearneysville. Eastside would eventually become part of Shepherdstown Elementary School in 1965 for those same grades. The seventh grade would be moved to Shepherdstown Junior High in 1972. Some of the faculty members included Dewitt Jacobs, John Harris, Sara Crane, Marion Johnson Reeler, Ira J. (Willis) Pendleton, and James Green Sr.

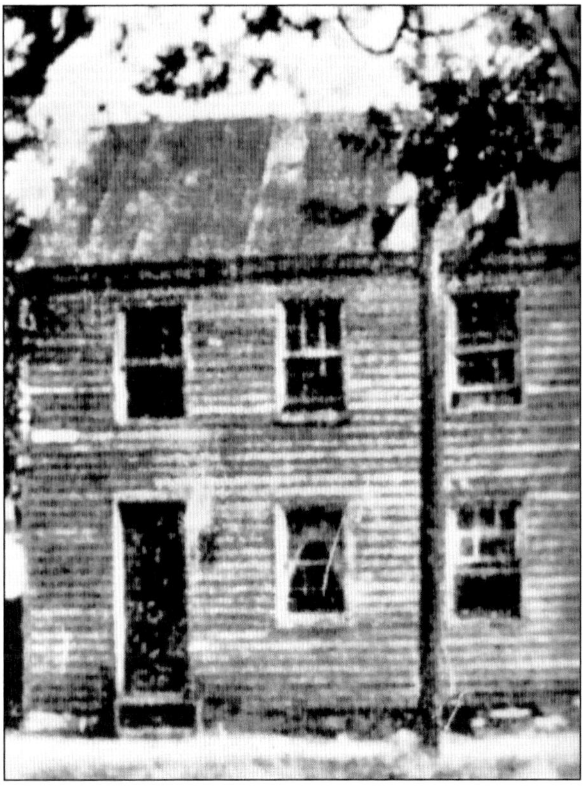

Archilles Dixon was one of 540 free blacks in Jefferson County in 1850. He and his wife, Ellen Dixon, owned a house and a blacksmith shop on the corner of Samuel and Liberty Streets in Charles Town. They allowed teacher Annie Dudley to use one room for her classroom. It was called the Liberty Street School and was used between 1867 and 1874, when the county began its own public school education for blacks.

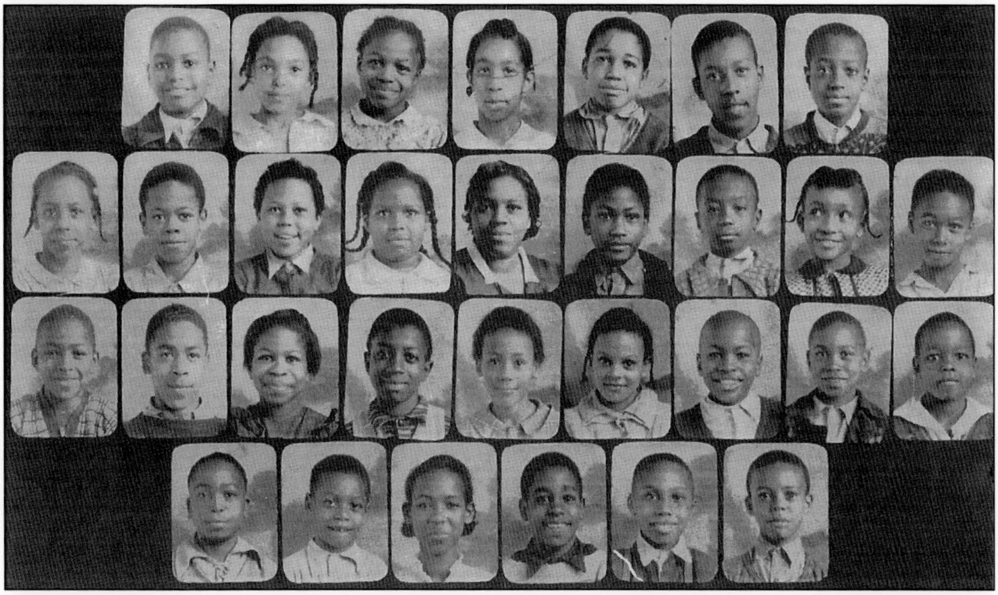

Pictured are students at Grandview Elementary School in the Harpers Ferry and Bolivar areas from the 1940s. This four-room school closed at the end of 1965. Prior to Grandview School, students attended classes in a two-room building on Ridge Street in Bolivar. When the school had outgrown those rooms, additional space in the basement of the Mount Zion Baptist Church was rented for $10 a month.

Students of Grandview Elementary School from Harpers Ferry, West Virginia, are pictured in this photograph. They were on a field trip to Luray Caverns in Virginia in the 1950s. Grandview was one of the earliest black schools in the Harpers Ferry District. Located in Bolivar on Ridge Street, it served black students for grades 1–8 and closed at the end of the 1965 school year. The last members of the faculty were Principal Robert Nunn, three teachers—Thomas Lee, Ruby Brown Reeler, and Betty Pleasant Taylor—and custodian Walter Fox.

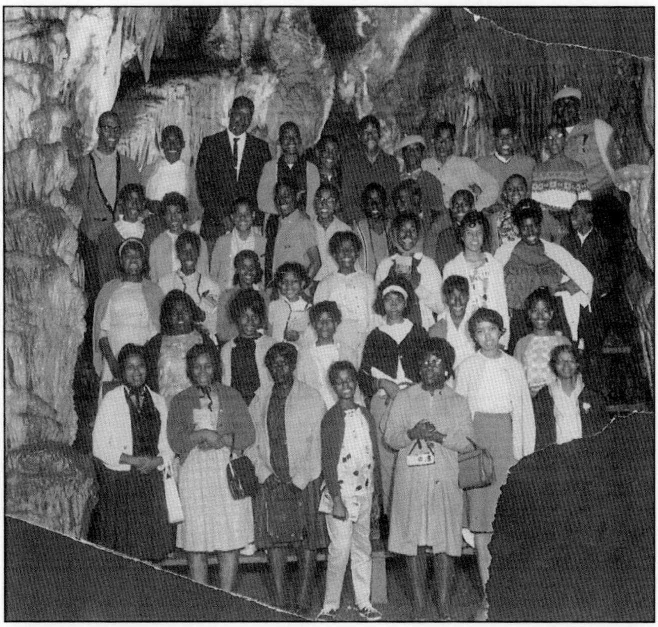

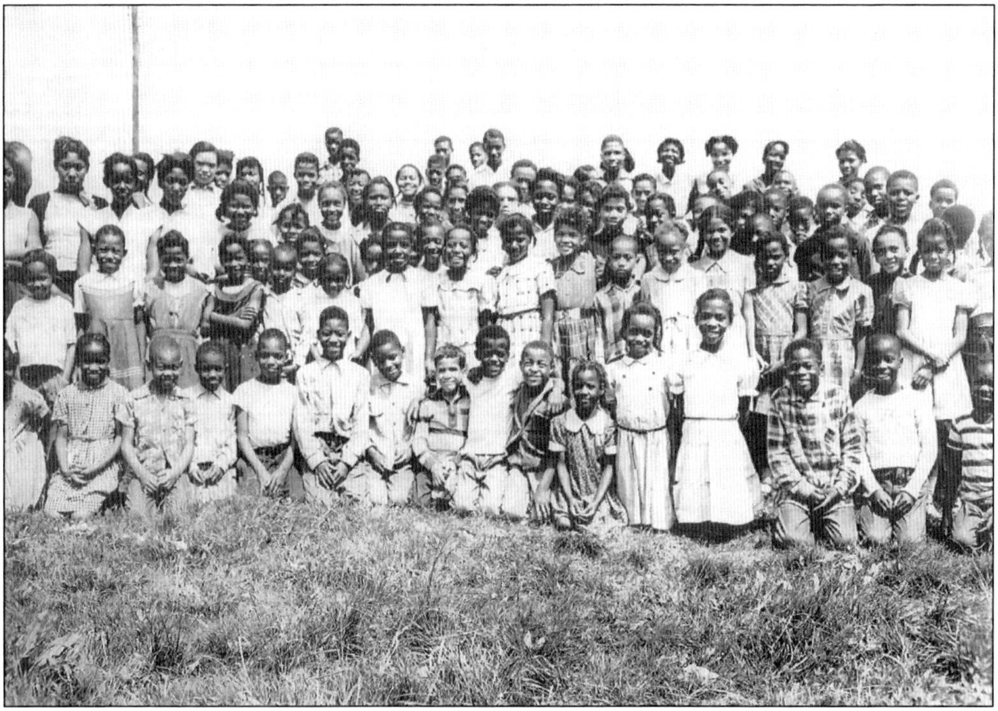

Students are pictured at Grandview Elementary School in the 1950s. The school started out as a four-room school that served black students from Bolivar and Harpers Ferry. Students from grades first through eighth attended. At the end of the school year in 1965, the school closed its doors. The last faculty members were Betty Taylor, Ruby Reeler, Thomas Lee, principal Robert Nunn, and custodian Walter Fox.

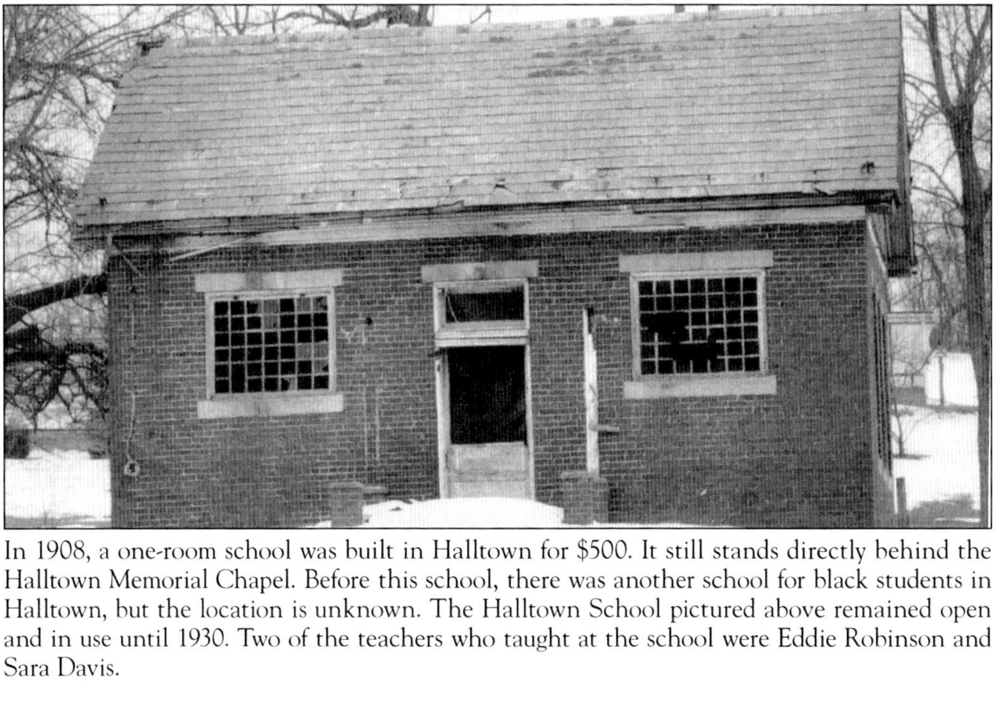

In 1908, a one-room school was built in Halltown for $500. It still stands directly behind the Halltown Memorial Chapel. Before this school, there was another school for black students in Halltown, but the location is unknown. The Halltown School pictured above remained open and in use until 1930. Two of the teachers who taught at the school were Eddie Robinson and Sara Davis.

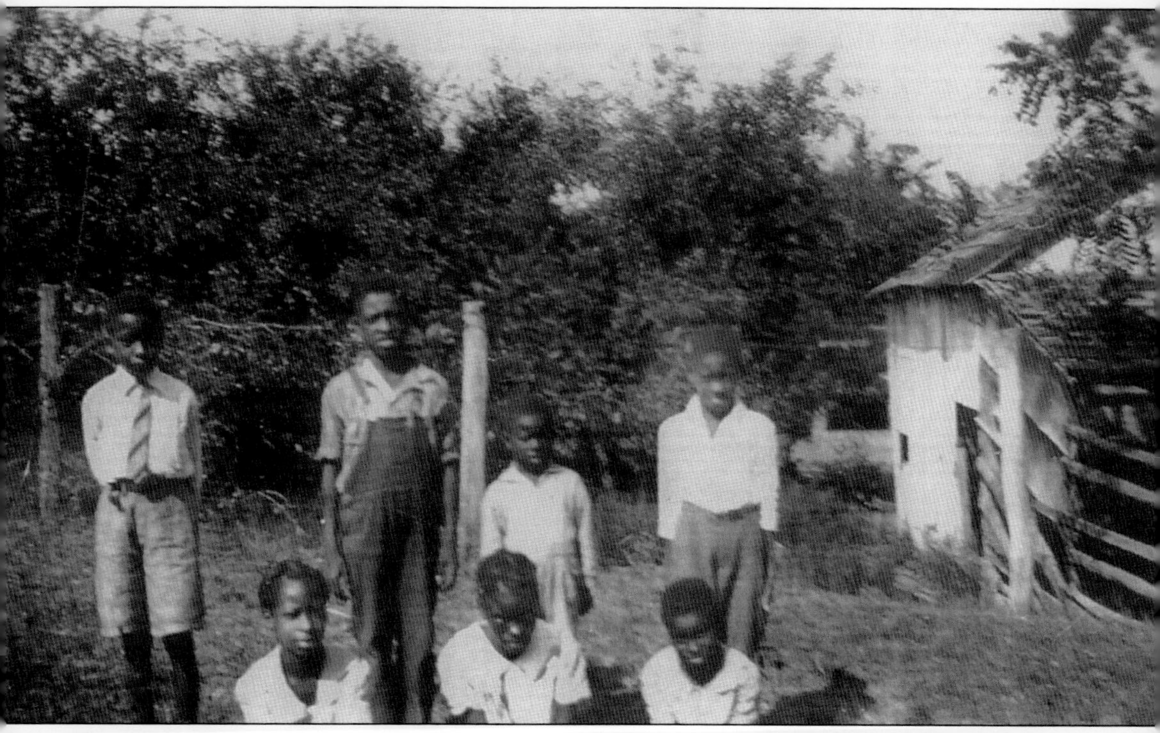

This 1930s photograph shows students from Mechanicstown Colored School. Elsie Clinton was the teacher when it closed in 1934. It was built in 1891 on land that John Myers sold to the board of education. At the time of its closure, the teacher and the students were transferred to the Eagle Avenue School in Charles Town. The building still stands on privately owned property on Route 9 South.

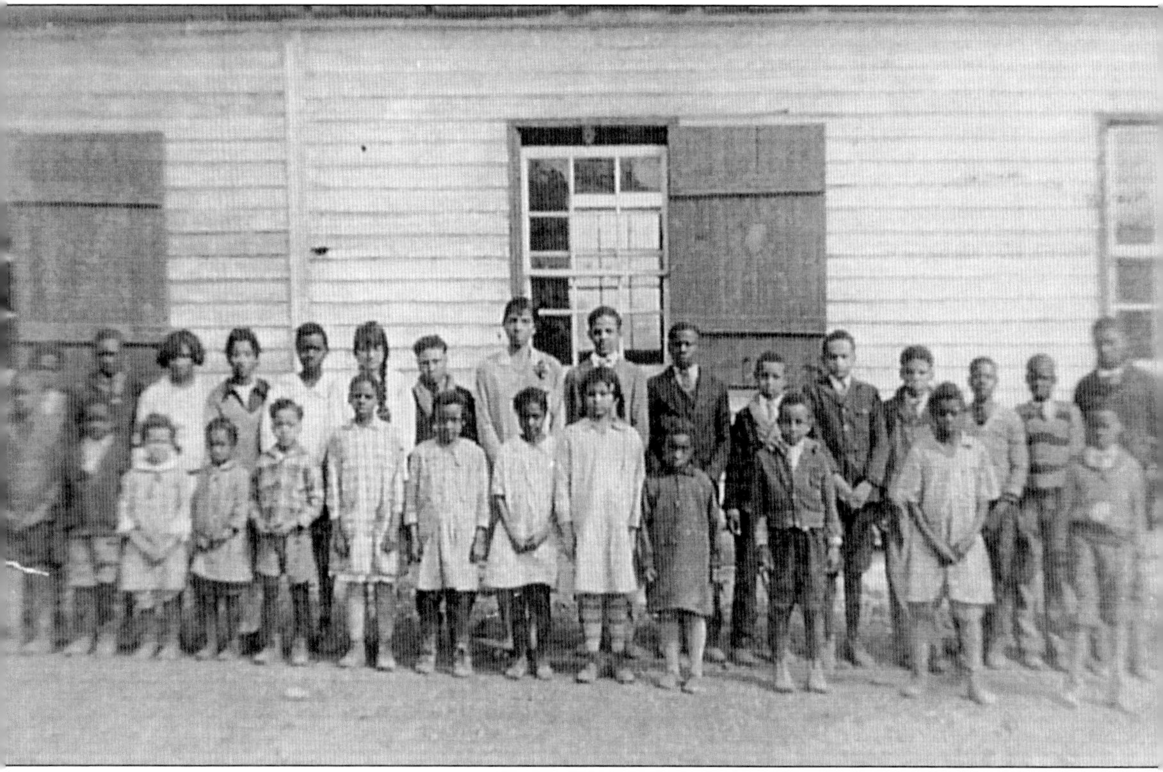

The first-known school for black students in Myerstown was built in 1875 on a lot purchased from Fisher A. Lewis. The building is no longer standing. Here students at the Myerstown Colored School are pictured with teacher Annie Watkins. The photograph was taken around 1920 in Jefferson County, West Virginia. Annie Watkins left this school and later taught at Eagle Avenue Colored School in Charles Town. Eventually the school was sold to Charles Sim.

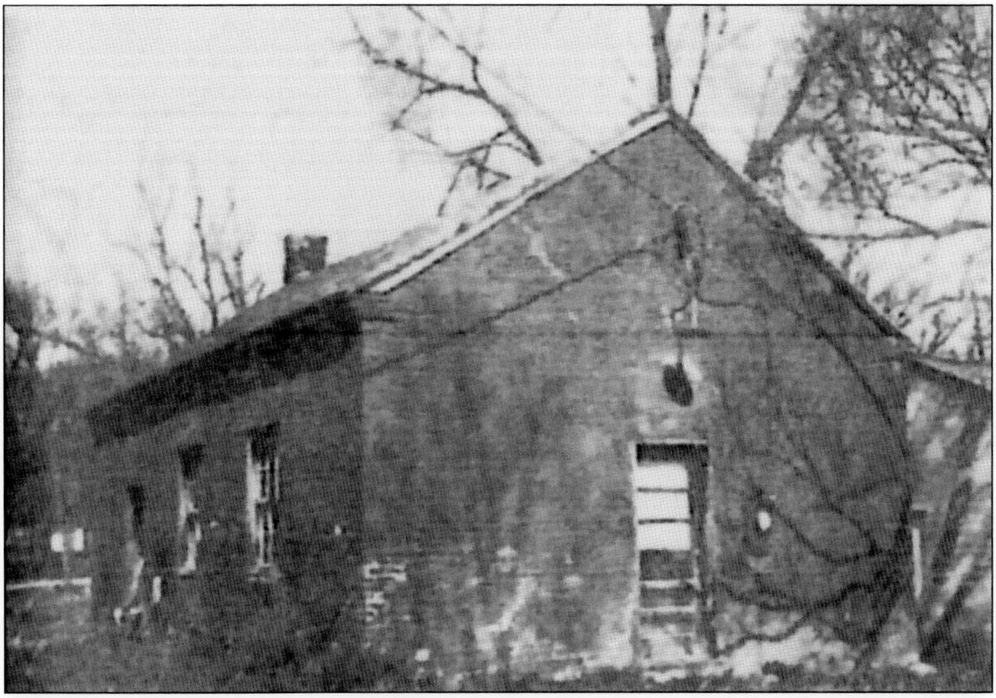

Pictured here is the Old School in Shepherdstown, which was the oldest school for black students in that town. It was the first black school in Shepherdstown and still stands on Brown's Alley. It operated until 1883 as a one-room school. Today it is used and owned by the Asbury United Methodist Church. Originally, classes were held both during the day and in the evening. During the day, there might be as many as 75 students, and at night as many as 35.

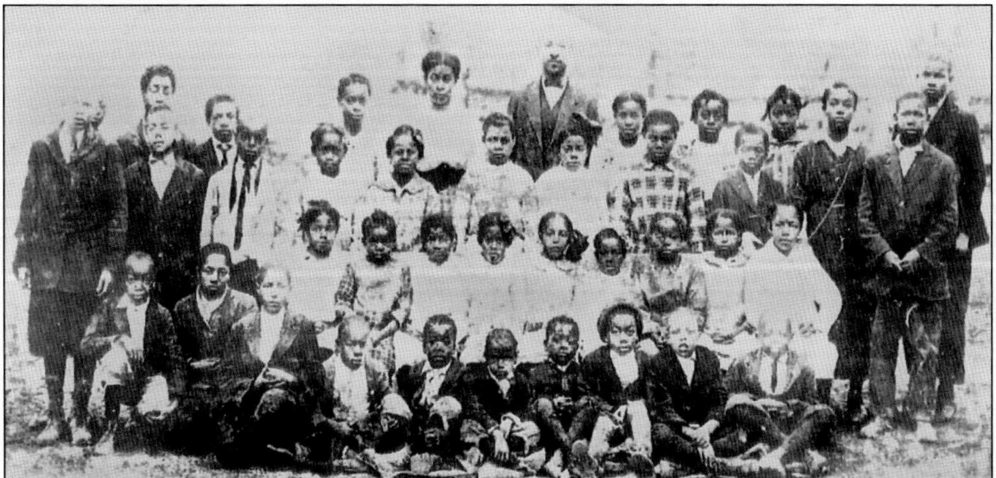

This c. 1918 photograph shows the students at Rippon Colored School with teacher Charles Arter in the back of the center row. The first school in Rippon for black students was a one-room country school located near the railroad tracks, exact date unknown. In 1900, the white Rippon School built in 1874 became the black Rippon Colored School because the white students moved to a brand-new brick building. The black school continued to serve the students until 1939, when they were transferred to Eagle Avenue School in Charles Town and the old building was sold.

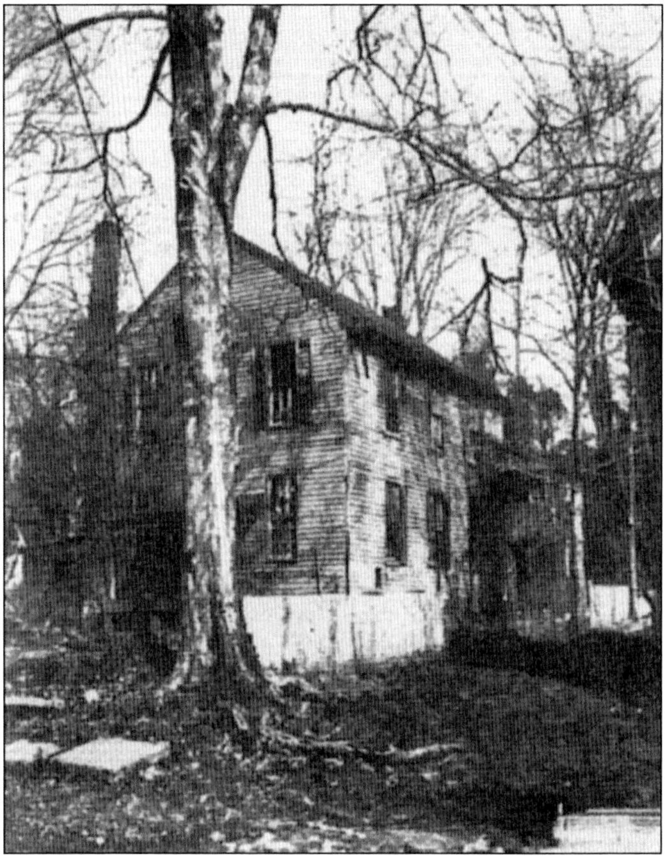

Shady Side Colored School was located on West High Street in Shepherdstown. The lot had been purchased for $65 from R. A. Hesey in 1883 by the school commissioners. This was the second school for black students in Shepherdstown. Eventually, the school would be replaced by Eastside Elementary in 1948. Sara Crane and John Harris were two of the teachers at this school.

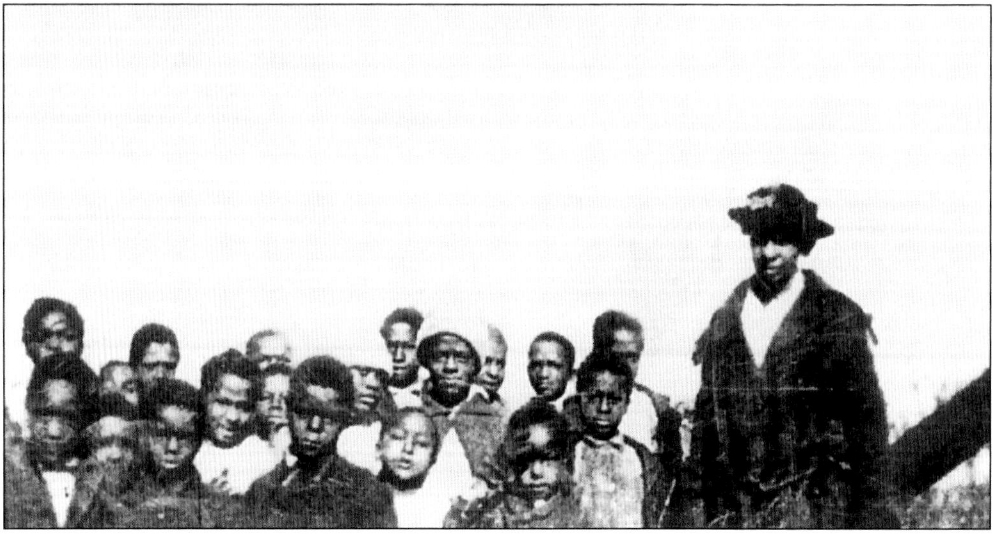

This 1930s photograph of Duffields School shows teacher Elsie Clinton and her students. The school was also known as Skeetersville Colored School. The exact opening date is not known—possibly 1930 when the Oak Grove School in Shenandoah Junction closed. Some of the teachers at this school included Elsie Clinton, John Harris, and Adora Payne. When the school closed, students were transferred to Grandview School (in 1935 or 1936).

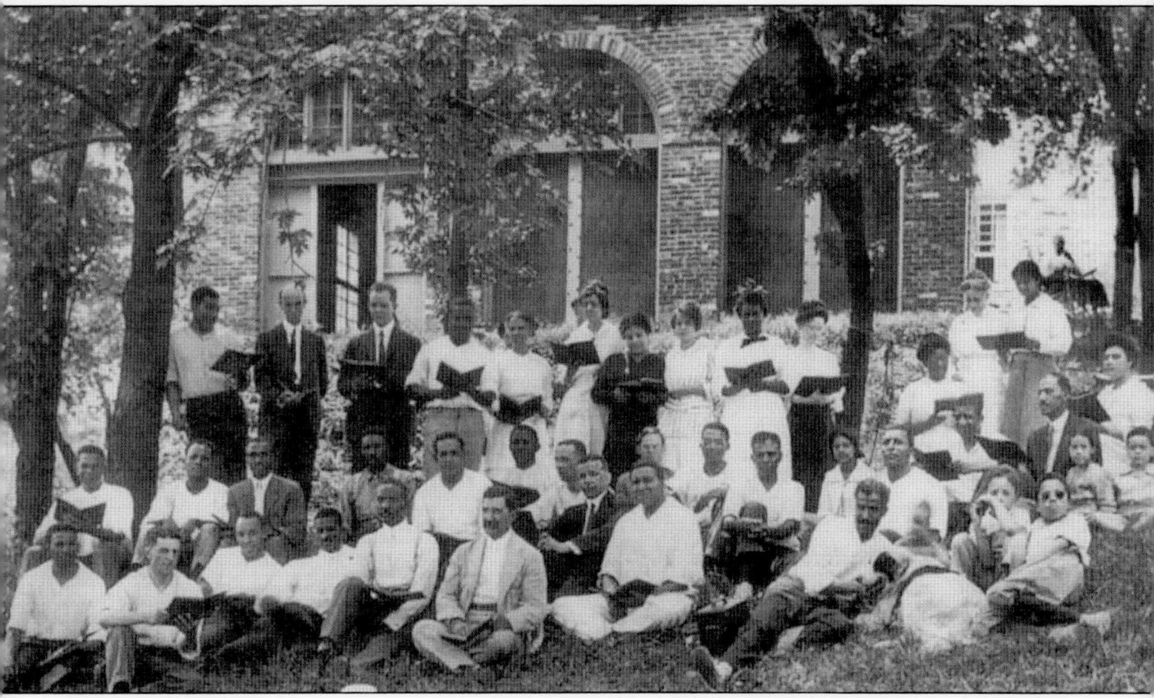

Pictured here are Storer College students, some children, and possibly some instructors. They all appear to be holding books, most likely hymnals, which makes one think this group is some kind of choir. There is a total of 47 people either standing or sitting. While none of the gentlemen appear to be wearing hats, the ladies do appear to be wearing long dresses, dating this photograph to the early 1900s.

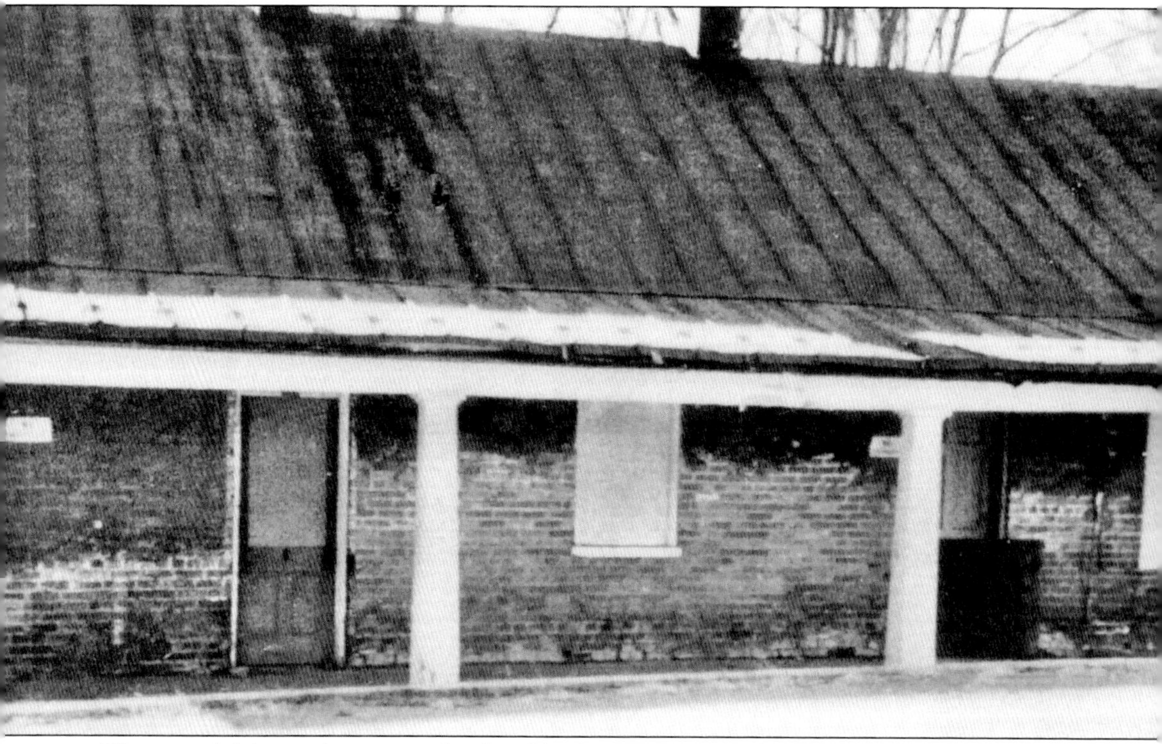

The second African American school in Charles Town is near the intersection of Summit Point and Middleway Roads. The lot was purchased for $100 from Thomas Davis by the Charles Town Board of Education. The school was known as the Charles Town District Colored School. The brick building still stands next to the Zion Baptist Church. Littleton L. Page was the first principal. After he retired for health reasons, Philip Jackson took over.

Five

Events and Entertainment

Some of the events that African Americans sponsored are festivals, horse shows, and dedication programs. At most events, there was some type of music to either lift the spirit or to provide entertainment. This music usually consisted of a singer, a choir, or a band.

In the early 1900s, individuals who could play a musical instrument would join with others, and soon a small band formed. Three of the most familiar bands during that era were the Thompson Stephenson Band, the Bunt Jackson Band, and the J. Wesley Tolbert Band. These bands played at the local juke joints, Fishermen Hall, and social affairs throughout the tri-state area. Sometime these bands would have dancers who would perform with them or perform solo. Two such dancers were Alyce Bradford Braxton and Cordell Thornton Bradford, later sisters-in-law, who often performed at the Fishermen Hall.

In the 1970s, the Jefferson County NAACP was responsible for the establishment and dedication of the Page-Jackson High School's room that houses Page-Jackson memorabilia. The room is presently located in the Jefferson County Board of Education's office building. Along with the room, a tree was planted in memory of all the students who attended the school.

The Jefferson County Black History Preservation Society was instrumental in having Lawrence Street's name changed to add "Martin R. Delany Place." The JCBHPS, along with the Page-Jackson Alumni Association, was responsible for getting the old Page-Jackson High School field designated as "E. M. Dandridge Memorial Field." E. M. Dandridge was the last principal of the Page-Jackson High School.

The dedication and placement of the John Brown plaque at the Storer College campus in Harpers Ferry was undertaken by the national office of the NAACP in 2006. The original plaque was rejected in 1932 by the then president of Storer College.

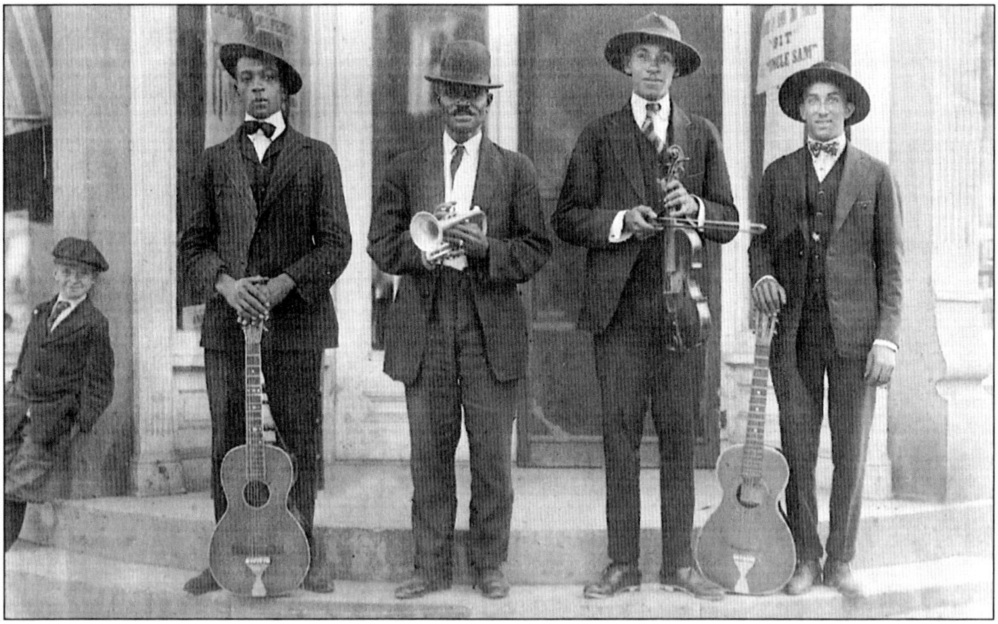

Pictured here are musicians Thompson Stephenson, two unidentified, and George Drew on a Charles Town street. The photograph was probably taken in the 1930s. During that time, there were quite a few bands in Jefferson County because once a year they had a Battle of the Bands event. These may have played for funerals, parades, and social events. At times, the bands would serenade people in white neighborhoods for donations.

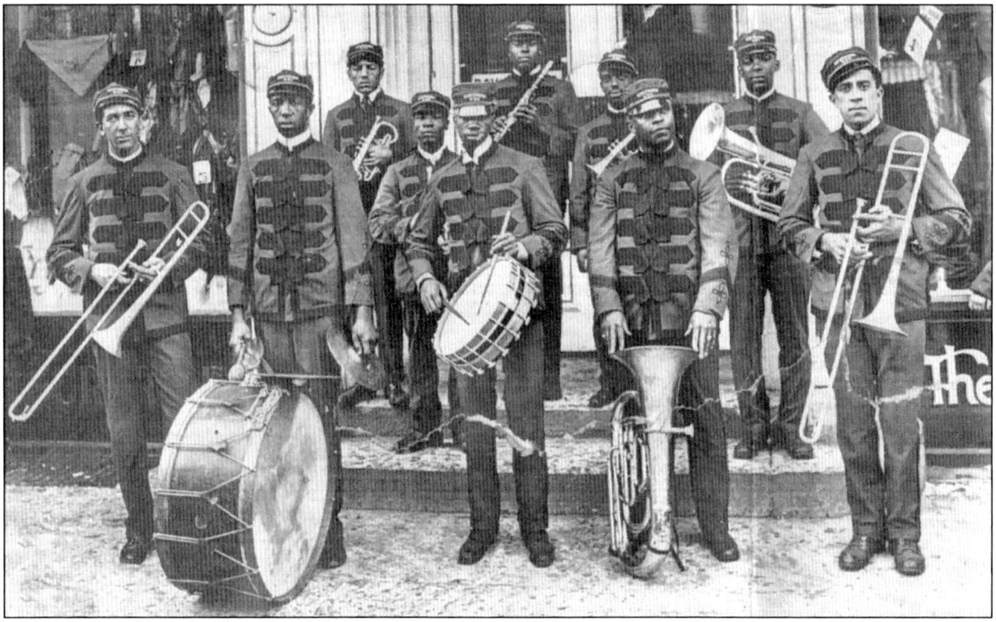

One of the organizers of this band was "Bunt" Jackson, pictured holding the trombone in the first row on the right. This African American band performed in Charles Town in the 1920s. The formation of African American bands was often dependent upon finances. In the case of this band, it could not only afford the instruments but the uniforms as well, which shows dedication and devotion to music.

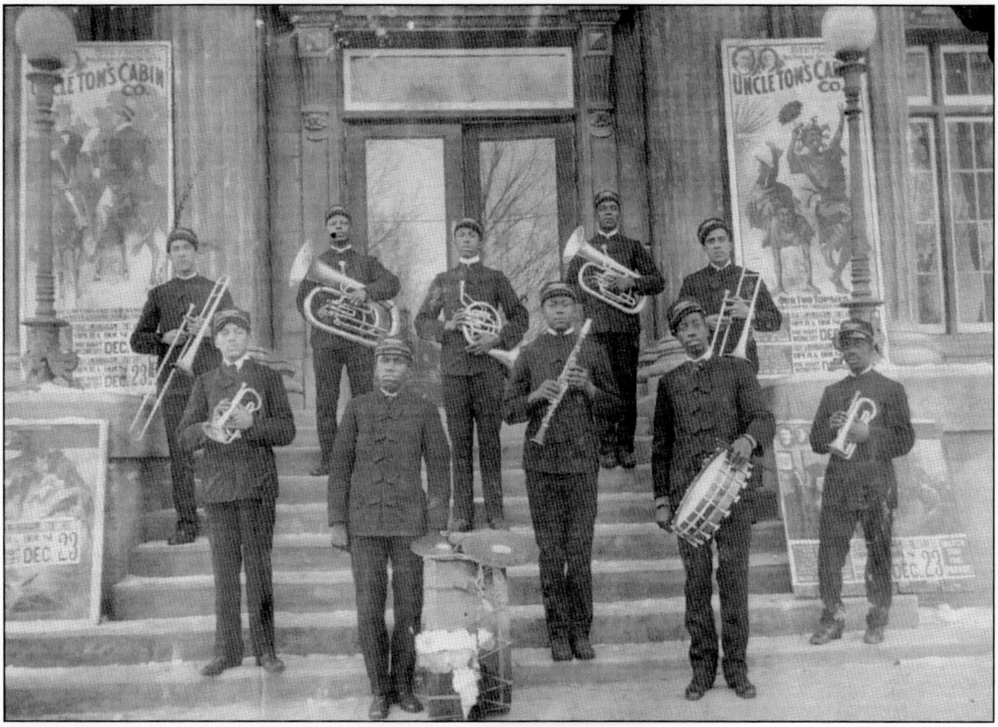

This picture probably dates from the early 1900s. There appear to be 10 members in this band. They are standing proudly, wearing their uniforms and holding their instruments. It is very likely these musicians were self-taught. If they had been to school, it is doubtful they were taught to play the instruments in school.

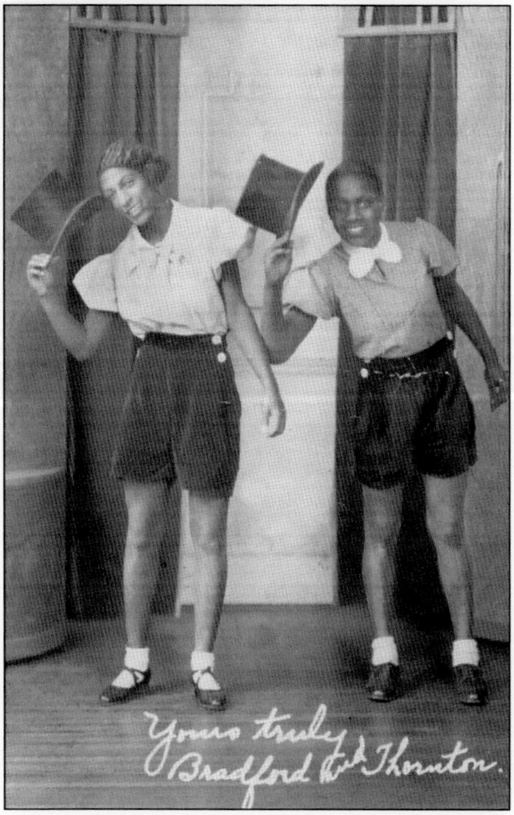

Alyce Bradford Braxton and Cordell Thornton Bradford are shown here dancing at the Fishermen's Hall Lodge located on South West Street in Charles Town. The two dancers would later become sisters-in-law. Various acts throughout the area performed on the Fishermen's Hall stage over the years.

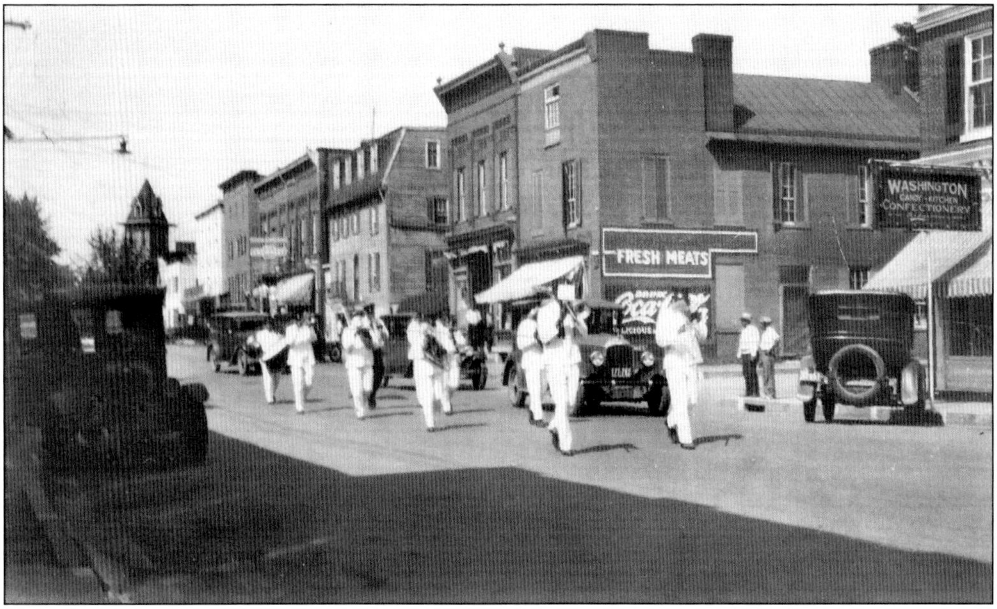

J. Wesley Tolbert's band marches proudly down the street in this photograph from the early 1920s. The band consisted of only black members. The exact parade date is unknown, but it was in the 1920s.

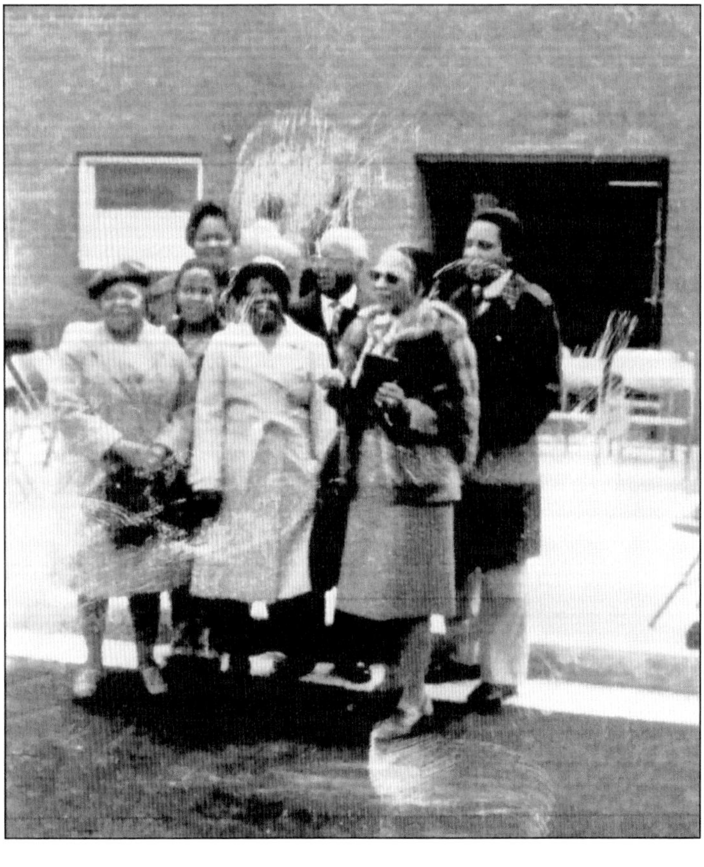

In January 1984, the "Page-Jackson Room" at the Jefferson County Board of Education in Charles Town was dedicated. A tree was planted and a marker placed to honor the former students. The building today houses the offices of the Jefferson County Board of Education and is located on Mordington Avenue/Page-Jackson Way. Pictured are former county teachers Marion Johnson Reeler (first row, far left) and Goldie Kemp Johnson (first row, far right).

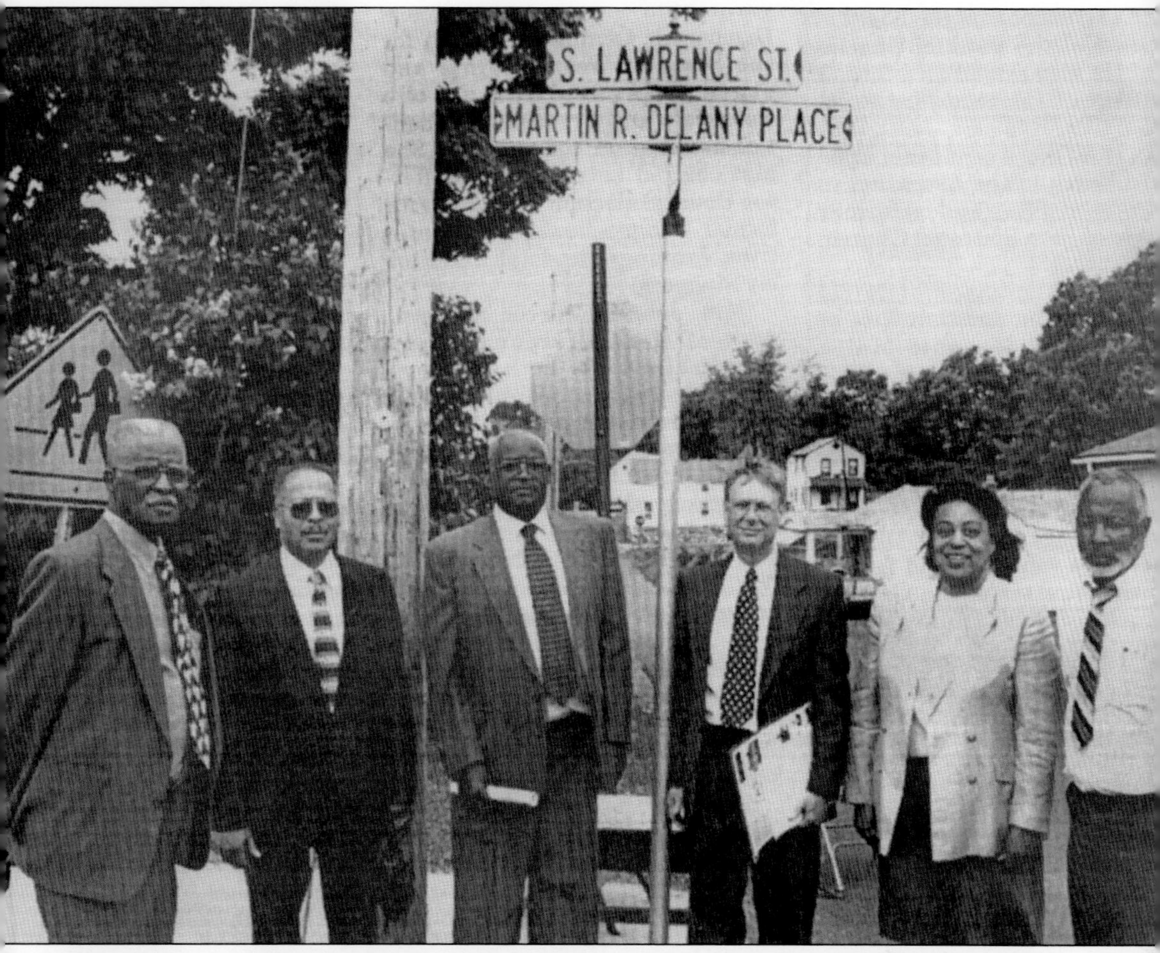

During the annual Founder's Day Celebration in Charles Town, the City of Charles Town added the sub-name "Martin R. Delany Place" to Lawrence Street. The event was hosted by the Jefferson County Black History Preservation Society. Shown from left to right are Nathaniel Downing, James Tolbert, James L. Taylor, Mayor Randy Hilton, Evelyn M. E. Taylor, and George Rutherford. Martin R. Delany was a famed black leader who was commissioned a major in the Civil War.

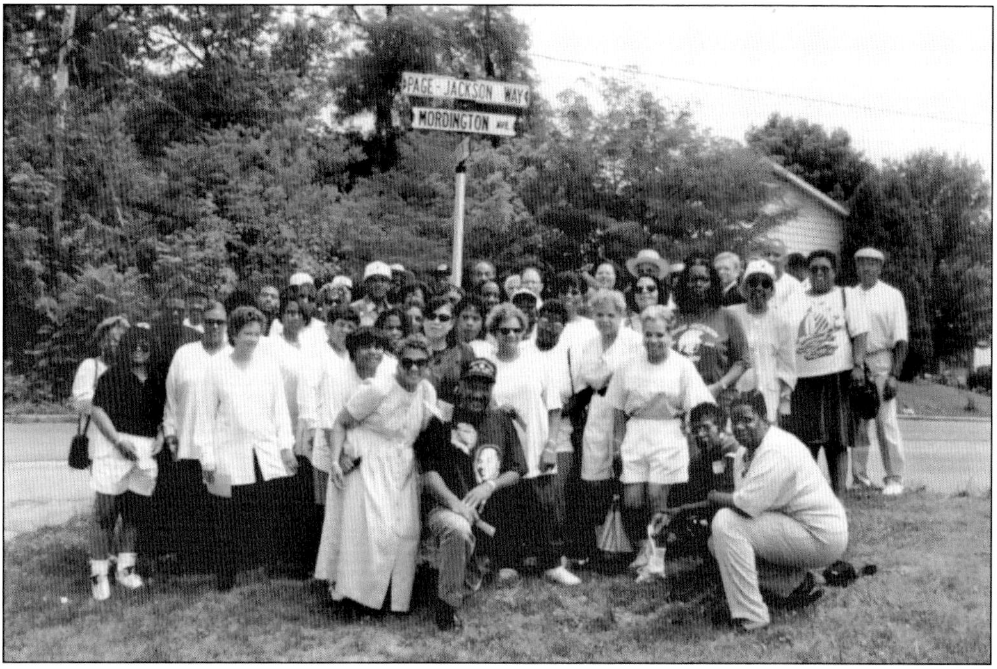

Pictured is the commemoration of the dedication of Page-Jackson Way, named after Littleton Lorton Page and Philip Jackson, who were influential and important in the early education of black students in the county. Page, born into slavery, became a principal and teacher at the Eagle Avenue School for 40 years. In 1887, Jackson was appointed to be Page's assistant. Page retired for health reasons, and Jackson assumed the position of principal and remained there until his death in 1937.

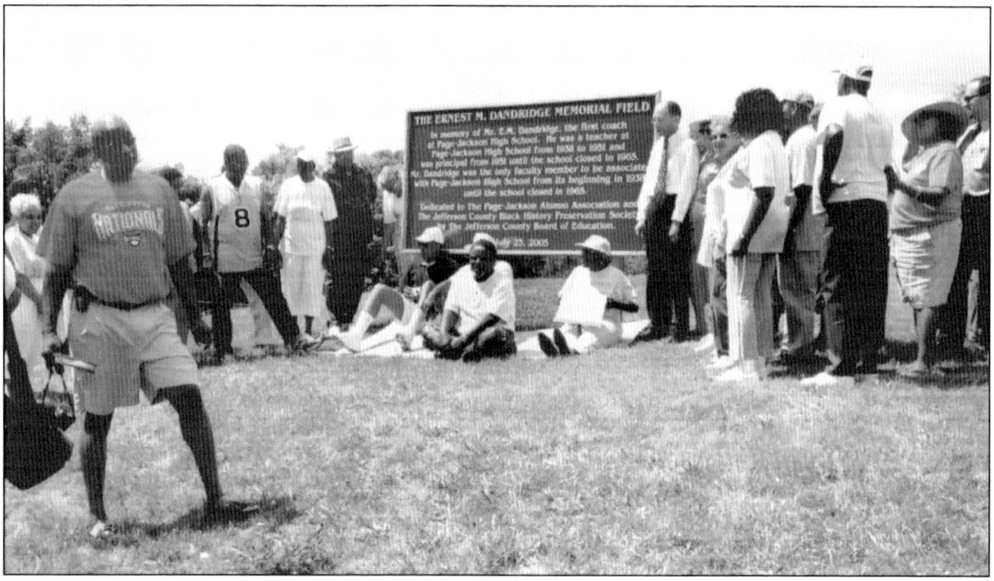

On July 23, 2005, the Ernest M. Dandridge Memorial Field was dedicated to the memory of E. M. Dandridge, the first coach of Page-Jackson High School. From 1938 to 1951, he served as a teacher and principal. From the school's beginning in 1938 until it closed in 1965, Dandridge was the only faculty member associated with the school for the entire time of its tenure.

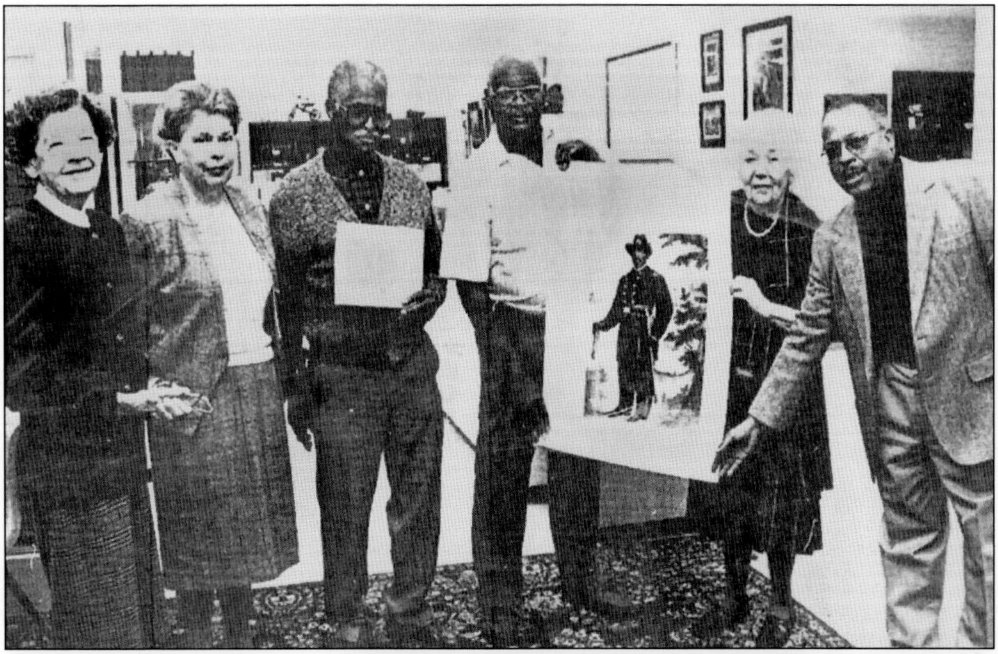

In this 2000 photograph, the Jefferson County Black History Preservation Society presents a portrait of Maj. Martin Robison Delany to the Jefferson County Museum in Charles Town. Pictured from left to right are Bettie Byrer, Sue Collins, Nathaniel Downing Sr., James Taylor, Mrs. J. Blackwell Davis, and James Tolbert.

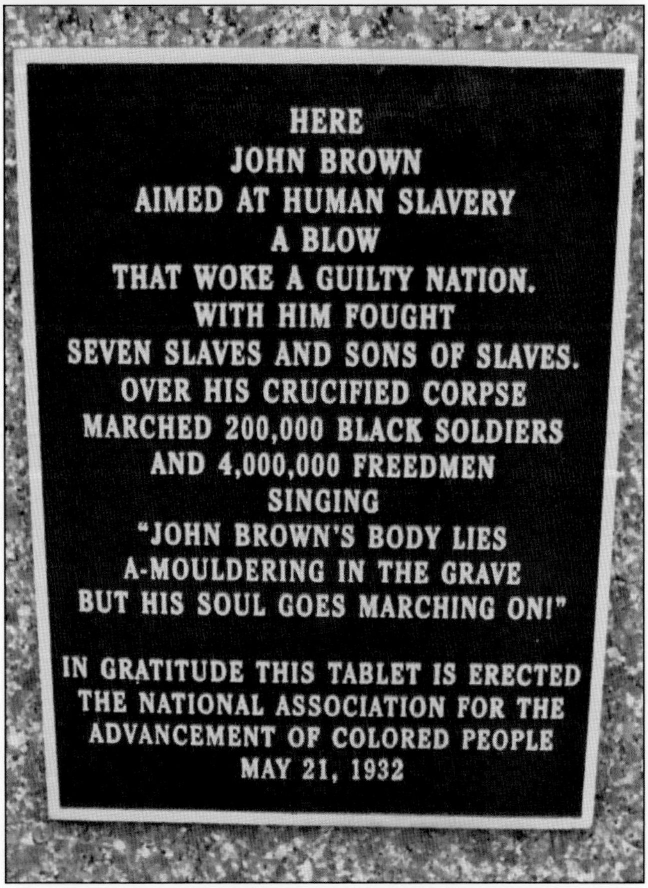

Pictured here is "The Great Tablet." The "Great Tablet" was erected on the former Storer College campus in July 2006. It had been refused for erection by the college in 1932 because it was thought that the placement of the tablet would cause social unrest. A pilgrimage from the NAACP's 97th-annual convention meeting in Washington, D.C., traveled to Harpers Ferry by train to erect the tablet in 2006.

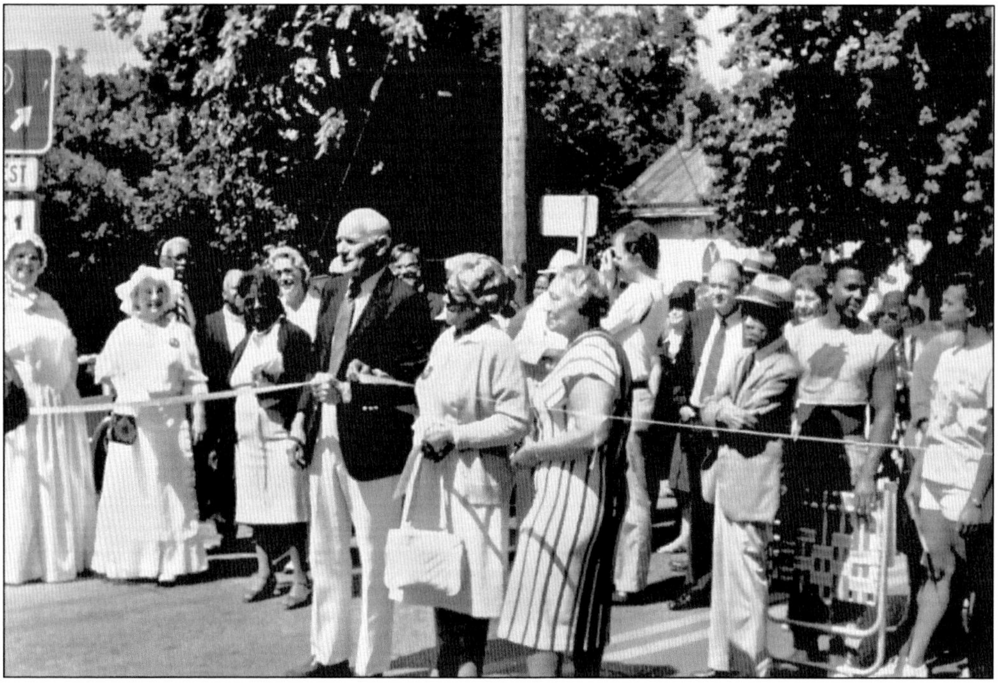

This monumental event shows dignitaries cutting the ribbon during the designation of "Dr. Martin Luther King Jr. Boulevard" in Charles Town. Three people are shown cutting the ribbon. Wearing the dark sport coat is D. C. Master, who was the mayor of Harpers Ferry. To the right of him is Susan Winston, to the left is Ollie Tolbert, and Audrey Morris is on the far right. Guests and spectators look on.

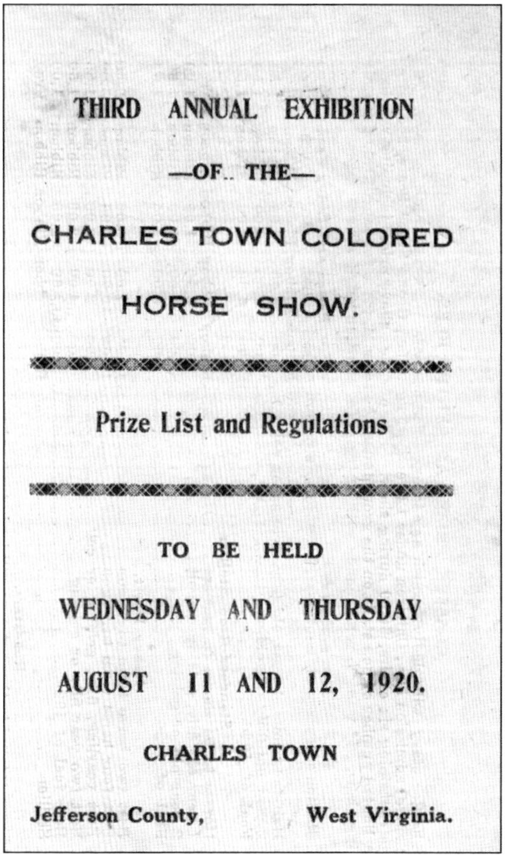

THIRD ANNUAL EXHIBITION

—OF.. THE—

CHARLES TOWN COLORED

HORSE SHOW.

Prize List and Regulations

TO BE HELD

WEDNESDAY AND THURSDAY

AUGUST 11 AND 12, 1920.

CHARLES TOWN

Jefferson County, West Virginia.

This is a copy of the program of the Colored Horse Show, held in Charles Town. Jefferson County was the only one in the country to offer a "Colored" horse show. It was chartered by the West Virginia secretary of state. The program for the show offered advertisements for local black businesses, such as Rideoutt Brothers (Cleaning, Pressing, and Dyeing), James Bradford (Good Eats), Chas. F. Payne (Payne's Cleaning and Pressing Shop), and William Williams (Home Cooking Restaurant).

Six

SOCIAL AND FRATERNAL ORGANIZATIONS

Most African Americans in Jefferson County feel the desire and need of belonging. Joining organizations fulfills this need. It is stated that this sense of need stems from the days of slavery when families were split and divided to never unite again. The joining of groups provided not only comfort but also encouragement and security. Groups varied, such as all boys or girls or all men or women.

In Jefferson County, the main youth group was the all-black Boy Scout troop that was widely supported by the parents, schools, churches, and the community.

The female groups included the Modern Maids and Matrons, the Jolly 15, the Zenith Club, the Loyal Ladies, and the Eureka Club. These were social clubs that met at different members' homes. They played games, planned social activities, and provided support to various activities in the black community. The Jolly 15 and the Zenith Club are still in existence today.

The prominent men's fraternal organization is the Prince Hall Masons. The first black Masonic lodge was organized in Charles Town in 1877. The lodge still operates today and is located in the historic Locke House located on South Lawrence Street/Martin R. Delany Way. The lodge hall serves as the community center for the black community. Many community groups, such as the all-black Marshall Holley Mason American Legion Post No. 102, use the lodge hall as their home and meeting place.

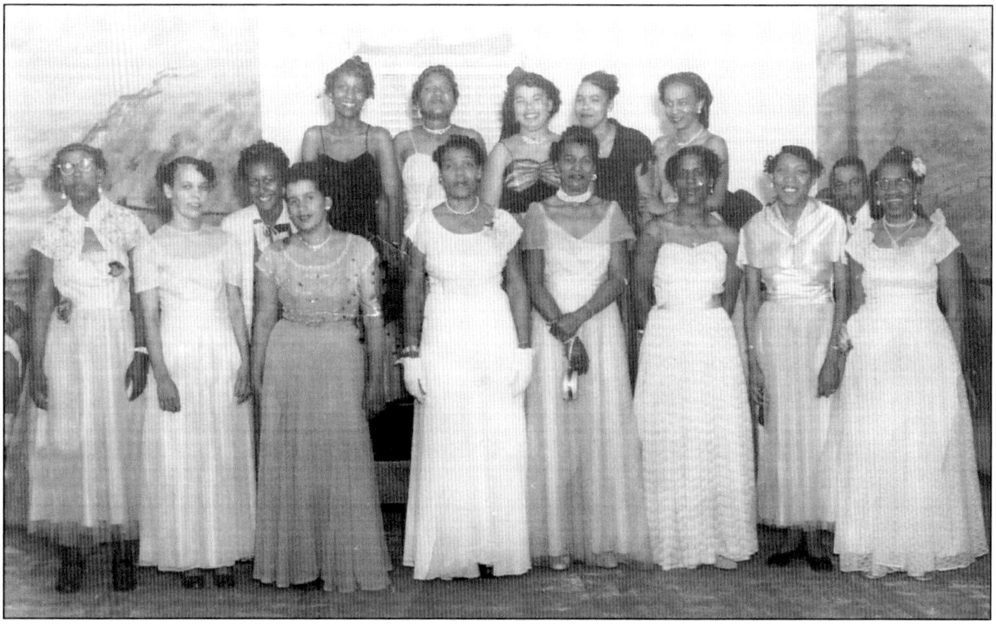

The Jolly 15 Club was organized in Kearneysville in 1949 with 15 members, and the club continues to meet today. In alphabetical order are Elsie Campbell, Naomi Carey, Selena Carter, Odell Clinton, Pauline Creamer, Annie Bell Ferguson, Fannie Hazelton, Hattie Bell Lee, Lucy Mason, Genevieve Ross, Marie Ross, Mary Twyman, Sara Walker, and Alice Washington. Not pictured is Theodisia McDowell. The man is unidentified.

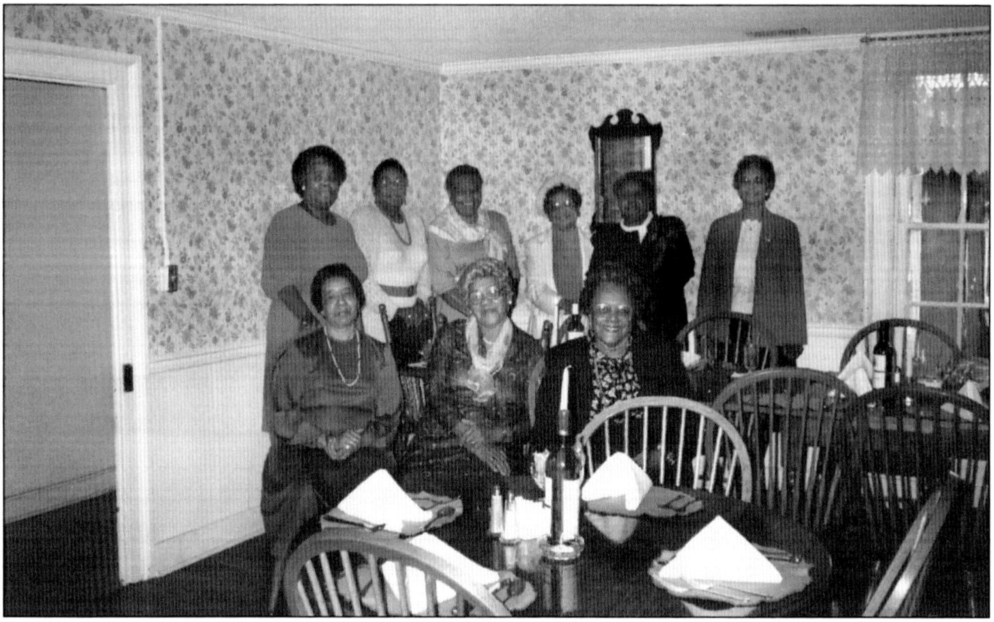

The Modern Maids and Matrons club was organized in Charles Town in 1946. From left to right are (seated) Dorothy Newman Clark, Ollie Lightfoot Tolbert, and Andrea Ewing Lewis. In the back row in alphabetical order are Vivian Heming, Margaret Grantham, Barbara King, Irma Snowden Patrick, and Betty Daniels Roper. Many social clubs were formed during the 1940s and 1950s because African Americans were not welcome in white groups.

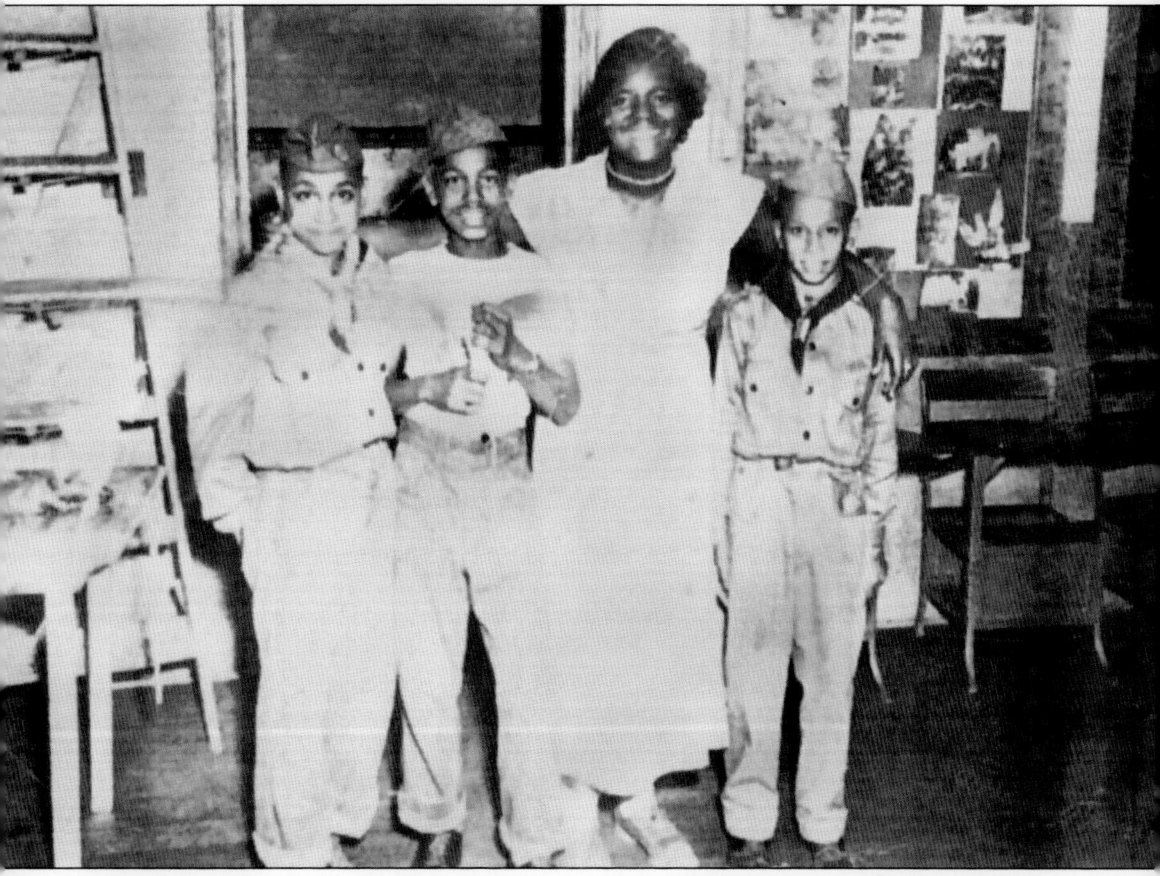

Pictured here is Mary Taylor Doakes, then an 11th grader at Page-Jackson High School. The boys are, from left to right, Randolph Johnson, Alfred Baylor, and Mervin Baylor, all members of Boy Scout Troop No. 31. E. M. Dandridge was the troop scoutmaster when this photograph was taken in 1952. Doakes went on to become a principal at Charles Town Junior High School.

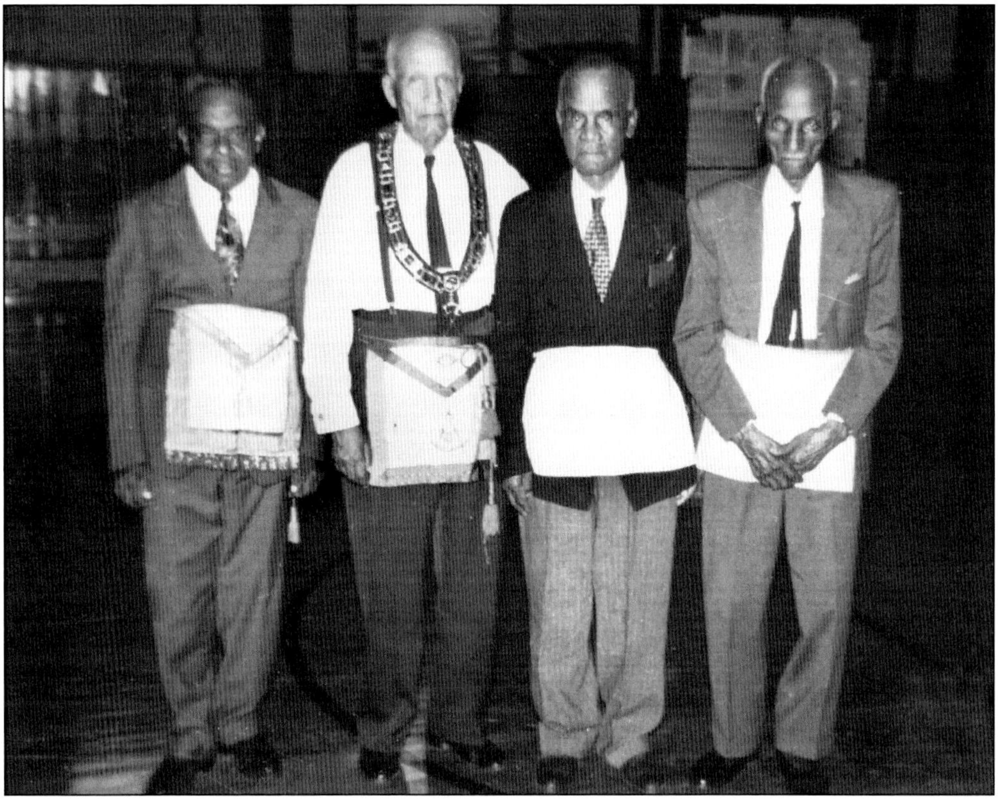

J. Frank Briscoe (second from left in this photograph), past master of Mount Pisgah No. 3 Lodge, West Virginia, meets with the senior members of the Star Lodge No. 1, Charles Town, in Martinsburg, West Virginia. From left to right are Charles Ross, J. Frank Briscoe, Lewis Rutherford, and J. Wesley Tolbert.

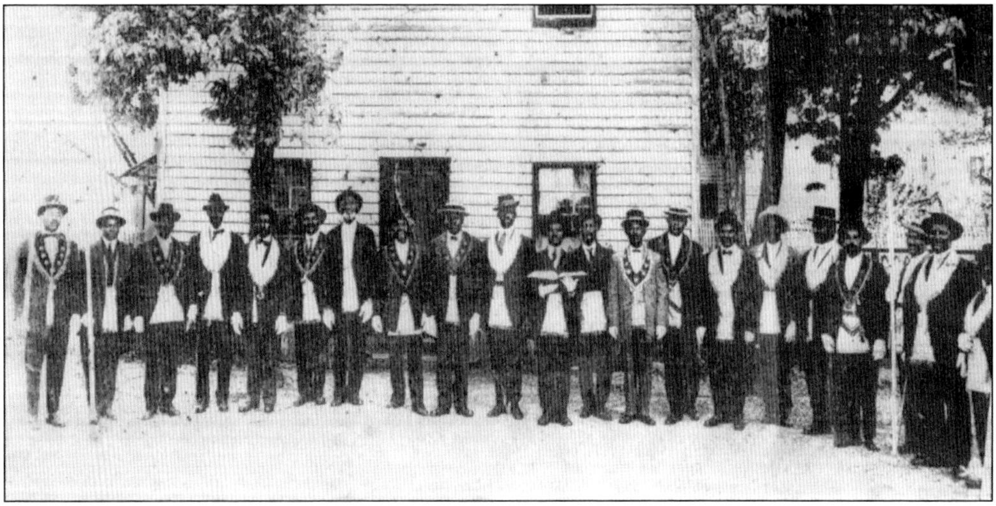

Pictured are the members of the Star Lodge No. 1 Prince Hall Masons, located at the intersection of East Liberty and South Seminary Streets in Charles Town. This photograph was taken in 1915. The house was the residence of Blanche Rutherford Jones, since demolished. The home of Mrs. Charles Baylor is now on the site.

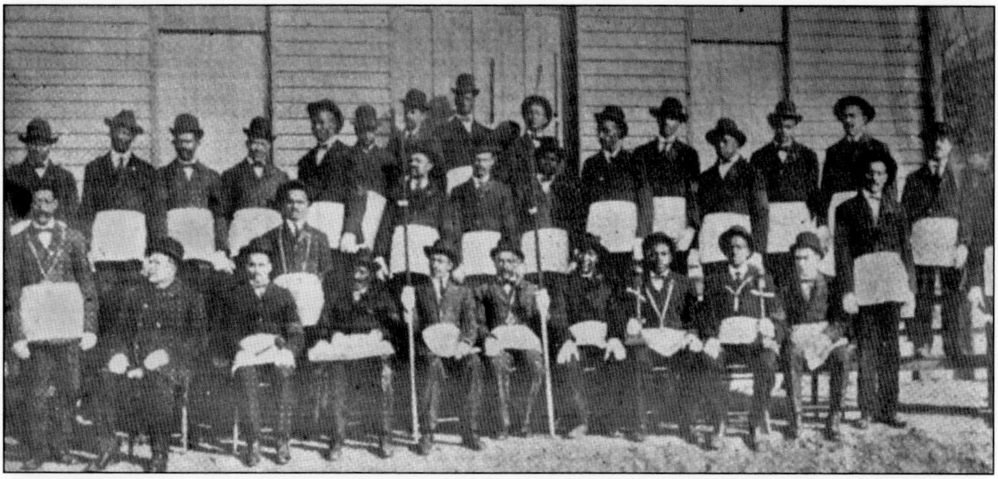

Star Lodge No. 1 Prince Hall Masons are shown at Fishermen's Hall, South West Street, around 1900. In no identified order are Thomas Young, Dan Carey, Tom Bailey, Louis Hill, Tom Nelson, Charles Snowden, Sam Dotson, J. Wesley Tolbert, Adam Taylor, Sam Galloway, Bunt Jackson, Charles R. Ross Sr., S. D. Taylor, James Twyman, William Ross, David Carey, Peter Brooks, Charles A. Ross, Ed Twyman, Sam Tucker, Earl Johnson, L. L. Page, and George Washington.

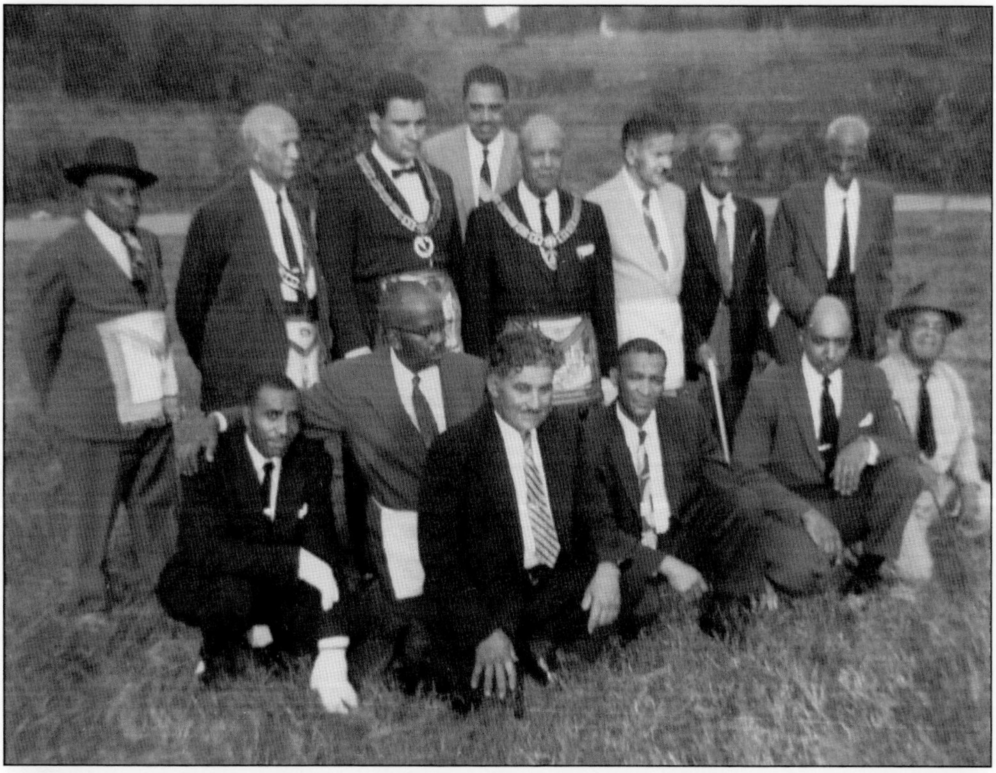

Pictured around 1951 are the Star Lodge No. 1, Free and Accepted Masons, along with the West Virginia Grand Lodge Officers, laying the cornerstone for Page-Jackson High School. From left to right are (first row) John Craig, Perry Arter, unidentified, George Mitchell, Herman Gaskin, and John Smith; (second row) Charles Ross, J. Frank Briscoe, Everett Barnett, Charles Taper Jr., Charles Taper Sr., unidentified, Lewis Rutherford, and J. Wesley Tolbert.

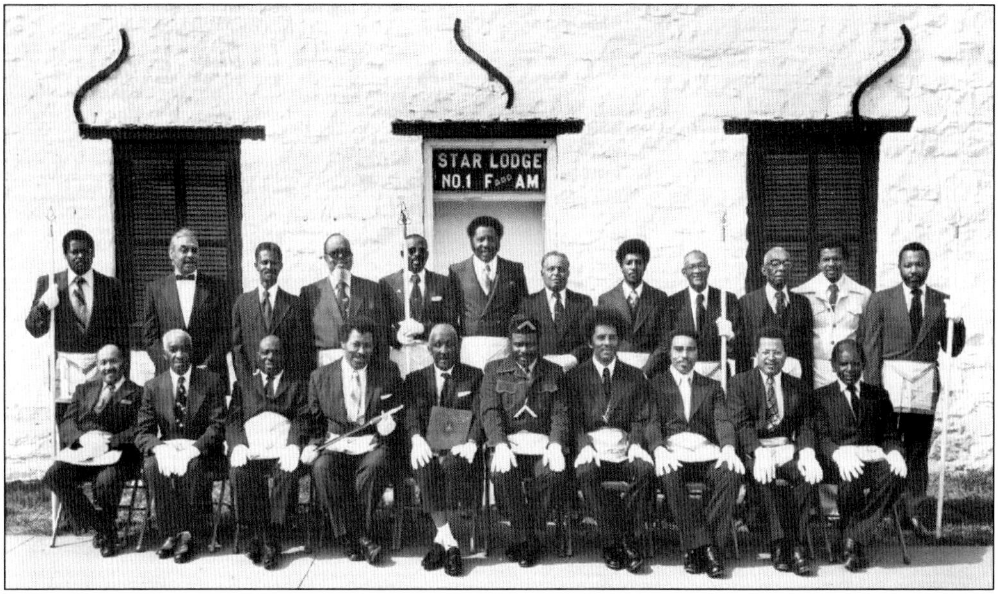

On Sunday, March 27, 1977, the Masons in Charles Town were, from left to right, (first row) James W. Nickens, Earl Edwards, Isaiah Allen, William Tolbert, Kelly Head, Daniel D. Jackson, Calvin L. Togans, Charles L. Newman, James A. Tolbert, and Philip Coley; (second row) James L. Taylor, Charles Baylor, Nathaniel F. Downing, Oscar D. Reeler, James Ford, Millard Dotson, Harry Green, Larry R. Creamer, George Mitchell Sr., George R. Rutherford Sr., Ernest Yates, and George C. Rutherford.

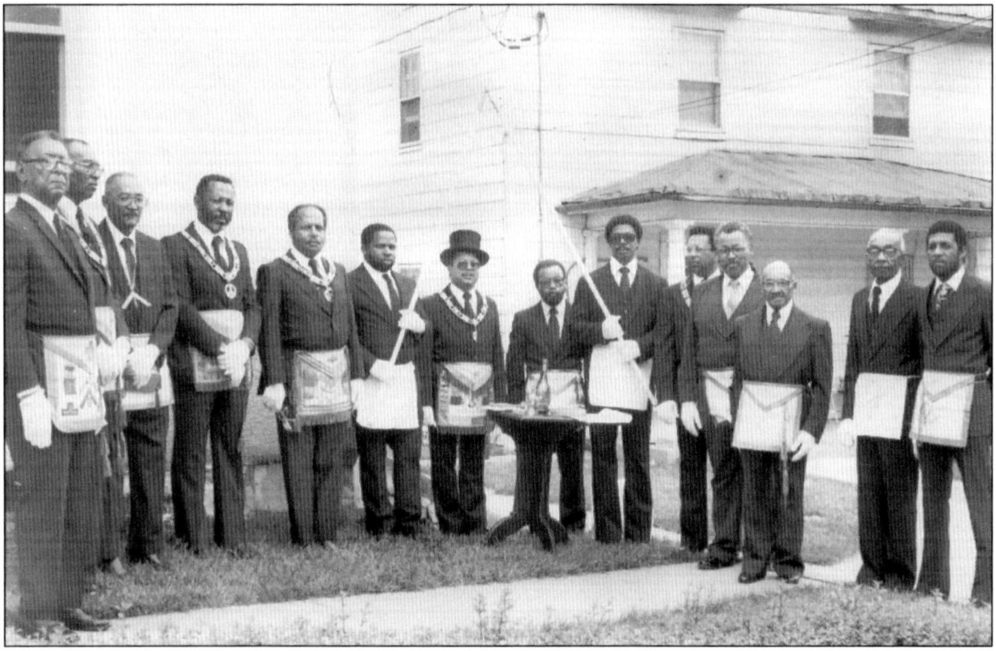

The event here is the 1984 re-laying of the cornerstone at St. Philip's Episcopal Church in Charles Town. From left to right are William Taylor, Charles Ferguson, George Mitchell, George C. Rutherford, Richard Burrell, James Brown, James Tolbert, Reginald Roper, Joseph Pinkcott, Harold Stewart, William Tolbert, James Nickens, George H. Rutherford, and Larry Creamer.

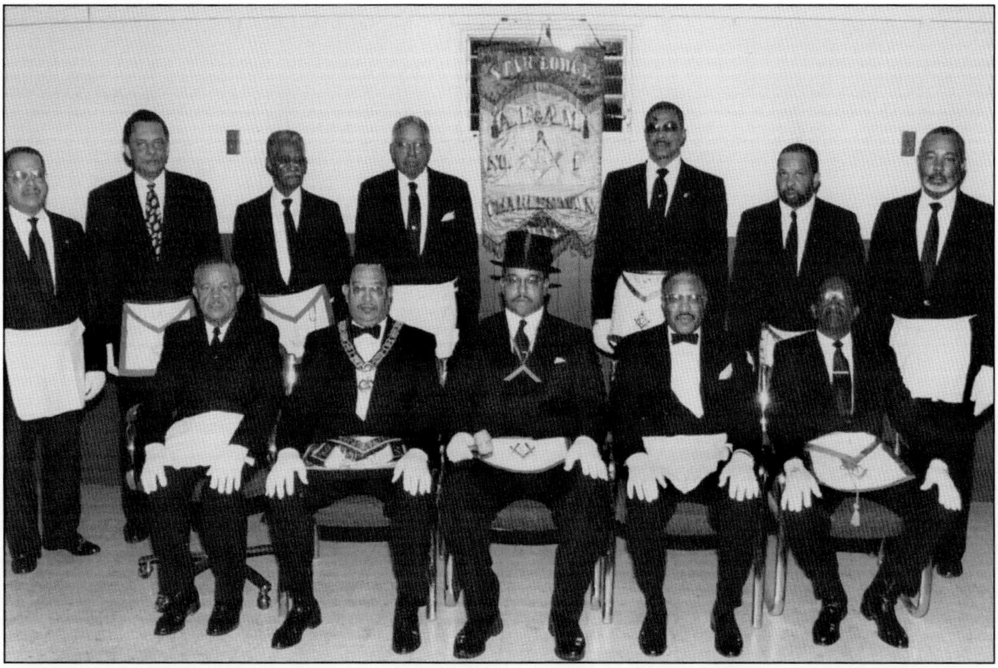

In this 1990s photograph are the Star Lodge No. 1 Masons at the lodge hall. From left to right are (first row) Claude Stanton, Harold Stewart, Warren Stewart, John Stevenson, and Alfred Twyman; (second row) James Tolbert, Larry Togans, Nathaniel Downing, Elvin Thomas, Joseph Pinkcett, James Brown, and George Rutherford.

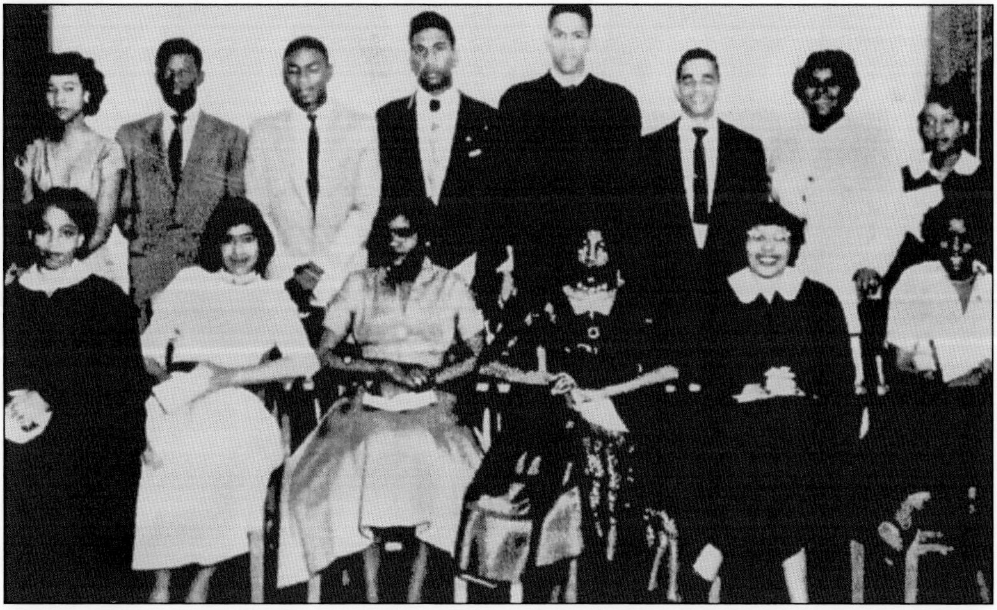

This c. 1953 photograph, taken at Storer College, is from the Dorothy Taylor Collection. It shows students who just received an award. From left to right are (first row) unidentified, Dorothy Young Taylor, Kathryn Jackson Norton, unidentified, Sylvia Spriggs Taylor, and Margaret Jackson Smelly; (second row) Lois Payne, five unidentified, Mary Taylor Doakes, and unidentified. All of the students identified are local Jefferson County students.

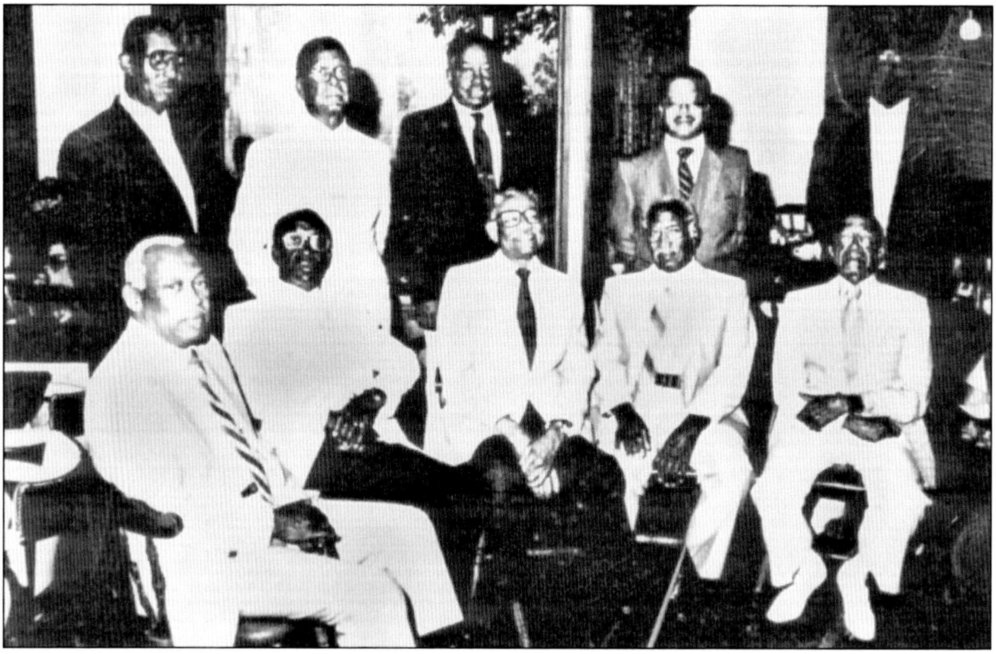

Pictured here is the Zenith Club of Jefferson County, West Virginia. From left to right are (seated) Q. D. Fleming Sr., Alfred Twyman Sr., Paul Austin, Edward Braxton, and James Hall; (standing) Charles L. Ferguson, William P. Taylor, Elvin Thomas, James A. Tolbert, and Lester Taylor. The Zenith Club was a social club for African American men in the county.

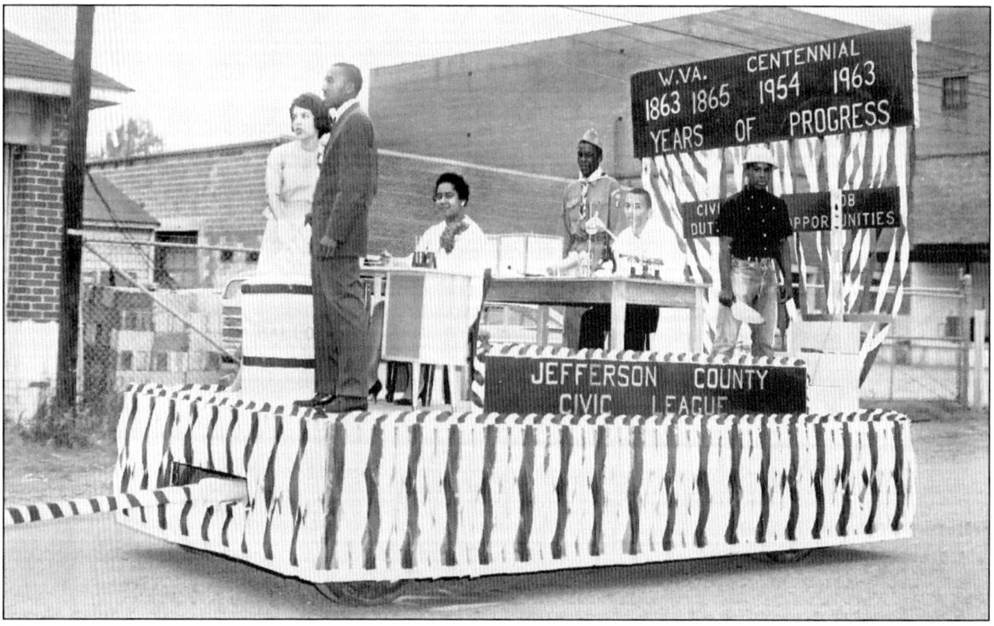

The Jefferson County Civic League float is pictured here. The float was in a parade celebrating the West Virginia centennial. Six people can be seen riding on the float, one of whom is a Boy Scout standing behind the young man wearing the white shirt seated at the table. The dates on the float represent important milestones in the fight for civil rights, starting with 1863 and the Emancipation Proclamation.

Seven

Sports

Sports were an important activity and social event for African Americans in Jefferson County, both for spectators and participants. Communities were able to use sports as "bragging rights." Baseball was probably the earliest and most important sport. Most communities had their own teams, but Shepherdstown had two semipro teams. Games were usually played on Sundays because most of the players worked six days a week.

In the late 1930s and 1940s, football became popular. After World War II, Charles Town had two semipro teams, named the Big Blues and the Homicide Kids.

Jefferson County can also boast that two African Americans played in the National Football League—William Craven with the Cleveland Browns and James Jett with the Oakland Raiders.

Basketball became popular when it was started at Page-Jackson High School in the late 1940s, and later several African Americans from Jefferson County played professional basketball. Larry Carr, William Lindsay, Vance Carr, and Lawrence Bailey were fortunate to play on European teams.

African Americans in Jefferson County found boxing to be very popular. There were both amateur and professional boxers. Many also participated in boxing in the military.

Storer College, which was located in Harpers Ferry, also had athletic teams such as football, basketball, and track.

Another sport enjoyed by many was horse racing. African Americans participated as owners, trainers, and jockeys. The Colored Horse Shows were also a part of the sports world for Jefferson County. In fact, the Charles Town Colored Horse Show was the first of its kind in the country. This was a yearly event and was totally sponsored by the blacks of Jefferson County.

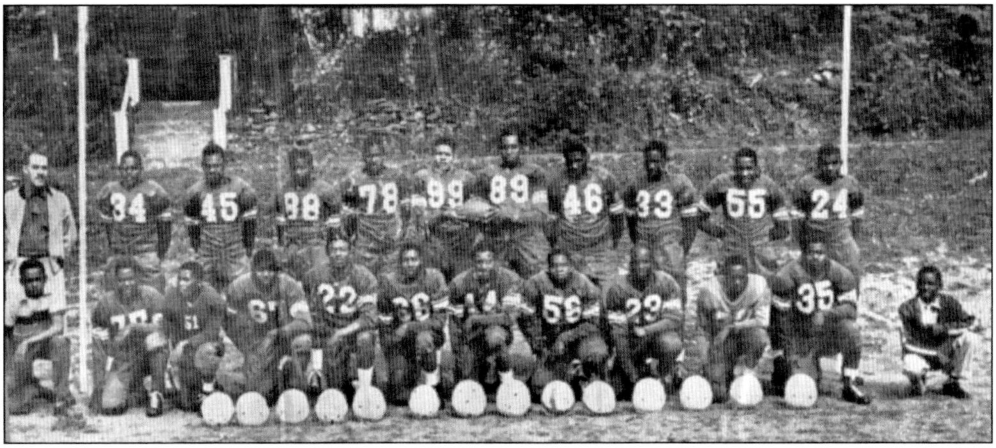

Page-Jackson High School's 1953 football team is shown with 20 team members suited up. Only 14 helmets are lined up in front of the team, which makes one wonder if the members had to take turns. Coach Adam Craven is in the back row on the far left. He was also a coach at Brown University, and Storer College. Later he served as the mayor of Harpers Ferry.

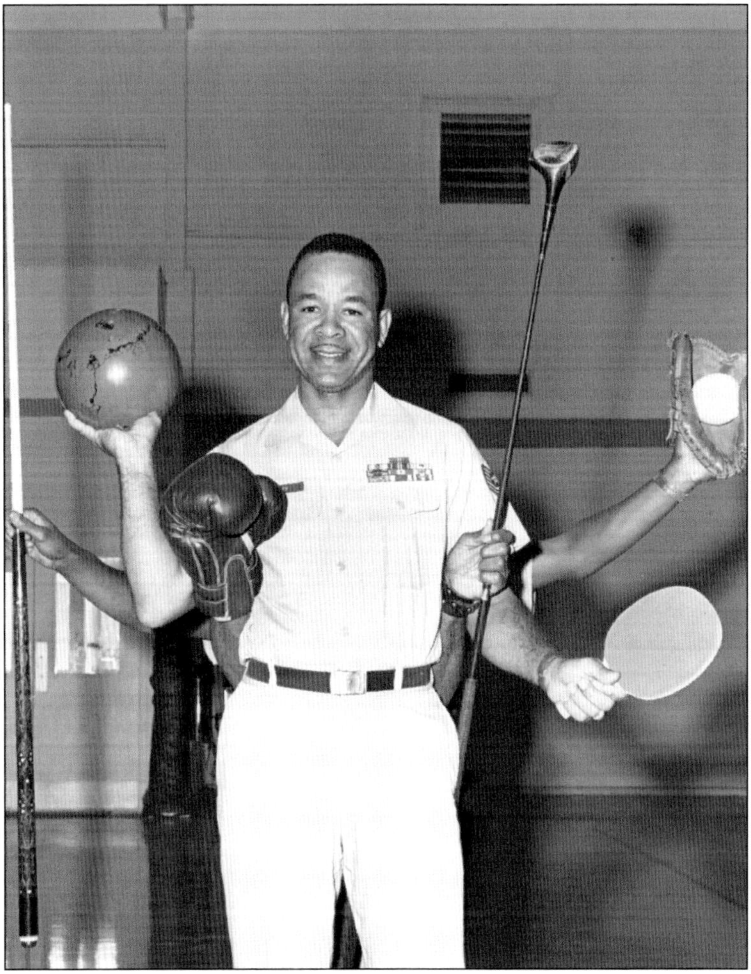

Johnnie Bailey, a graduate from Page-Jackson High in 1952, holds all the equipment of sports in which he excelled. He served in the military and received a Bronze Star. The Bronze Star was established by Executive Order 9419 on February 4, 1944. It is awarded to those who distinguished themselves by heroic or meritorious achievement of service while serving in any capacity with the U.S. Army.

The boys' basketball team of Page-Jackson High School is pictured in the 1960s. Coach Jim Taylor is in the center, top row.

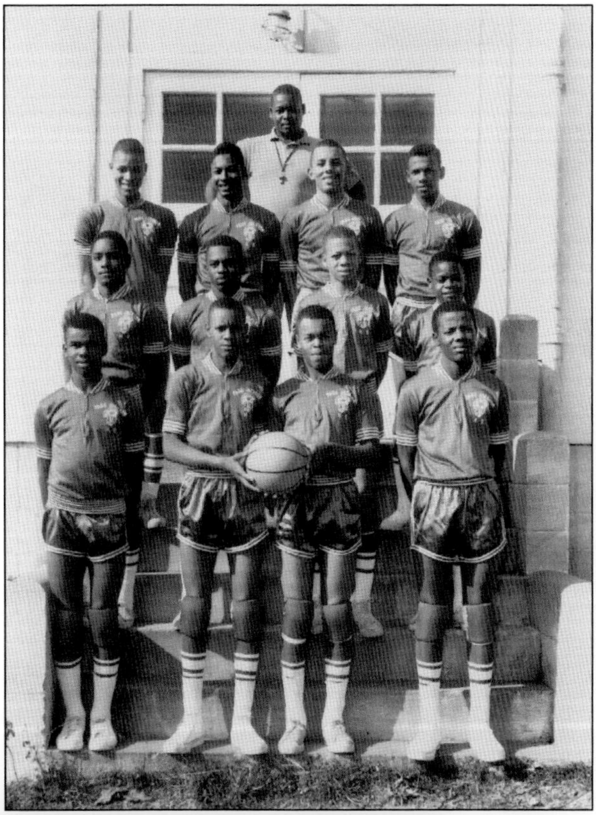

This 1960s photograph shows the Page-Jackson High School boys' basketball team with coach Jim Taylor (first row, left). Taylor was a graduate of Page-Jackson High School in 1951. In addition to coaching, he was also a teacher. He is also a published author, having written *African Americans of the Lower Shenandoah Valley 1700–1900* and *A History of Black Education in Jefferson County, West Virginia 1865–1966*.

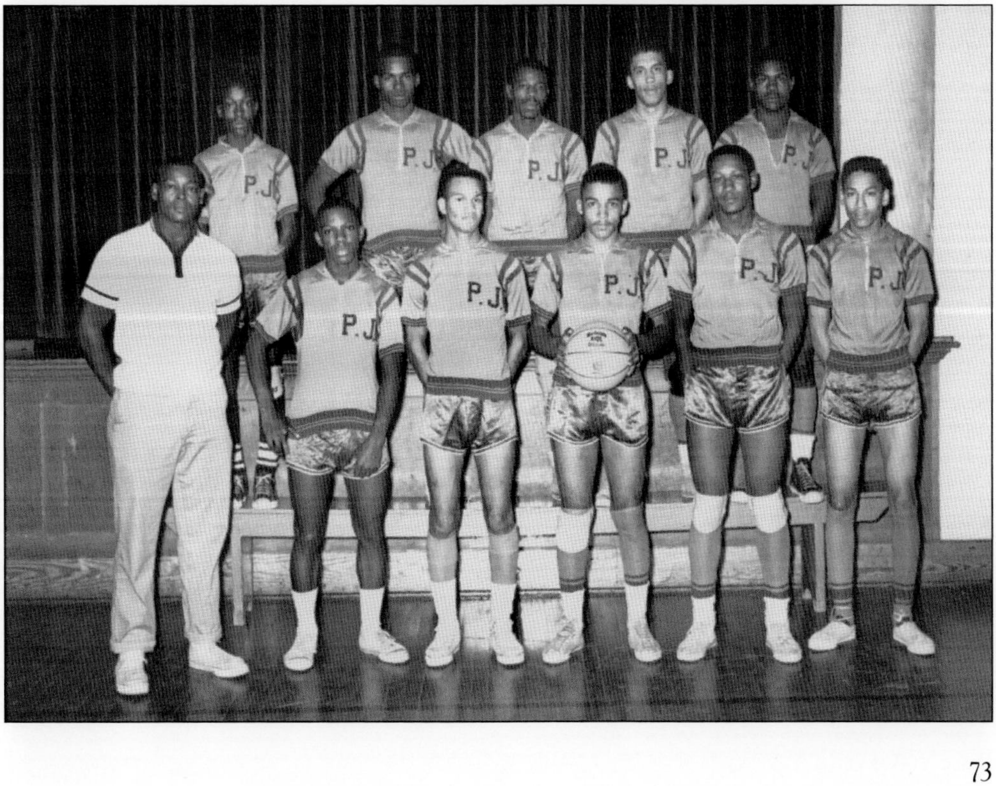

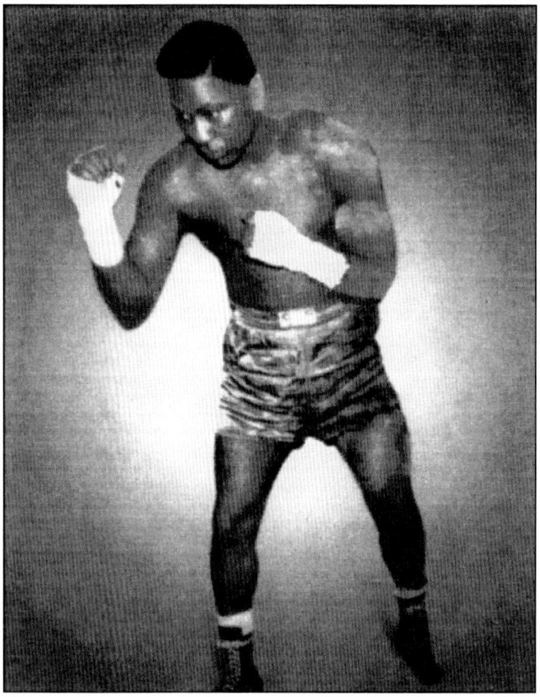

Jackie ("Kid") Harris is pictured here in a boxing pose. His wrists are taped, and he appears ready to take on his opponent. Jackie was a highly regarded international light-heavy to heavyweight professional fighter. His manager was Harry Shephard. He fought in London and the United States. In addition, he was a singer with the Glenn Miller Band. He also attended Page-Jackson High School.

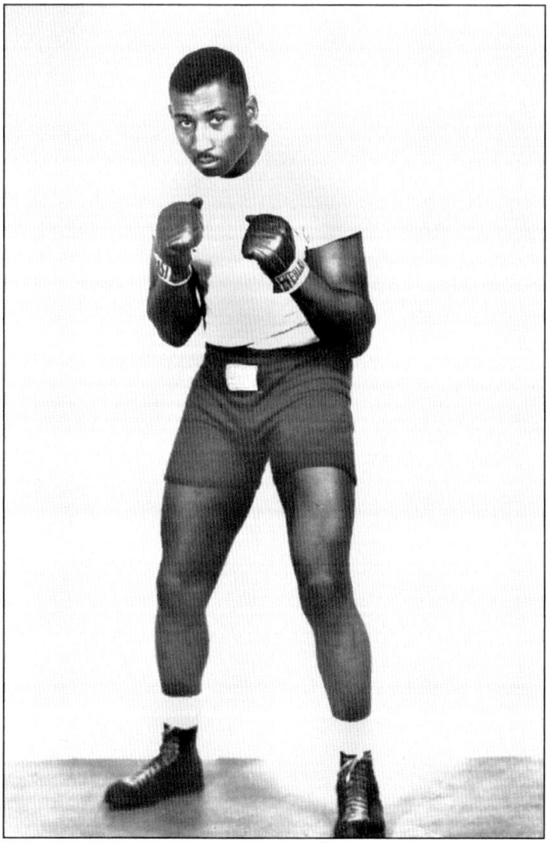

James E. Taylor poses in this photograph from the 1950s. Known as "Jimmy" Taylor and a Page-Jackson High School alumnus from Charles Town, he fought his first fight on a military base in the 1950s and went on to become a professional boxer. He was also listed under the "Owners and Trainers" section of the "Thoroughbred Horse Racing Industry" listing in the *The Black Book*.

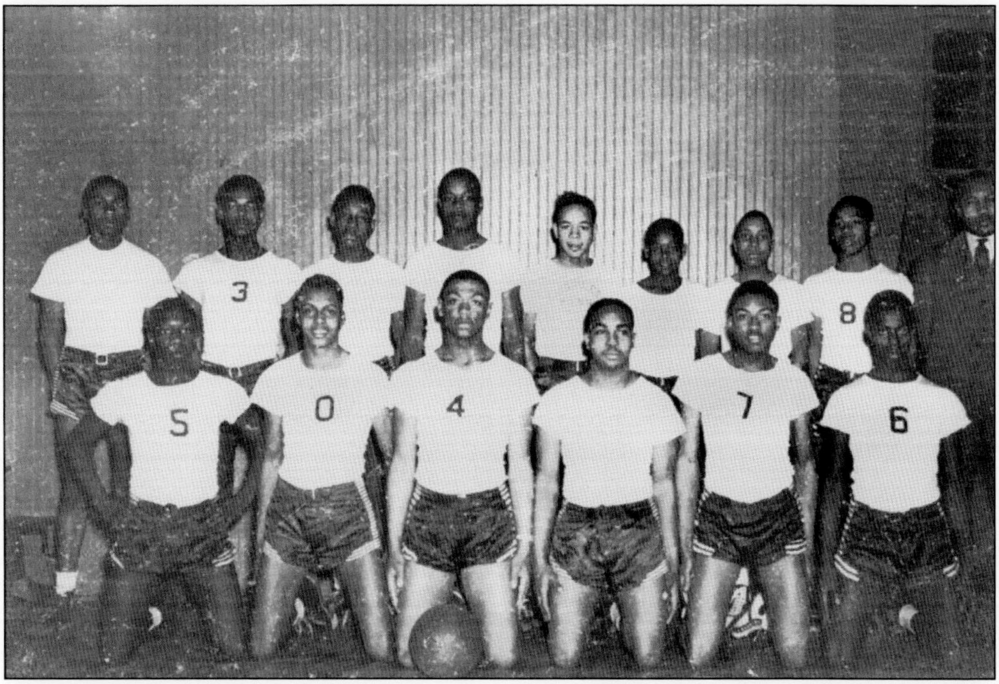

Page-Jackson High School's boys' basketball team poses in this 1947 photograph. These young men comprised the first basketball team for the first all-black high school in the county. The school had graduated its first class in 1942, but it was not until five years later that they had both a basketball coach and the enrollment numbers necessary to begin a basketball team.

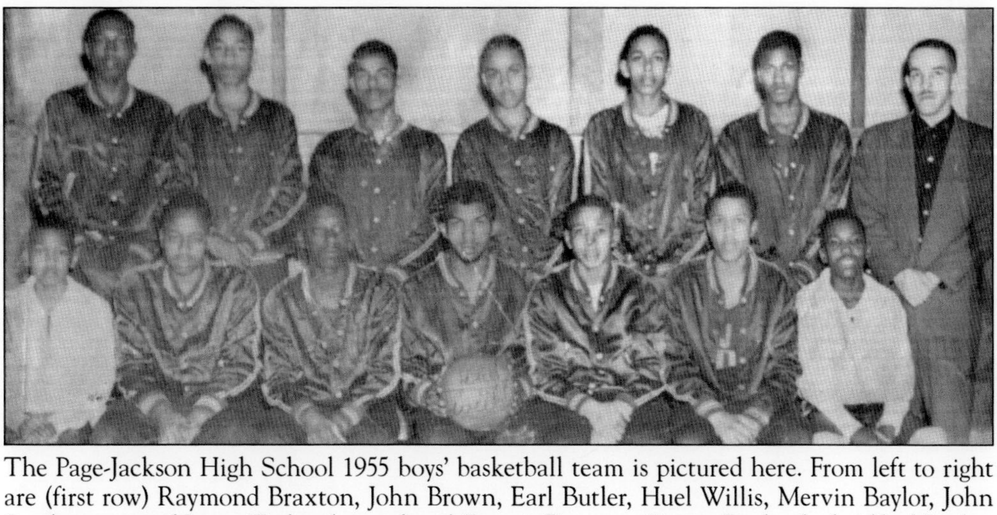

The Page-Jackson High School 1955 boys' basketball team is pictured here. From left to right are (first row) Raymond Braxton, John Brown, Earl Butler, Huel Willis, Mervin Baylor, John Stephenson, and James Taylor; (second row) Francis Braxton, George Rutherford, Alfred Baylor, Randolph Johnson, John Berry, David Newman, and coach Adam Craven.

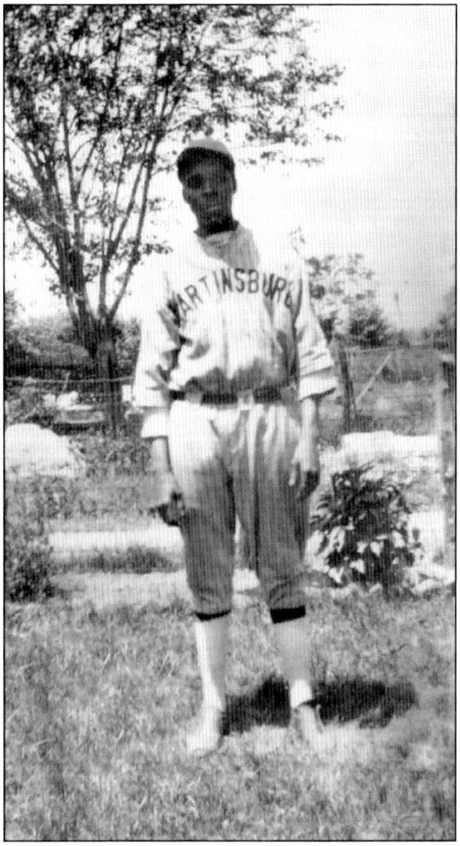

Pictured is Jim Washington, who played for the all-black Martinsburg baseball team. This type of team had been established as early as 1861. Even the sons of Frederick Douglass played ball on amateur teams. The National Baseball Colored League was formed in 1887. A racially mixed team was formed in 1912 by J. L. Wilkinson. The color barrier in Major League Baseball was finally broken by Jackie Robinson in 1947.

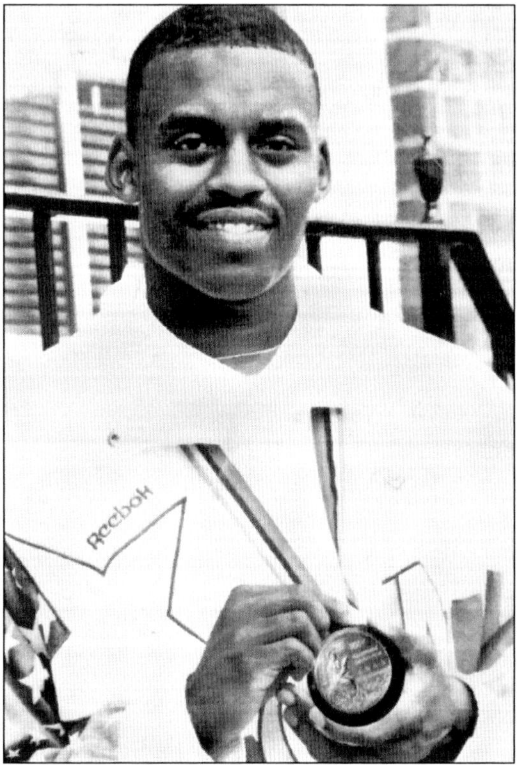

Olympic Gold Medalist James Jett, former Jefferson High School and West Virginia University star athlete, was an All-American Athlete at West Virginia University in track. He was inducted into the West Virginia University Hall of Fame. In Barcelona, Spain, in 1992, he won the Olympic Gold Medal for the 400-meter relay for the United States. He played professional football for the Oakland Raiders in the NFL.

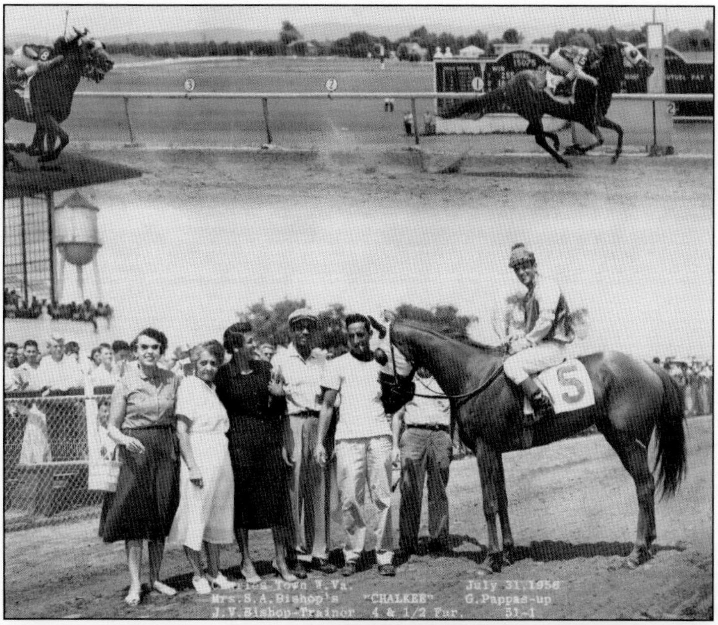

This July 31, 1956, photograph shows Sylvia Rideoutt Bishop (third from left), first African American female Thoroughbred racing trainer in the United States. She is flanked by her sister, Irma Rideoutt Berry, and mother, Bertha Snowden Rideoutt, on her right, and her husband, John Bishop, and John E. Berry, her brother-in-law, on her left. Sylvia Bishop's accomplishment came a long way from the first Charles Town Colored Horse Show in 1917.

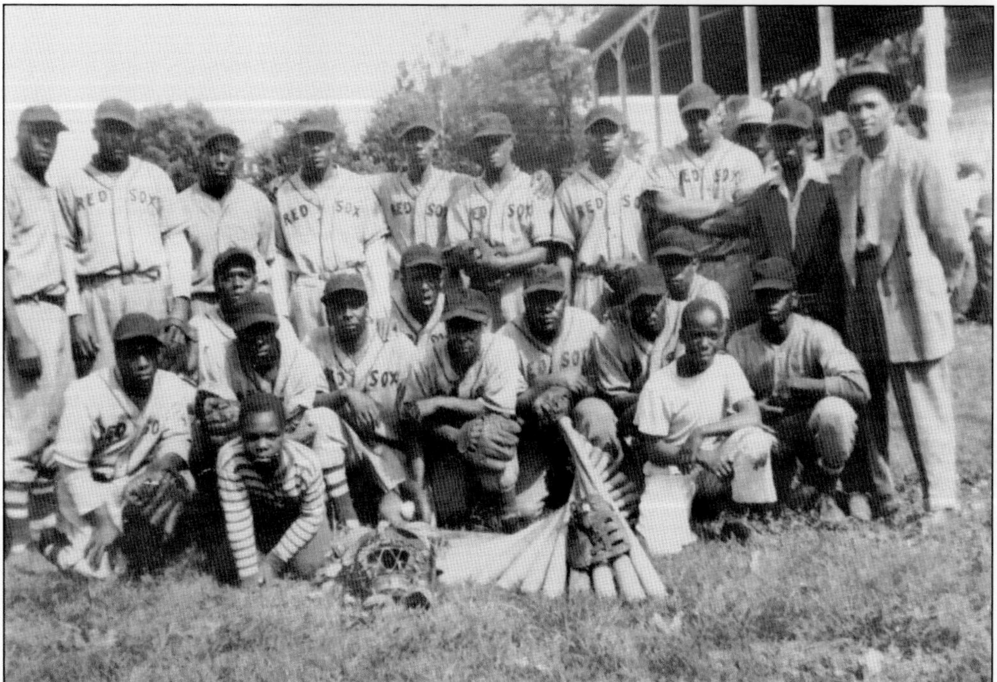

Shepherdstown Red Sox baseball team in 1946 included, from left to right, (first row) Jake Monroe, William Grantham, George Holmes, Mike Swann, and Charles Cook; (second row) King Washington, Tom Brooks, Newton Washington, Charles Washington, and Leslie Clark; (third row) Johnny Washington, Jimmy Brown, Arthur Washington, Pete Washington, Warren Clark, Clarence Holmes, Joe Washington, Buddy Brown, and managers Charles Boyd, Robert Stubbs, and (background) DeWitt Jacobs. Absent were Jackie Boyd, Burton Brown, and batboys Mack Washington and Jim Branson.

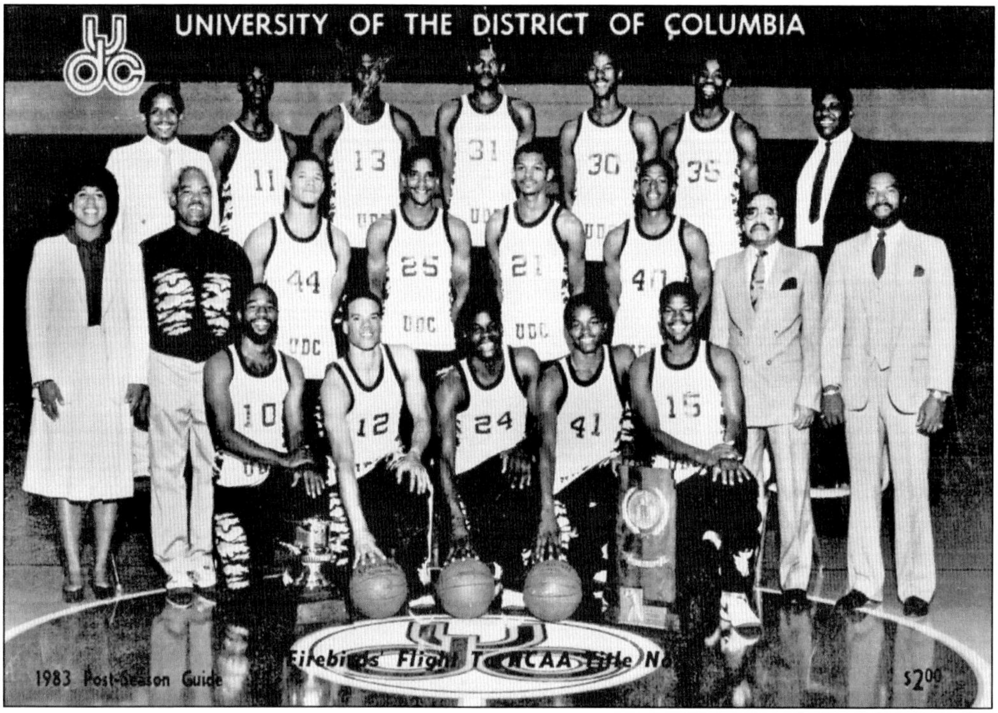

Cheryl Roberts, the first female in the country to serve as an assistant coach on a men's college basketball team, was only 24 years old when she was so designated at the University of District of Columbia. As a first in her profession, she was interviewed on *Good Morning America* twice. In 1960, the year she graduated from West Virginia's Shepherd College; she was also named Outstanding Young Woman in the State of West Virginia.

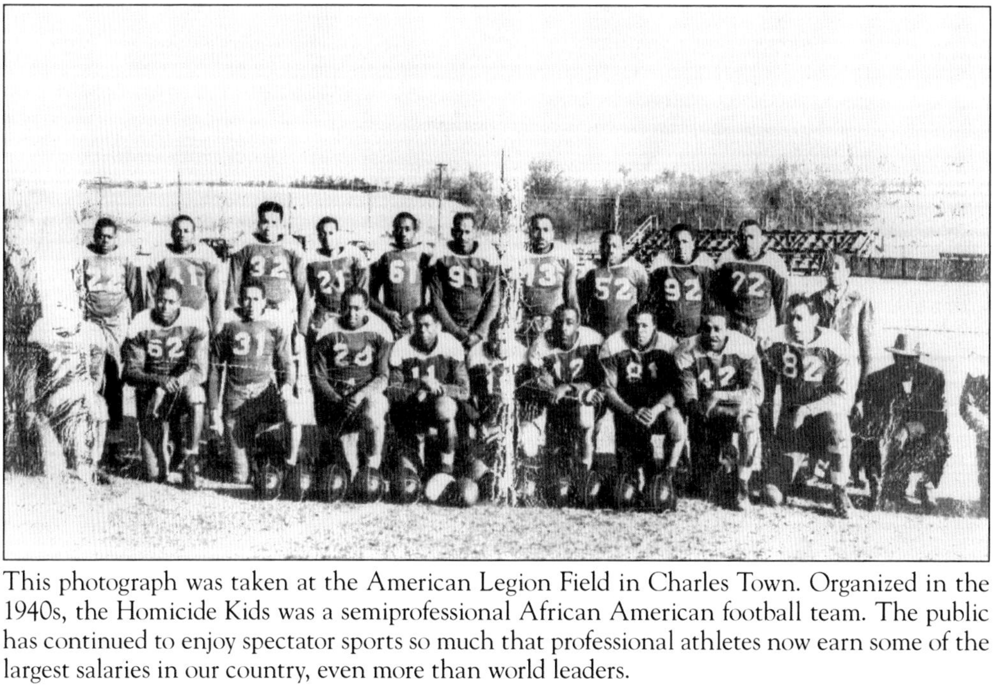

This photograph was taken at the American Legion Field in Charles Town. Organized in the 1940s, the Homicide Kids was a semiprofessional African American football team. The public has continued to enjoy spectator sports so much that professional athletes now earn some of the largest salaries in our country, even more than world leaders.

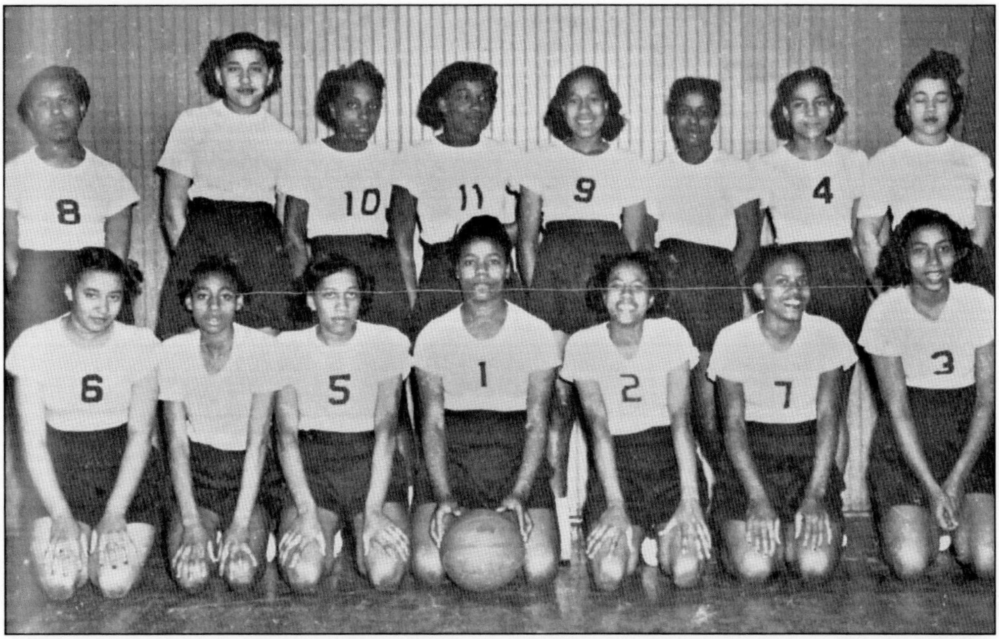

Pictured here is the first girls' basketball team at Page-Jackson High School in 1946. From left to right are (first row) Dorothy Newman, Ella Carr, J. Wesco, Margaret Washington, Ruby Brown, Ollie Robinson, and Dorothy Taylor; (second row) Louise Campbell, Mary Walker, Josephine Butler, Anna Belle Hosby, Mildred Roy, Anna Posey, Corrine Jackson, and Dorothy Davenport.

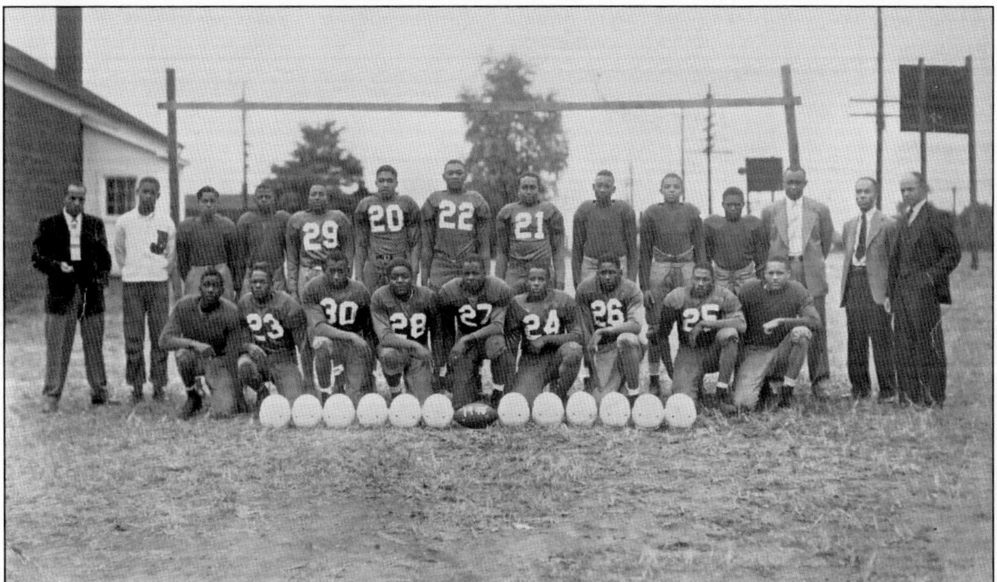

The *c.* 1947 Page-Jackson High football team included, from left to right, (kneeling) George Hosby, Donald Taylor, James E. Taylor, Horald Pinckney, Pinckney Willis, John Brown, Ralph Wilson, Frank Wilson, and Clifford Payne; (standing) George V. King (coach), Wilbur Clinton (manager), Raymond Harris, Ronald Blackwell, Rodye Butler, Willard Jones, Austin Clinton, Lionel Reeler, Thomas Doleman, Maurice Taylor, Richard Strother, Q. D. Fleming (coach), E. M. Dandridge (coach), and Steward Payne (principal).

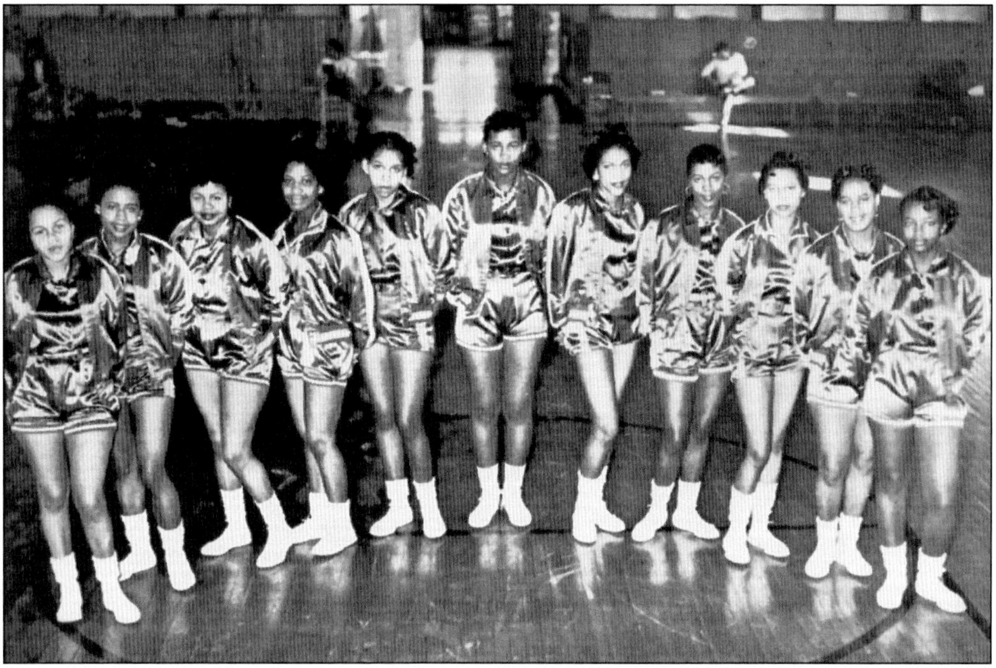

In 1957, the girls' basketball team consisted of these young women. From left to right are Lamour Jackson, Pauline Campbell, Sheila Jackson, Viola Bailey, Ardalia Johnson, Joyce Carr, Brenda Washington, Francine Russ, Morrisey Rutherford, Jean Lee, and Willa Mae Thomas. Many of these girls played on previous or subsequent teams at Page-Jackson High School, proudly wearing the school colors.

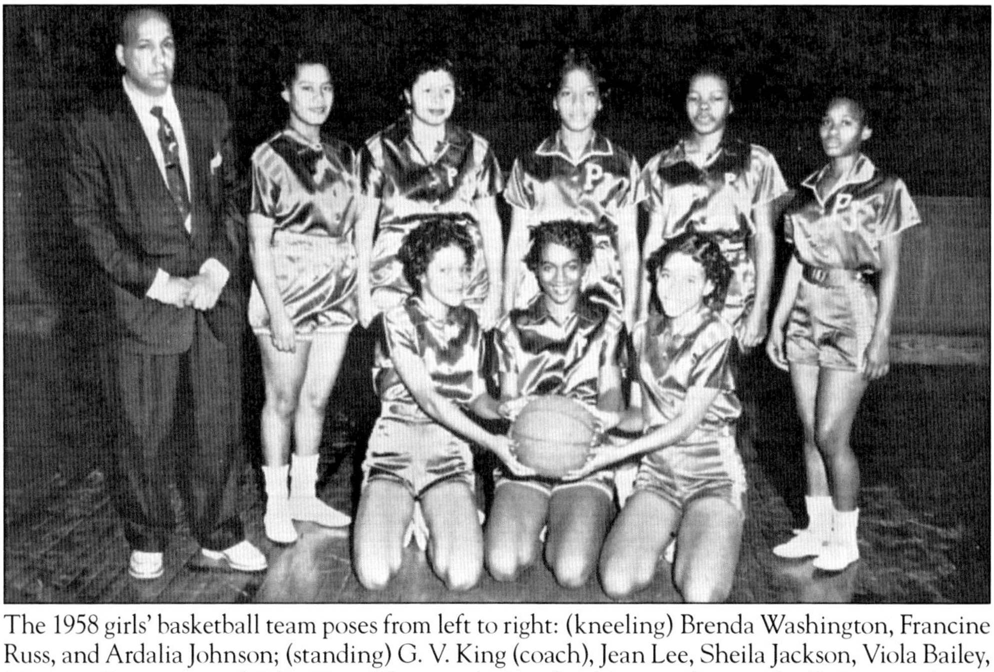

The 1958 girls' basketball team poses from left to right: (kneeling) Brenda Washington, Francine Russ, and Ardalia Johnson; (standing) G. V. King (coach), Jean Lee, Sheila Jackson, Viola Bailey, Margaret Ramseur, and Julia Carr. The popularity of girls' sports has gradually increased over the years.

Eight

Page-Jackson High School

Until 1938, the only education provided to black students was grades 1–8. Students who wished to complete high school attended the high school program at Storer College. In 1938, Storer discontinued that program, which left students with no local means of completing high school. The Jefferson County Black PTA approached the county school board and asked for a high school. The board explained that because of the Depression, they were unable to build a high school at that time.

The PTA asked the school board again and pleaded for a high school because of the high enrollment at Eagle Avenue Elementary; a number of students were eager to start high school. The board told the PTA that if they could find a way to start a high school, they could do so. The PTA then started to make plans. It was decided to use the Eagle Avenue building for both the elementary and high schools because it was the largest black school in the county.

Donald Wingo, who was the principal at Eagle Avenue Elementary at the time (1938), resigned at the beginning of the school year to take a job in Virginia. O. M. Stewart was then hired as principal. The board decided that the PTA had to find the necessary equipment and find teachers willing to take on extra duties for the high school because the board was not willing to do so. Once all plans were finalized, the board named the school Page-Jackson High School in honor of two early outstanding black educators in Charles Town, West Virginia: Littleton Lorton Page and Philip Jackson.

In 1941, the PTA asked the board to build an addition to Eagle Avenue for the growing number of students. The board agreed, and an annex was added to accommodate the increased enrollment.

In 1951, a separate high school was built on Mordington Avenue in Charles Town for black students. In 1965, Page-Jackson was closed. It is believed to be one of the last black high schools to close in the state. The building is still being used and is occupied by the Jefferson County Board of Education.

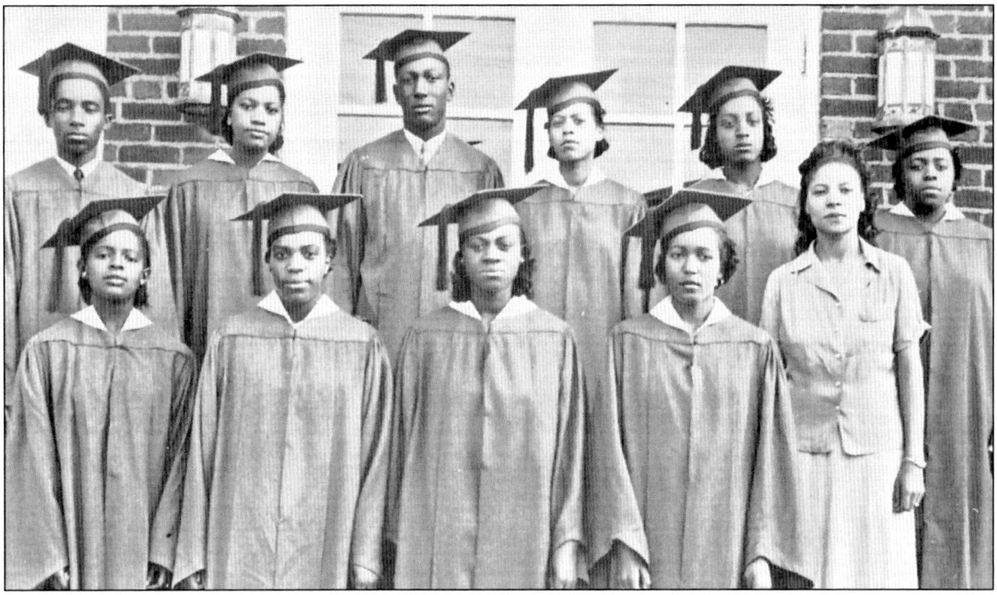

The first graduating class at Page-Jackson High was 1942. Here they stand proudly with their adviser, Goldye Johnson. In alphabetical order, the students are Raymond Brooks, Bertha E. Fox, Nannie B. Fox, Theodosia Lewis, Emma McCann, Dorothy Moats, Beatrice Russ, Katherine Shelton, Christine Spriggs, and Lester Taylor. In 1951, PJHS got a building to call its own when it opened on Mordington Avenue with Prof. E. M. Dandridge, principal.

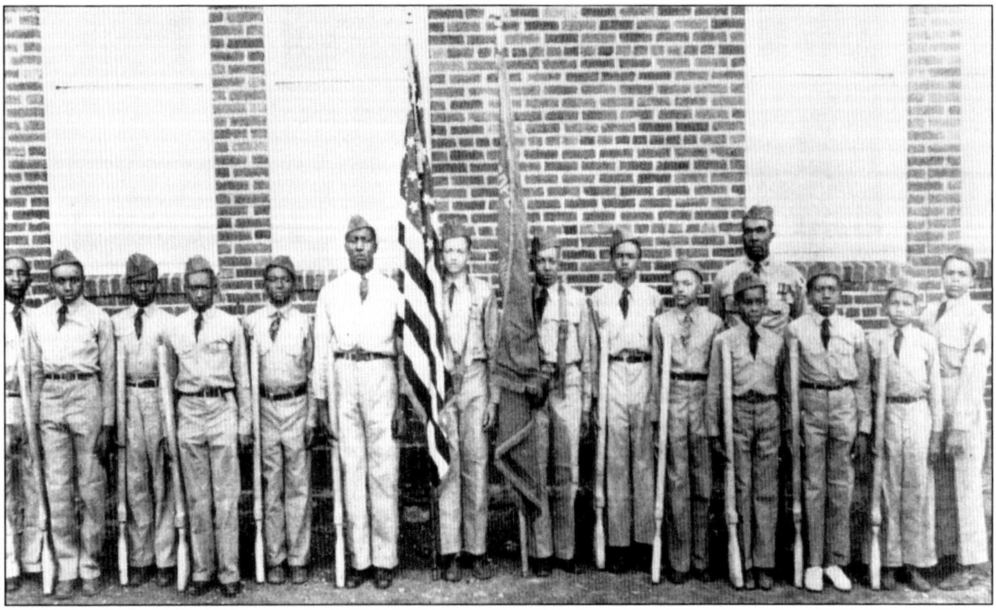

In this 1942 photograph can be seen the Page-Jackson High School "cadets." Commandant E. O. Morgan led the group. In 1941, Page-Jackson was the first high school in Jefferson County with a quasi-military unit. In 1942, the United States was involved in World War II and would be for three more years, which explains the interest in military groups for the young people.

The 1943 Page-Jackson High School class consisted of only four members, of which only three are pictured. From left to right are Frances Twman, Madeline Lawson, and Doris Beals. Classmate Mary Posey is not pictured. This was a small class because the country was in the middle of World War II, and many young men had enlisted or been drafted to serve in the military.

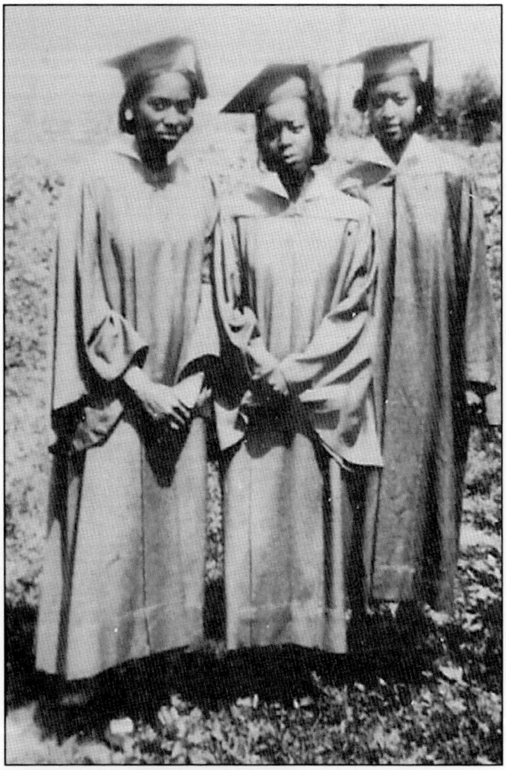

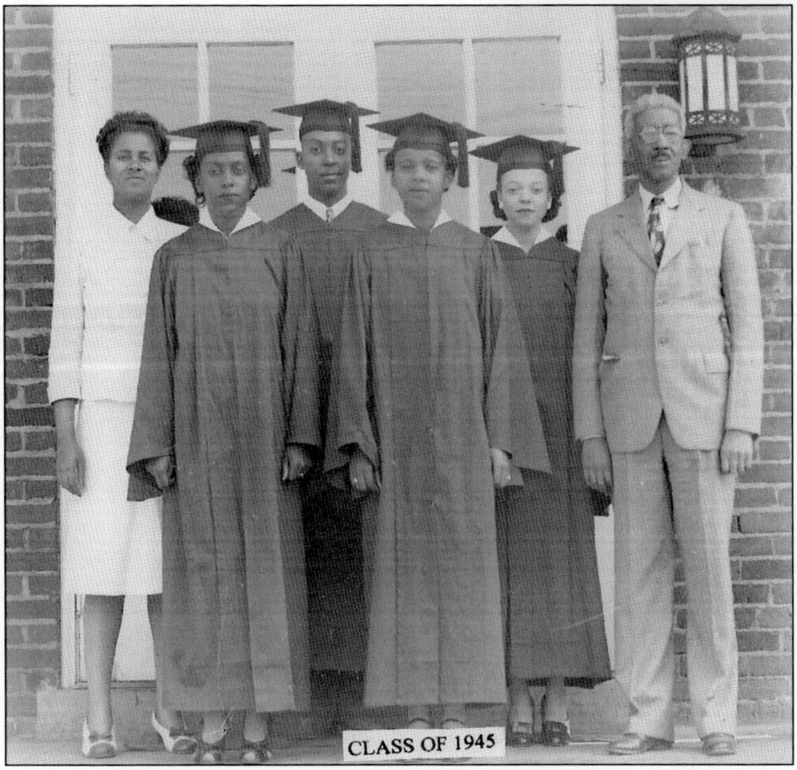

Here are four of the members of the 1945 graduating class of Page-Jackson as well as the principal and a teacher. The complete list of graduates in alphabetical order is Brucilla Fox, Pearl Fox, DeWitt Jacobs, Sarah McCann, Grafton Napper, and Houston Snowden. The class was not larger partly because many young men joined the military to serve in World War II.

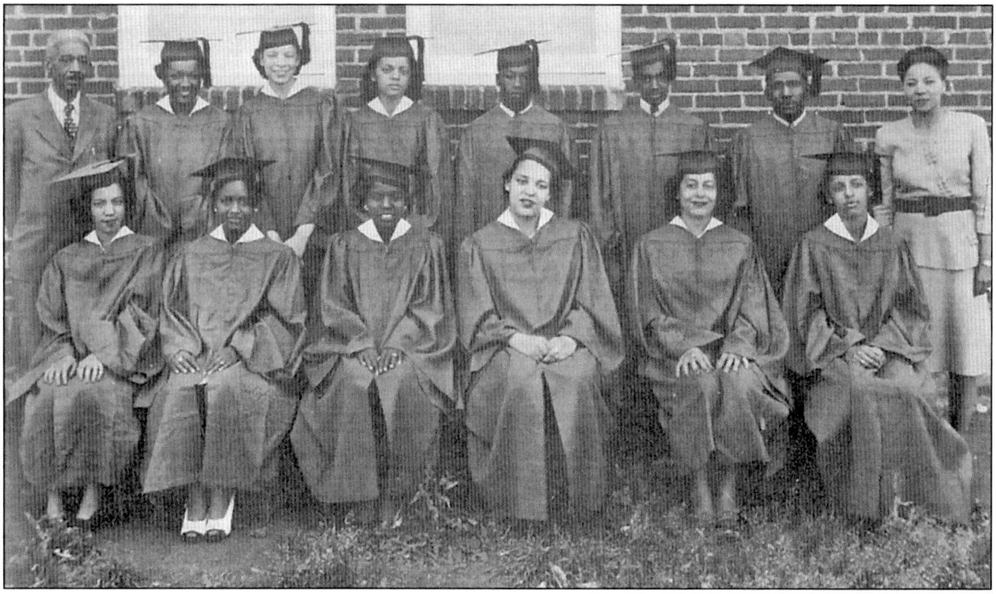

Pictured here are 12 of the 13 members of Page-Jackson High School class of 1947. Listed alphabetically are Chauncey Allen, Delores Berry, Zada Berry, Ellen Blakely, Thelma Campbell, Betty Dyson, Delores Jackson, Jacqueline Jackson, Nellie Lawson, Robert Stewart, Bernard Taylor, Gladys Walker, and Roland Willis. The two adults located at either end of the back row are O. M. Stewart, principal (left), and Goldye Johnson, class sponsor (right).

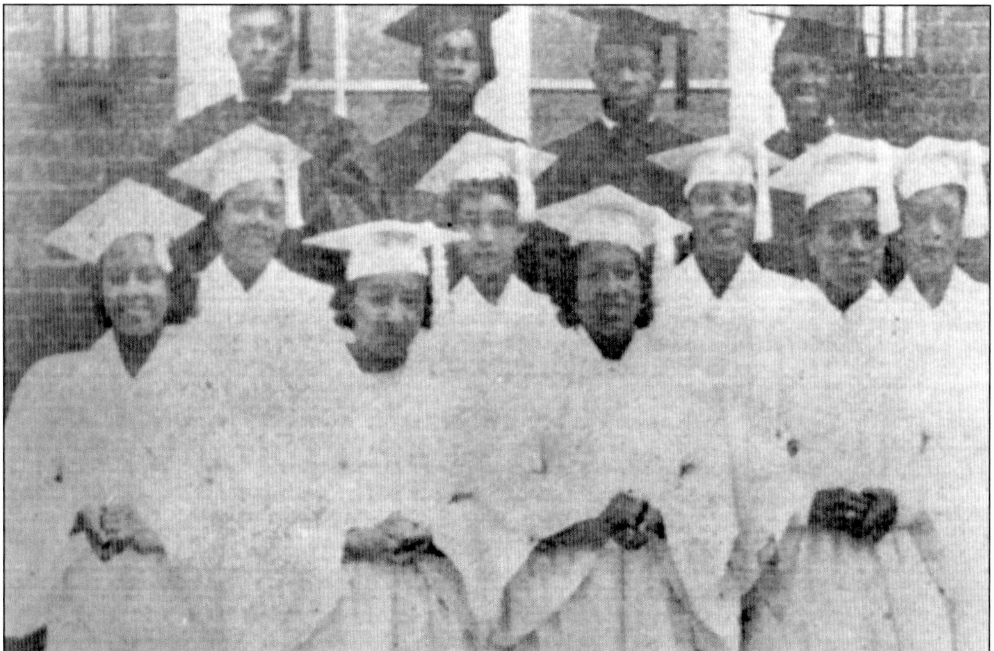

The graduating class of 1948 of Page-Jackson High School stands proudly, all prepared for entrance into the adult world. Students pictured are, in alphabetical order, Ruby Brown, Essie Campbell, John Lee, James Lindsey, Charles Mayberry, Dorothy Newman, Ollie Robinson, Mildred Roy, Peggy Tolbert, Robert Twyman, Jerry Wesco, and Alice White.

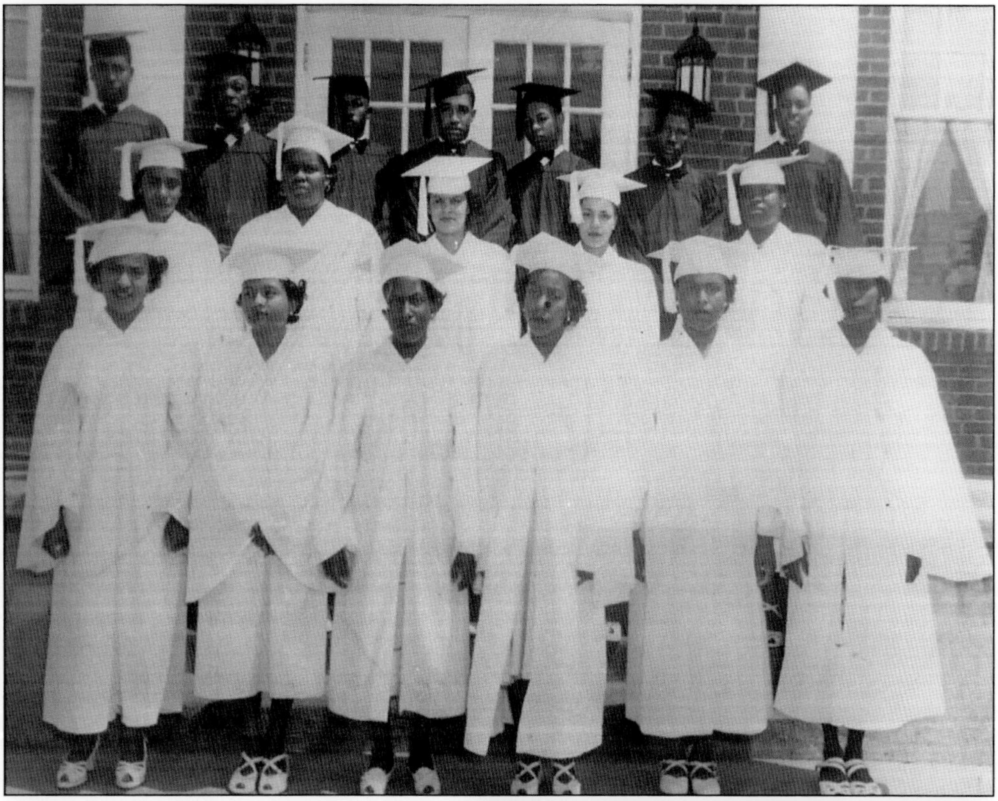

Graduating members of the class of 1949 at Page-Jackson included 18 students. In alphabetical order, they are Estelle Bailey, Karilla Brown, Rodye Butler, Helen Campbell, Louise Campbell, Austin Clinton, Wilbur Clinton, Dorothy Davenport, Janet Jacobs, Willard Jones, Yvonne Jones, Louise McCann, Nannie Morris, Lionel Reeler, Dorothy Taylor, Eugene S. Taylor, Leon Washington, Ira Jean Willis, and Frank Wilson.

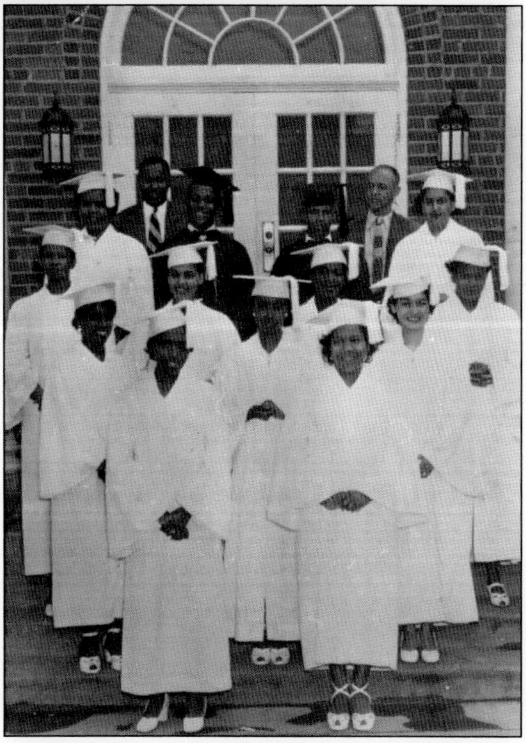

The graduating class of Page-Jackson High School in 1950 had 11 women and only two men. The students in alphabetical order were John A. Brown, Josephine Butler, Carol Dennis, Annabelle Hosby, Barbara Kemp, Helena McCann, Helen E. Parker, Anna P. Posey, Georgiane Schley, James A. Tolbert, Mary Walker, Margaret Washington, and Margaret Willis. The year after this class graduated, the school would move to its new location on Mordington Avenue.

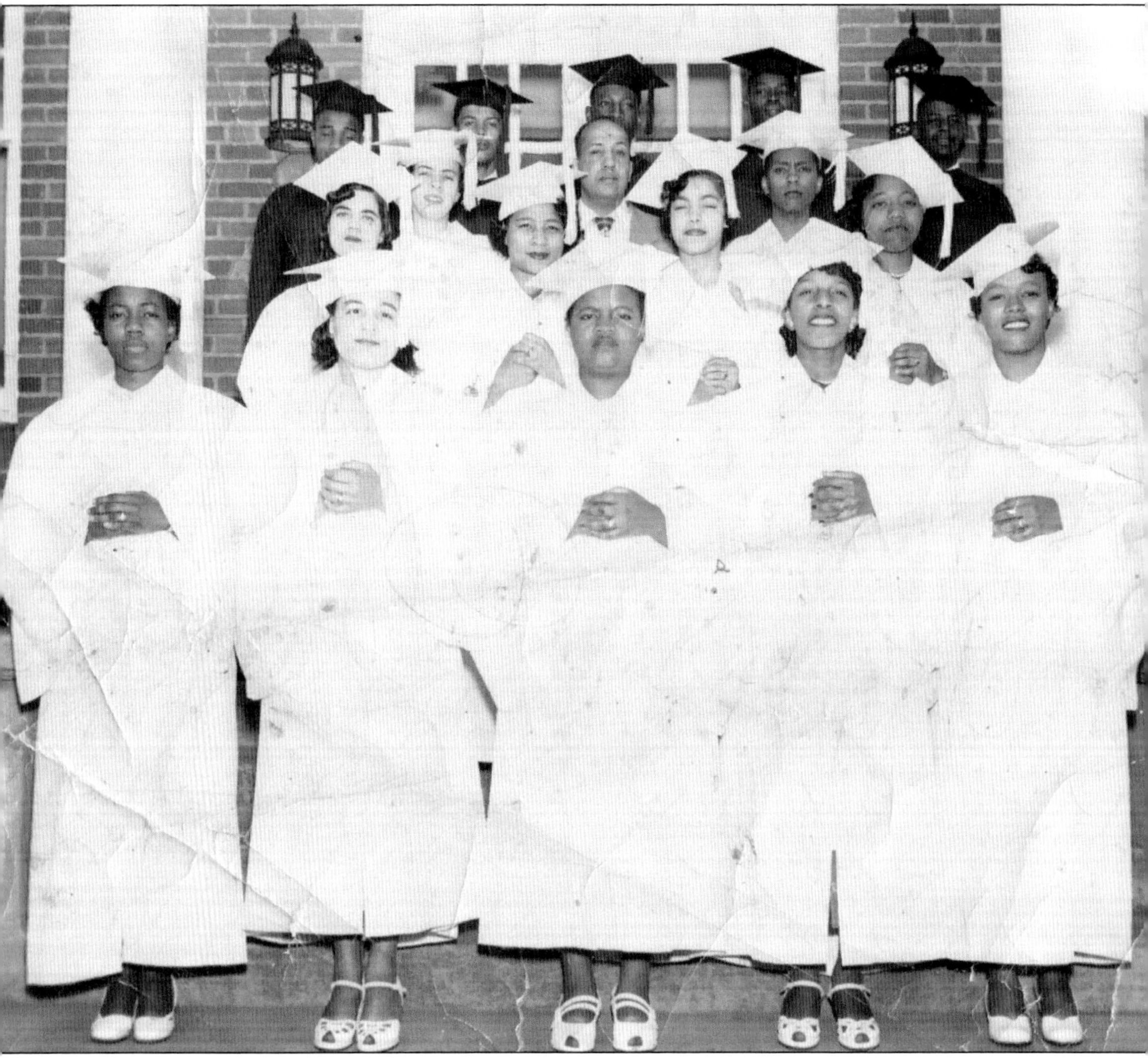

The class of 1951 of Page-Jackson stands proudly. From left to right are (first row) Willa Pinckney, Madelene Fox, Beatrice Williams, Edith McDaniel, and Marie Allen; (second row) Esther Johnson, Helen Brooks, Mary C. Dennis, and Phyllis Jackson; (third row) Marlene Willis, G. V. King, and Frances Lewis; (fourth row) Nathaniel Hall, Raymond Harris, Thomas Doleman, James L. Taylor, and Ronald Blackwell.

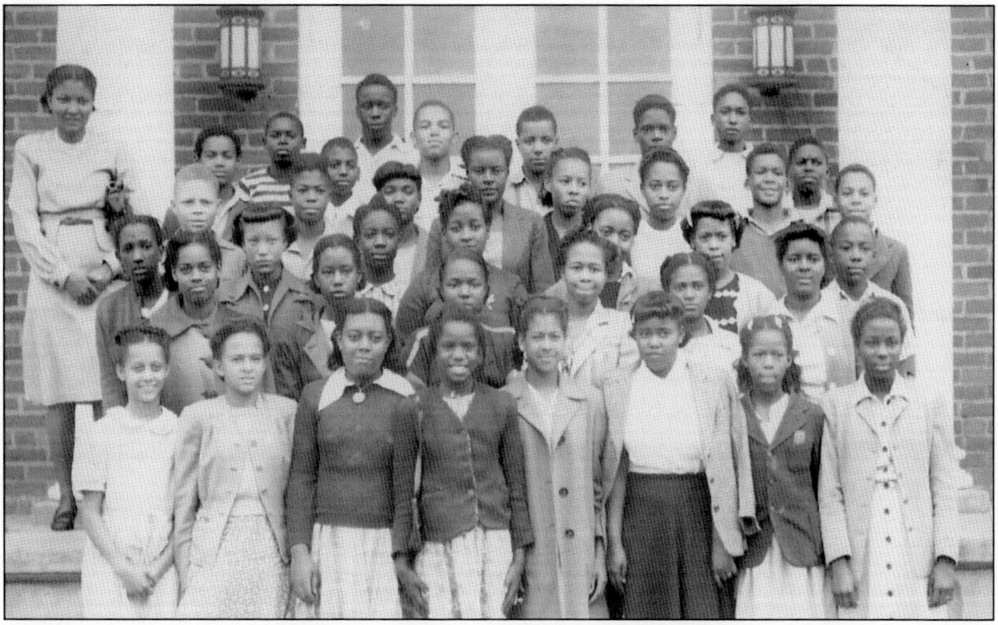

This is an early photograph of the members of the PJHS graduating class of 1953. The group would change over the years prior to graduating. The school had an auditorium-gymnasium with a capacity of 300 with a stage, lockers, and showers. It also had an outside athletic field. The school had been founded in 1938 as the first black high school in the county. Its last class graduated in 1965.

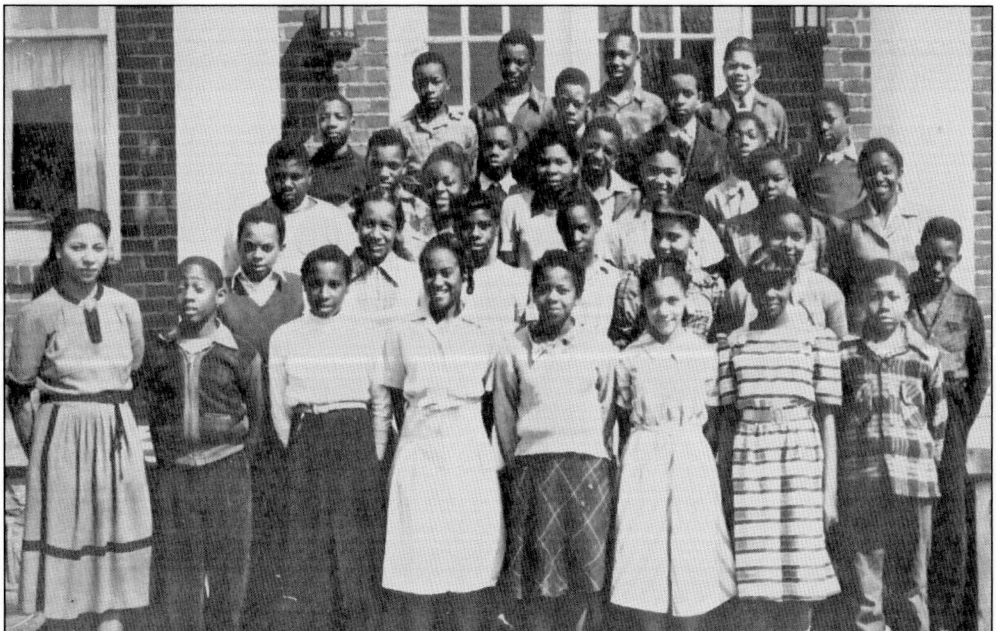

Goldye Kent Johnson stands with the students at Eagle Avenue School. Johnson was the class sponsor. This group of students would later be the class of 1954 at Page-Jackson High School. Johnson was also a teacher at Grandview Elementary School. Grandview School would close after the 1965 school year.

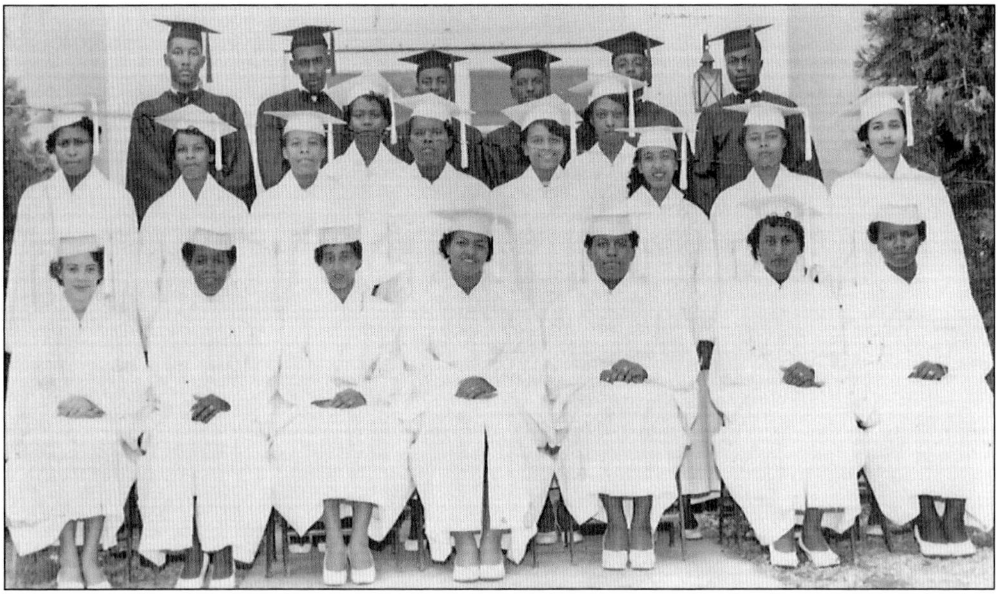

Class of 1955 of Page-Jackson High School members beam with pride. Students in alphabetical order are Jesse Brooks, Yvonne Brooks, Alma Brown, Lincoln Brunswick, Earl Butler, Emma Butler, Phyllis Curry, Evelyn Dozier, James Frye, Marva Hughes, Delorse Jackson, Helen Johnson, Phyllis Lane, Lucy Napper, Doris Puller, Irvin Rector, Sylvia Robinson, Deloris Scott, Lillian Stevenson, Blanche Washington, Rose L. Washington, Daniel Weaver, Geraldine Willis, and Georgene Winston.

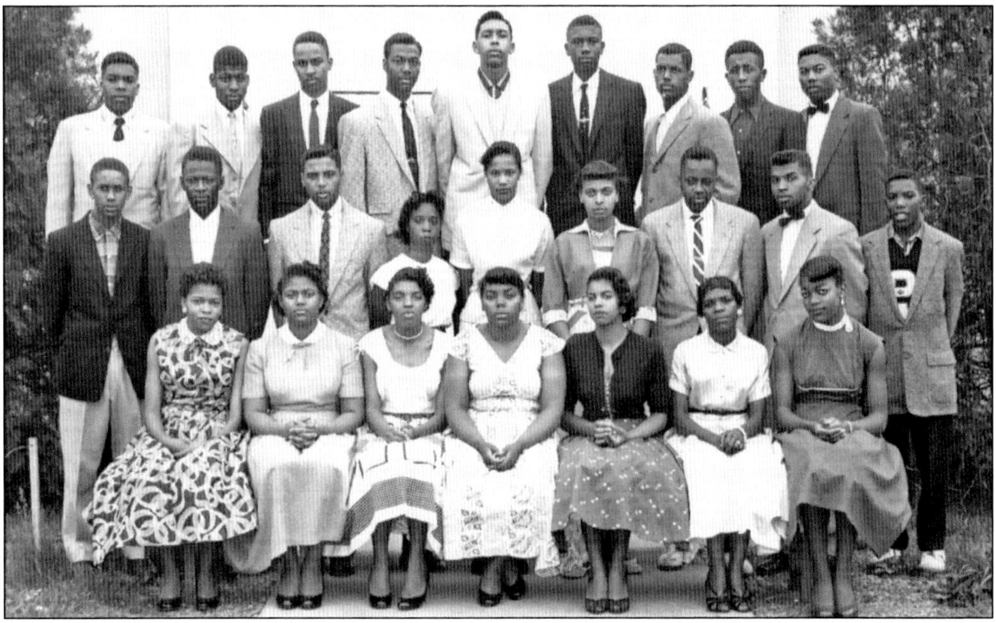

The class of 1956 included, in alphabetical order, Alfred Baylor, Mervin Baylor, John Berry, Grafton Blue, Rose Branson, Ernest Braxton, Oliver Braxton, Arianne Brown, John Brown, Mary Green, Leo Harri, Randolph Johnson, Elizabeth Morris, Kathryn Pinckney, Mary Robinson, Thelma Robinson, Charles Ross, Floyd Rutherford, Harry Shelton, Anna Stanton, James Taylor, Averill Washington, Eleanor Washington, John Washington, and Huel Willis.

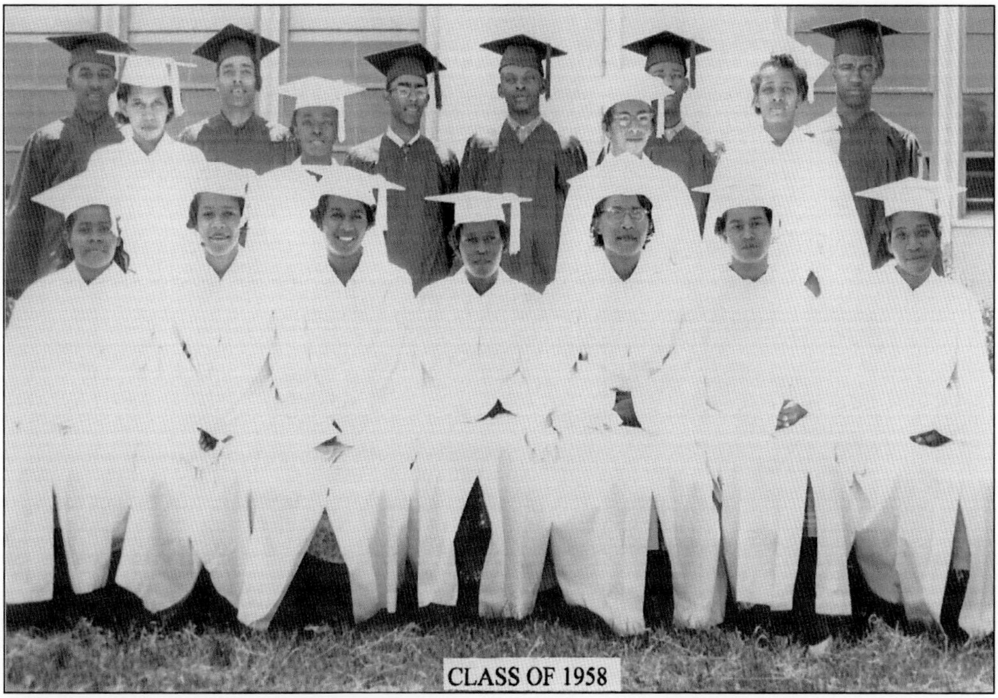

Pictured is most of the 1958 graduating class of Page-Jackson High School. The entire list of class members, in alphabetical order, was Kirk Baylor, Maurice Braxton, Barry Burns, Mary Galloway, Charles Grantham, Anna M. Jenkins, Ardalia Johnson, Stephen Luckett, Violet Morris, Magruder Rideoutt, Janet Robinson, Francine Russ, Morrisey Rutherford, Robert Smith, John Stevenson, Audry Twyman, Brenda Washington, and William Woodford.

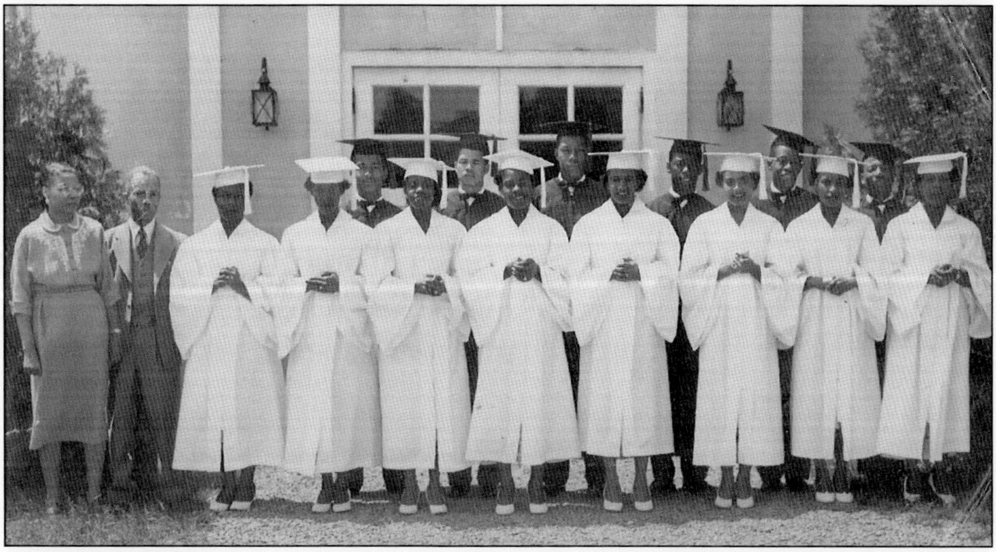

At left are Goldye Johnson, advisor, and Principal E. M. Dandridge. The Page-Jackson High School class of 1954 consisted of 14 students. The names in alphabetical order are Kenneth Braxton, Betty Brown, Allen Butler, Daniel Campbell, Gladys Campbell, Arlene Curry, Morolyn Doleman, Richard Green, Joyce Harris, Charles Jackson, Thomas Johnson, Esther McDaniel, Ruth McDaniel, and Robert Taylor.

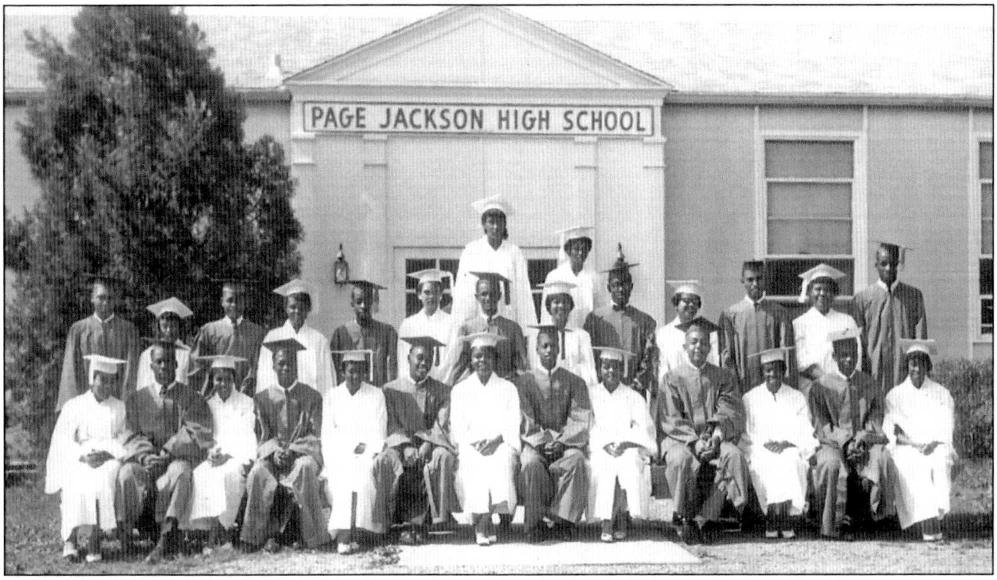

The graduating class of 1960 is pictured. Members of the class in alphabetical order were Bernard Bailey, Barbara Branson, Charles Branson, Philip Braxton, Albert Brown, Marcel Brown, Pauline Brown, Betty Clark, Richard Clark, George Dozier, Mae Edwards, Shelia Jackson, Helen Johnson, Venning Johnson, Edgar Kidrick, Norm McDonald, Henry Paige, Doris Payton, Cornelia Stanton, Harriet Taylor, James Twyman, David Weaver, Mary White, Romanda Williams, Elizabeth Yates, and Phyllis Young.

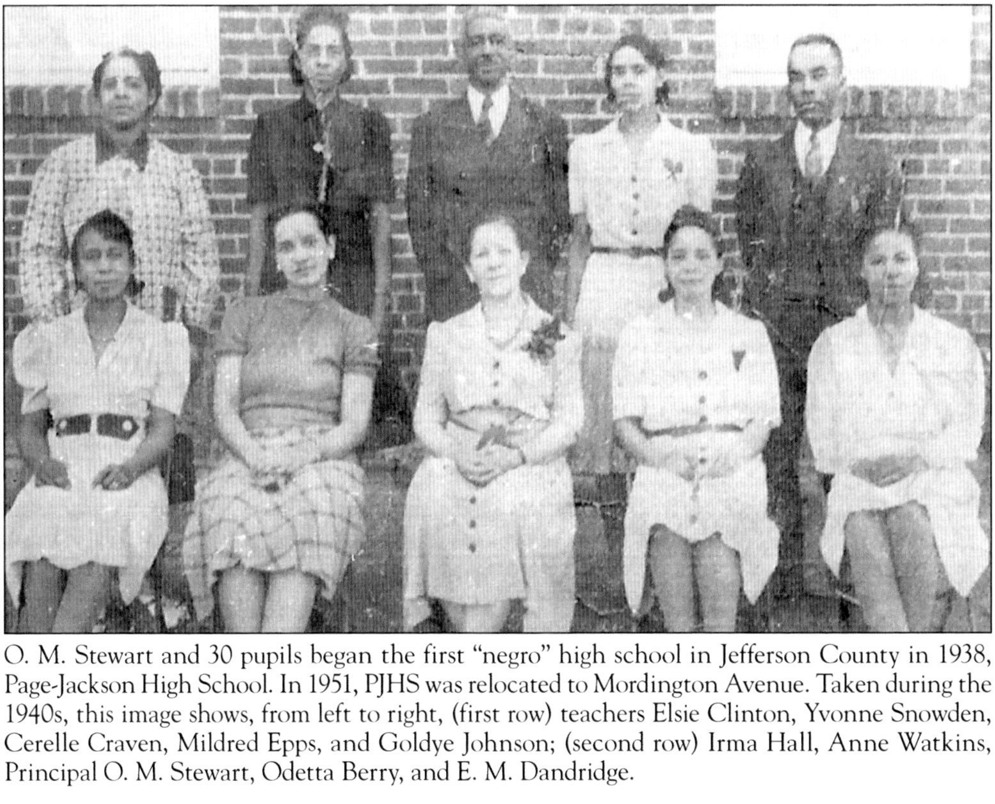

O. M. Stewart and 30 pupils began the first "negro" high school in Jefferson County in 1938, Page-Jackson High School. In 1951, PJHS was relocated to Mordington Avenue. Taken during the 1940s, this image shows, from left to right, (first row) teachers Elsie Clinton, Yvonne Snowden, Cerelle Craven, Mildred Epps, and Goldye Johnson; (second row) Irma Hall, Anne Watkins, Principal O. M. Stewart, Odetta Berry, and E. M. Dandridge.

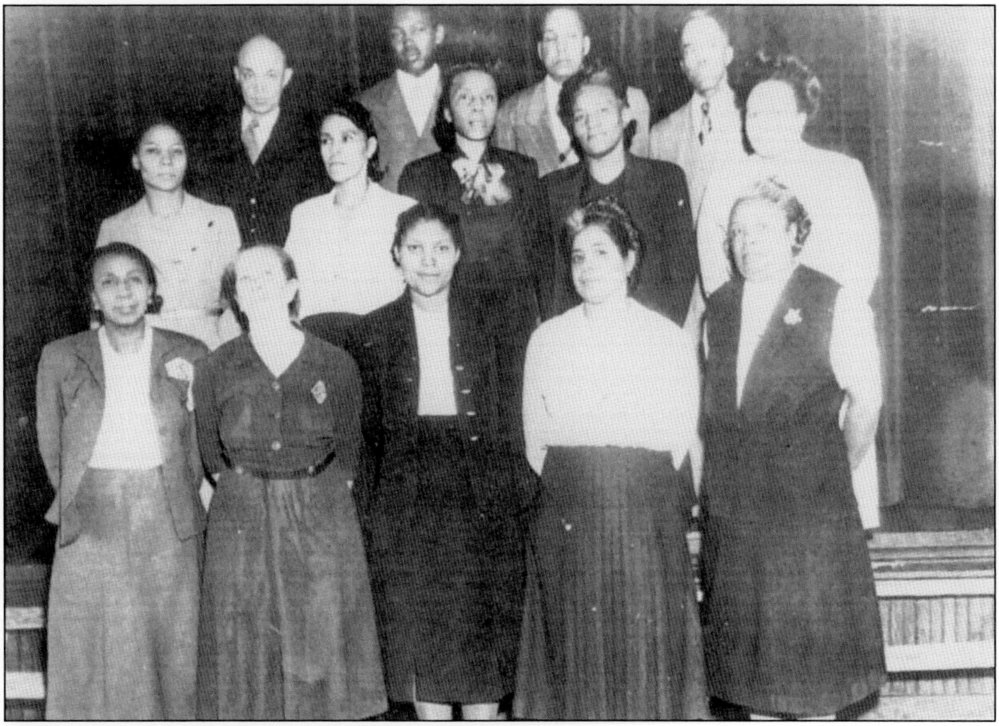

The faculties of Page-Jackson High School and Eagle Avenue Elementary School in 1949 included, from left to right, (first row) Elsie Clinton, Cerelle Craven, Vivian Fleming, Irma Patrick, and Lucy Green; (second row) Goldye Johnson, Odetta Berry, Anne Watkins, Lucy Saunders, and Adrea Lewis; (third row) Principal Stewart Payne, O. D. Fleming, George J. King, and Ernest Dandridge. Eagle Avenue Elementary was located on Eagle Avenue. The original edifice burned in 1966.

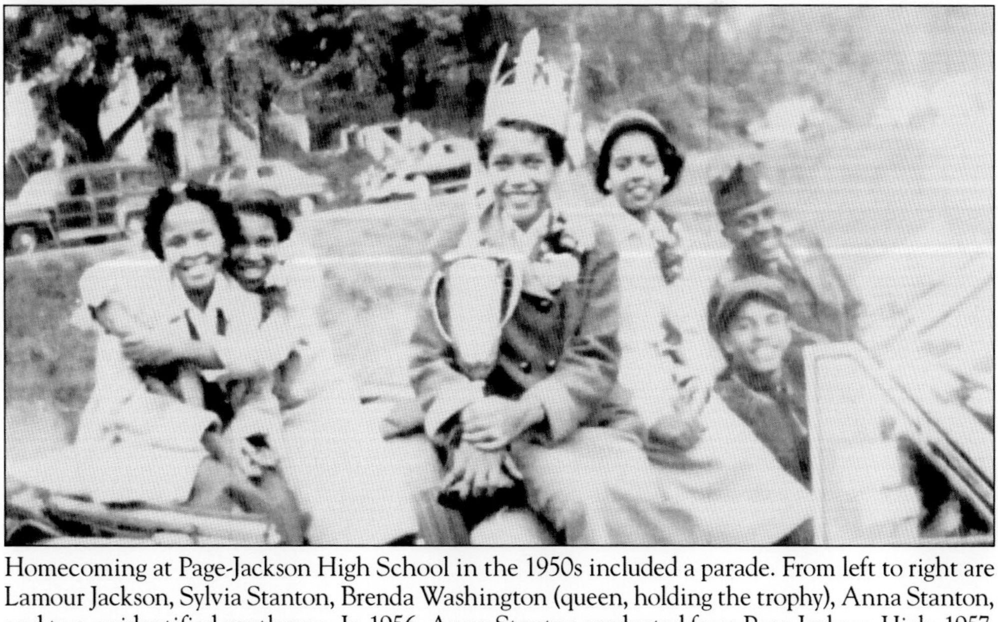

Homecoming at Page-Jackson High School in the 1950s included a parade. From left to right are Lamour Jackson, Sylvia Stanton, Brenda Washington (queen, holding the trophy), Anna Stanton, and two unidentified gentlemen. In 1956, Anna Stanton graduated from Page-Jackson High; 1957, Lamour Jackson; 1958, Brenda Washington; 1959, Sylvia Stanton.

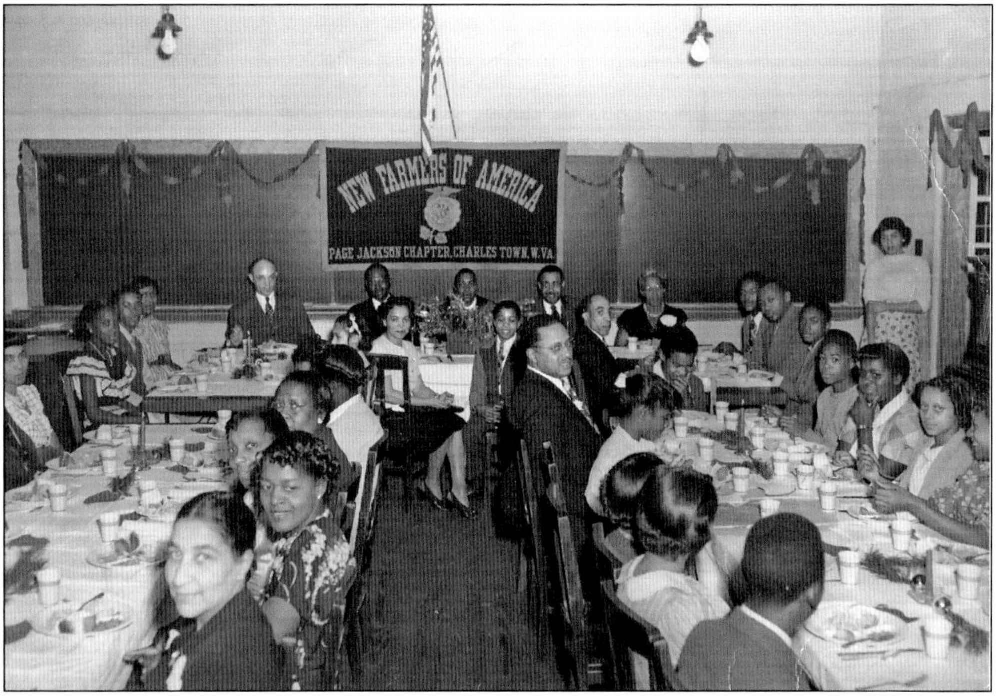

The Page-Jackson High School Father/Son and Mother/Daughter Banquet in 1949 was held by the New Farmers of America (NFA) and the NHA. The school would move into a new building in 1951. Once in that new building, they did not have to move again. Page-Jackson stayed open until 1965, when it was closed because of integration. The Page-Jackson High School building became the offices for the Jefferson County Board of Education.

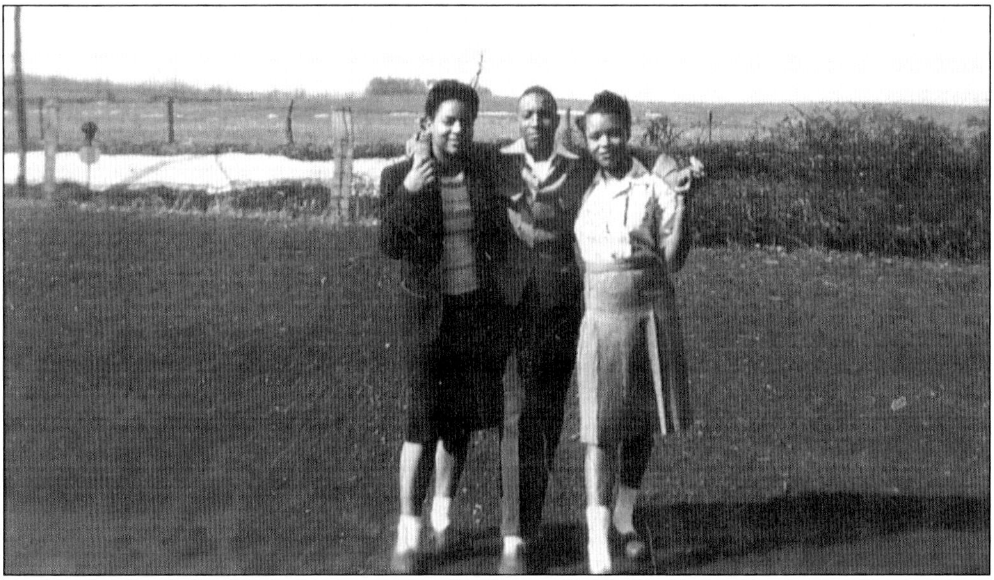

Page-Jackson High School started their classes at Eagle Avenue School. The building would come later. Pictured from left to right are Corrine Jackson, Rodye Butler, and Marie Allen around 1949. Rodye Butler graduated 1949; Marie Allen, 1951. Rodye went on to veterinary school and became a doctor of veterinary medicine. He also served as a U.S. Army major.

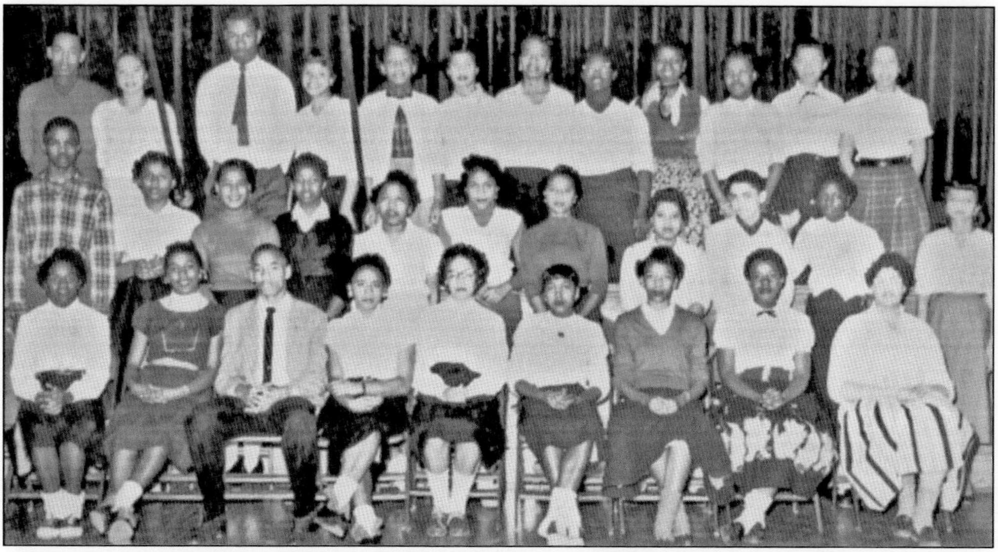

These Page-Jackson High School students pose here in the 1950s. This very likely is a photograph for their yearbook. The school itself does not exist any longer. However, the building that was constructed for Page-Jackson High School now houses the Jefferson County Board of Education. One room is set aside in the building to house the archives of the Page-Jackson High School Alumni Association.

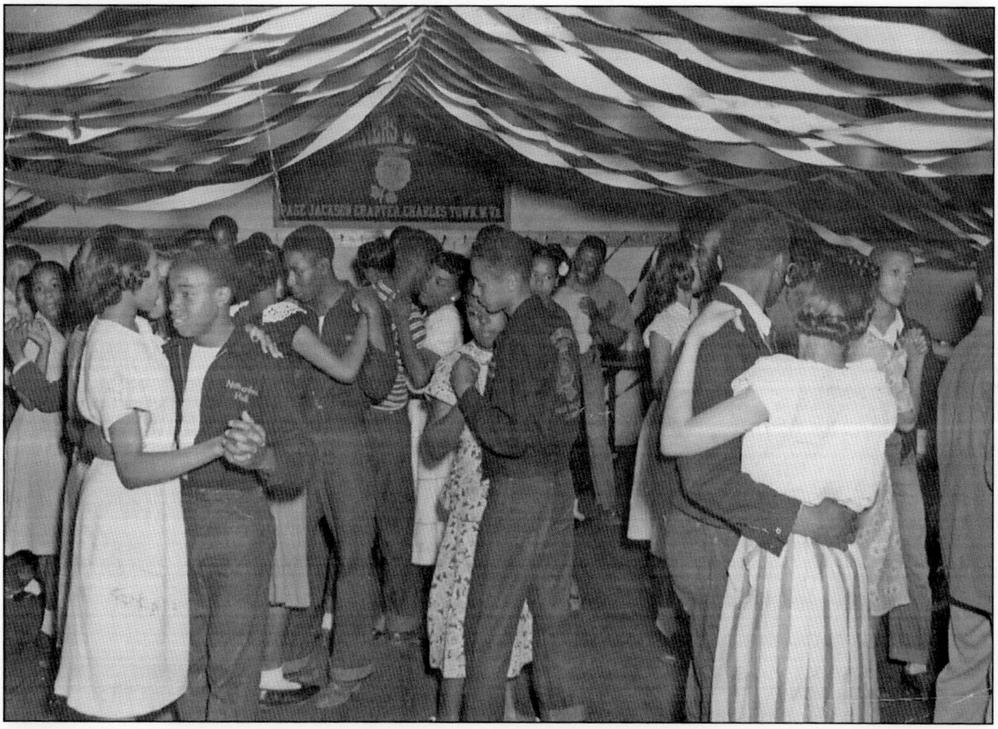

The "fabulous 1950s" were a great time to be young. Pictured here are students of Page-Jackson High School at the NFA Ball in 1950. The school was still part of Eagle Avenue School in Charles Town. While Page-Jackson High School had been started as the first black high school in the county, it would not be in its own building until 1951. It closed in 1965.

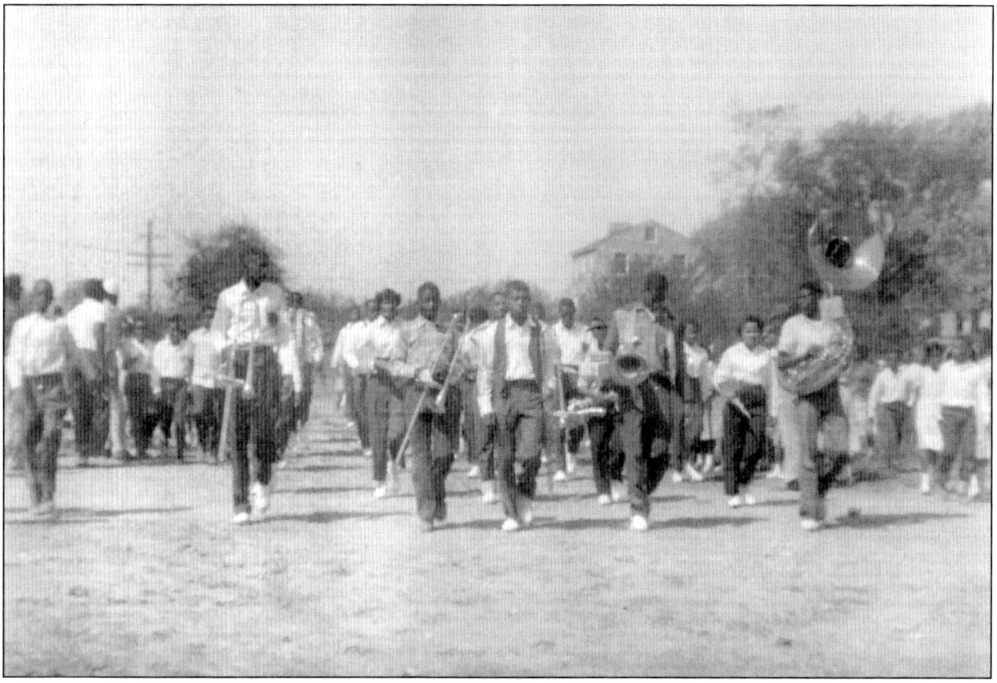

Page-Jackson High School marching band is pictured in the 1950s. They are practicing some of their marching routines. Marching bands have been popular in high schools, junior high schools, and colleges for many years. John Philip Sousa is the best-known name in American band music and earned the name "March King" because he composed so many marches.

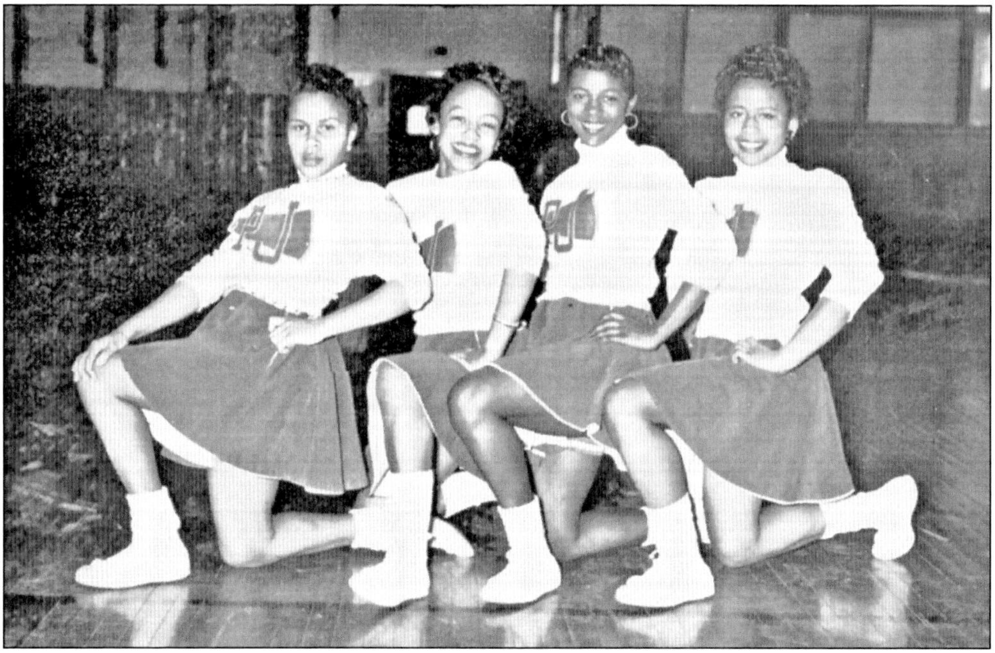

This photograph was taken in the 1960s and shows the cheerleaders of Page-Jackson High School from Charles Town, West Virginia. The sponsor was Delores Jackson, who is at center in the back row. Jackson was a graduate of Page-Jackson High School in 1955.

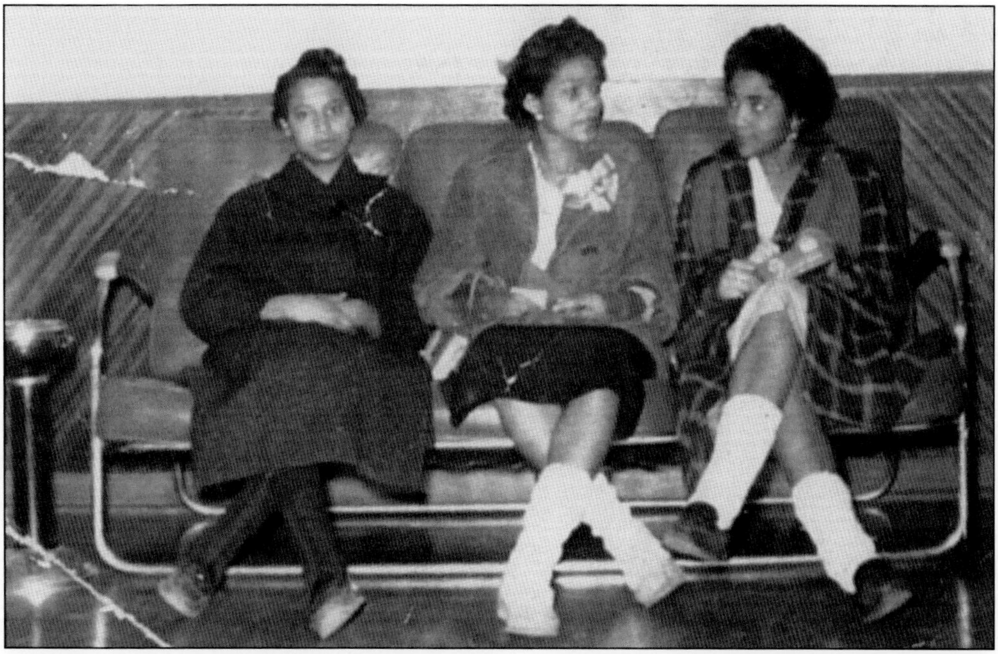

From left to right are cousins Morrisey Rutherford, Brenda Washington, and Ora Jean Washington. The date and location are unknown, but it was probably at Page-Jackson High School in the 1950s. Morrisey graduated in 1958, Brenda in 1958, and Ora in 1961, all proud graduates of Page-Jackson High School. The school they loved so dearly closed in 1965.

The Page-Jackson High School majorettes practice with the marching band on their practice field. Members appear to be standing at attention, waiting for directions from their band director. This photograph might have been taken before they purchased marching band uniforms because they all seem to be dressed alike, with white tops and dark bottoms.

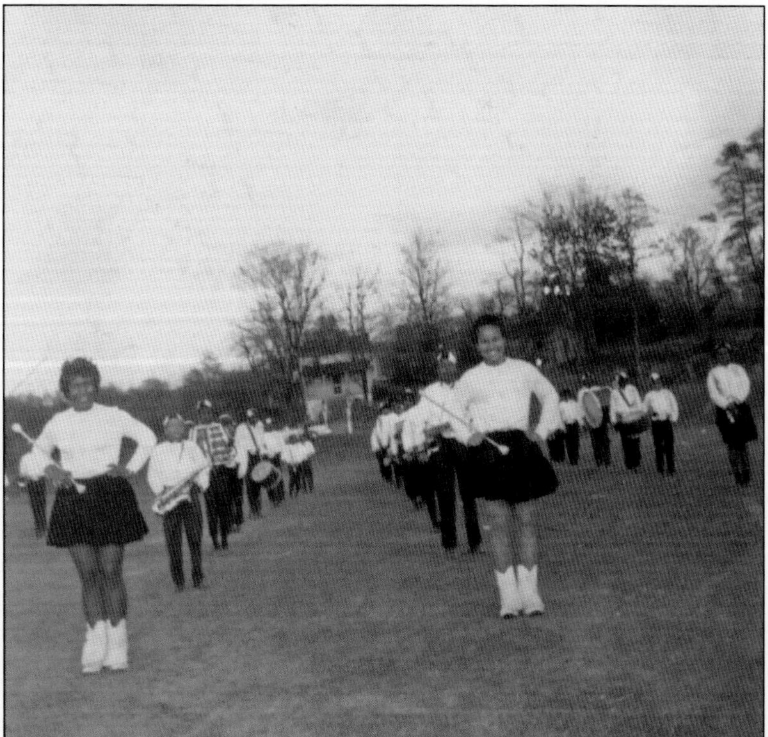

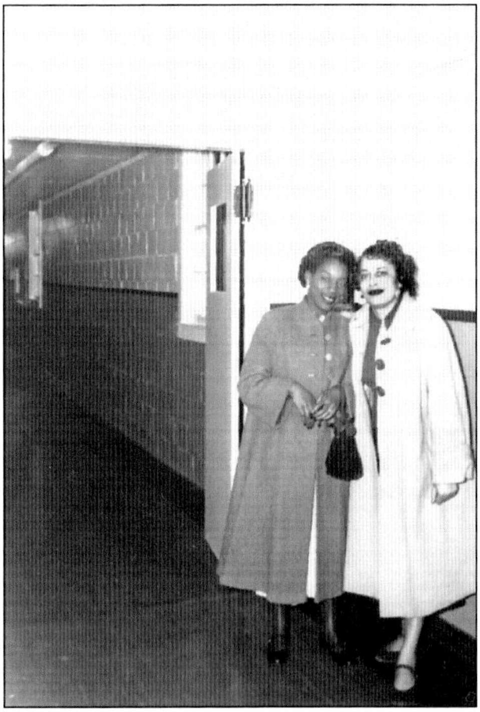

Annabelle Hosby is on the left and Gladys Walker is on the right in this 1950s picture. Annabelle graduated in 1950 and Gladys in 1957. Page-Jackson was the only all-black high school in Jefferson County. It closed in 1965. The building today houses the board of education offices on Mordington Avenue.

Marion Newman sits proudly in the seat of honor as the 1961–1962 Future Farmers of America "Sweetheart" in this photograph. The national FFA was founded in 1928. The goal is to reflect the expanding career field of agricultural education and the motto of FFA: "Learning to Do, Doing to Learn, Earning to Live, Living to Serve."

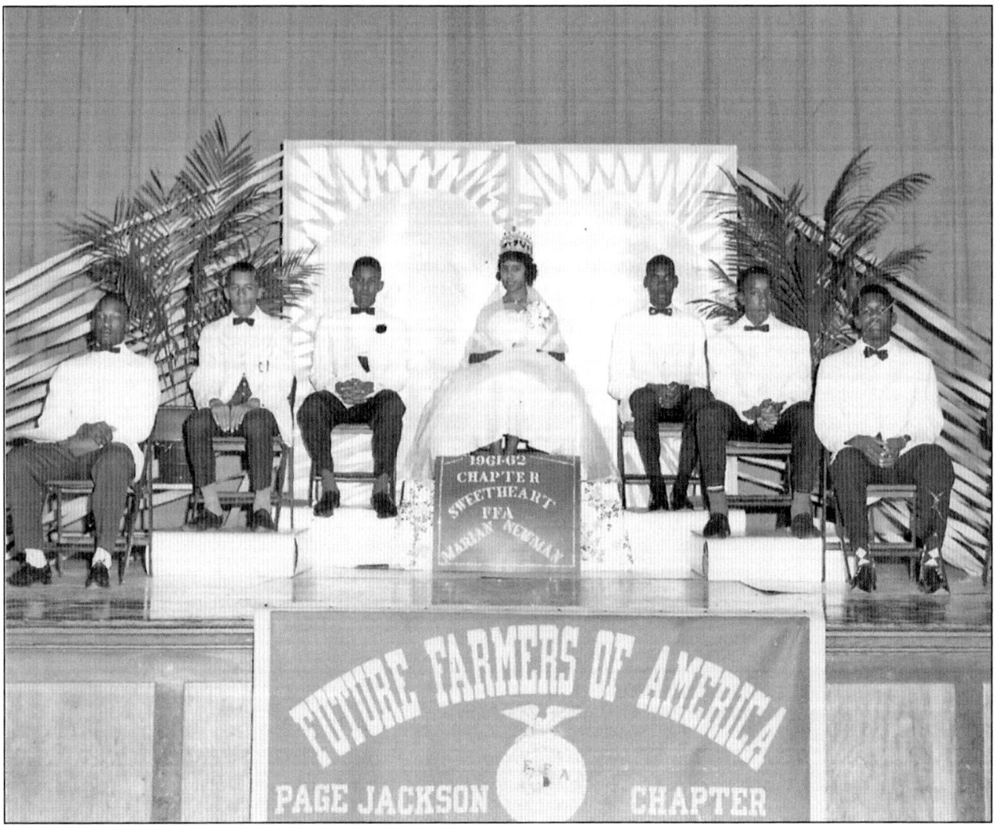

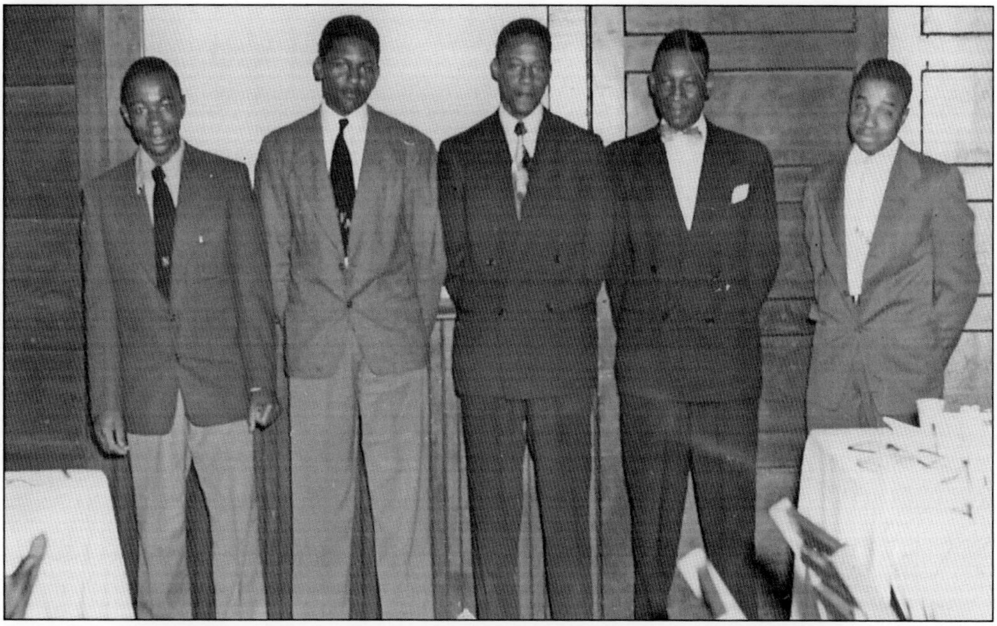

St. Philip's Parish House was the location of the New Farmers of America (NFA) Awards Night. The photograph dates from the early 1950s. Pictured from left to right are George Rutherford, Ralph Wilson, Robert Brown, Thomas Doleman, and Nathaniel Hall. All five gentlemen graduated from Page-Jackson High School: George Rutherford, 1953; Ralph Wilson, 1952; Robert Brown, 1952; Thomas Doleman, 1951; and Nathaniel Hall, 1951.

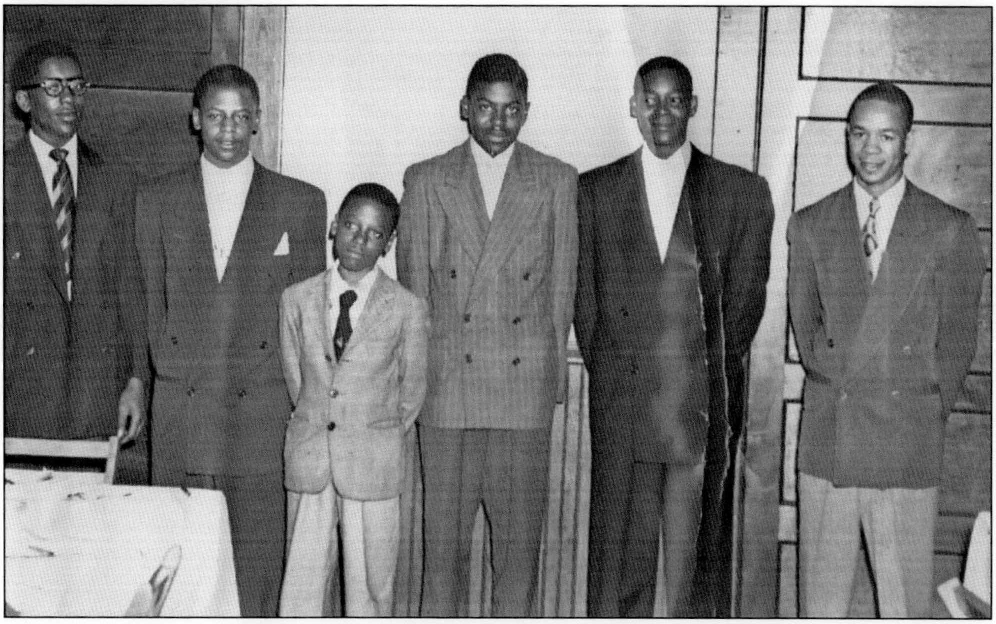

NFA awards night was held at St. Philip's Parish Hall. From left to right are Robert Hosby, Ronald Blackwell, Earl Butler, Charles Brunswick, James L. Taylor, and Johnnie Bailey. Ronald Blackwell graduated from Page-Jackson High School in 1951, as did James L. Taylor. Charles Brunswick graduated in 1953 and served in the U.S. Army as a lieutenant. Johnnie Bailey graduated in 1952, and he earned the Bronze Star.

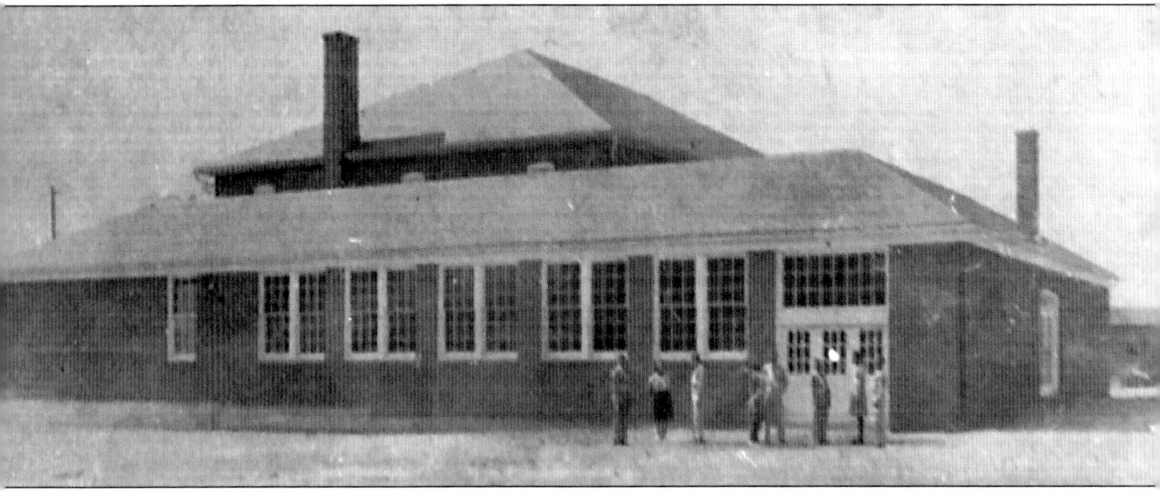

Eventually, the parents, teachers, and students all realized that they needed more space and more equipment to meet the demands of a growing attendance. By 1942, the school board had found the money and work began. The new annex contained two classrooms, a chemistry laboratory, a shop, a lunchroom, a kitchen, and a home economics room. Those facilities would be used until the new Page-Jackson building would be completed in 1951.

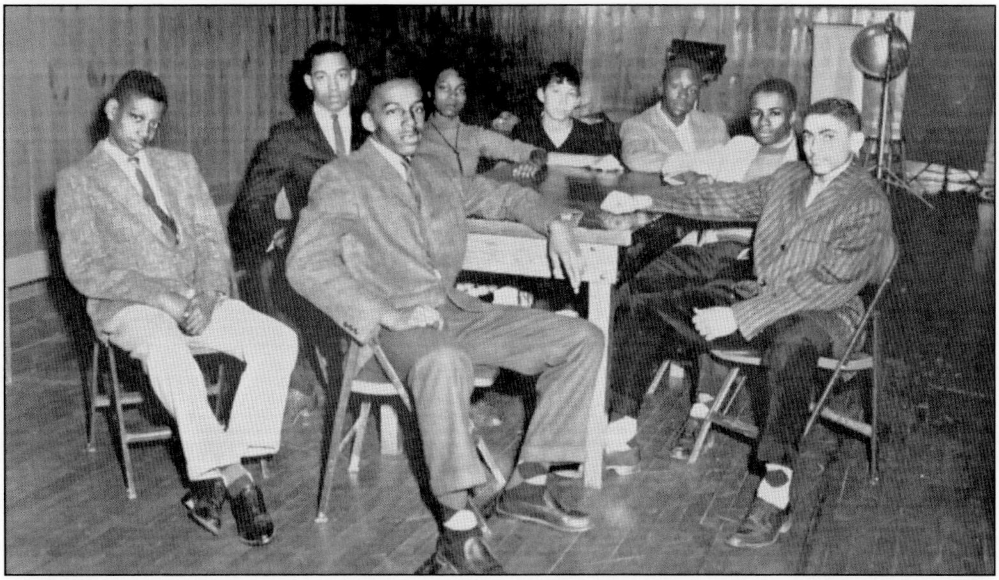

Student government representatives are the leaders selected by their peers. This picture shows the Page-Jackson Student Government Association in 1959. Starting at the far left (young man with light slacks) and going clockwise around the table are Phillip Braxton, Kirk Baylor, Emma Butler, Betty Sims, George Dozier, George Mitchell, Paul Sims, and Maurice Braxton. Fellow classmate Barry Burns provided the identification 50 years later—quite a memory.

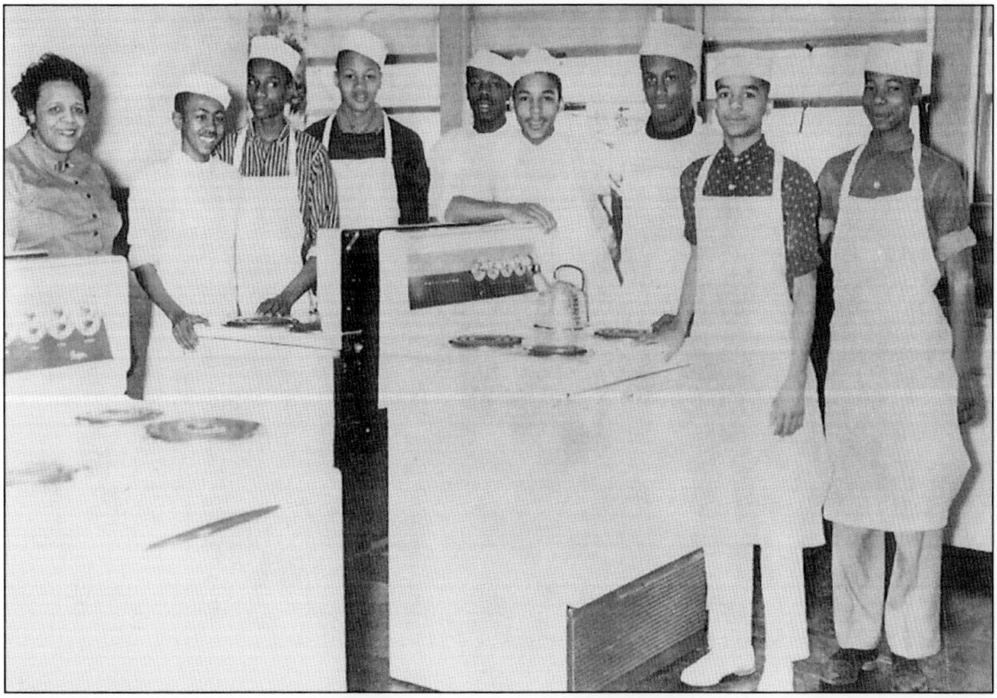

Students who took the boys' cooking class at Page-Jackson High School in the 1960s pose. It was the first class of this type in Jefferson County, which was a progressive move because prior to this, cooking classes were for girls only. The teacher pictured behind the students, third from the left, is Andrea Lewis. Aprons and hats were required for all when they were in the kitchen.

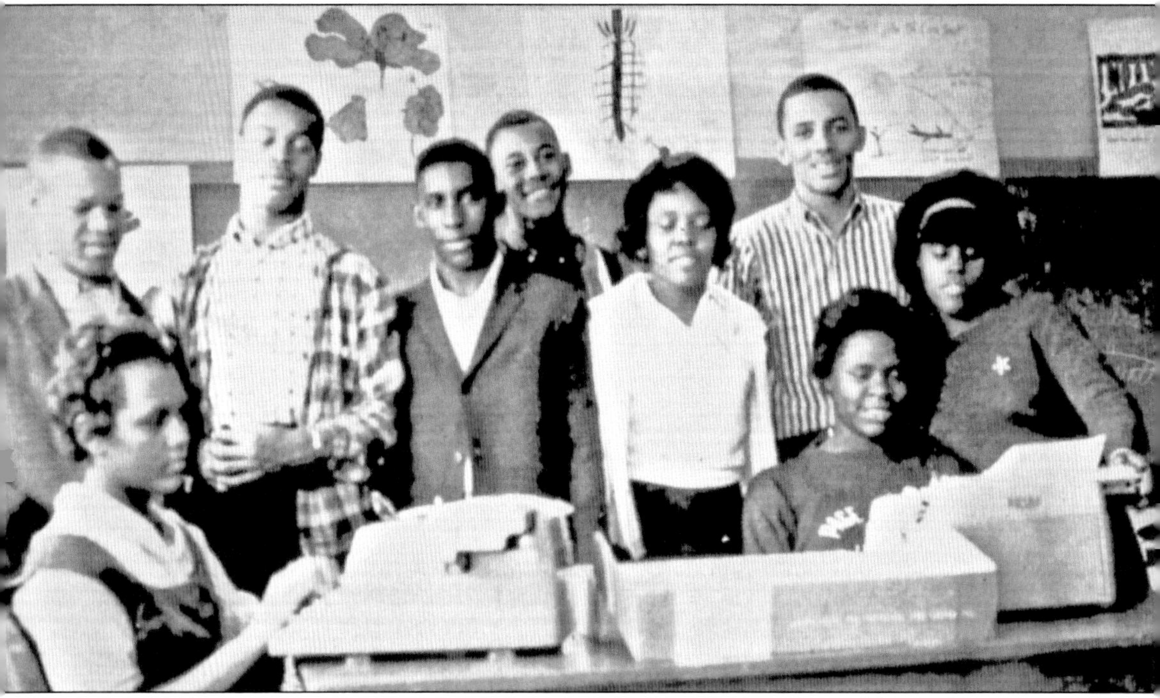

Pictured here are seniors at Page-Jackson High School working on the yearbook for 1965. From left to right are Patricia Winston, James Payton, Samuel Jones, James Butler, John Weaver, Cora Berry, Amelia Lindsay, Larry Togans, and Joyce Taylor. The process of putting a yearbook together begins in the fall and continues up to distribution day. It involves long hours of dedicated work both by the students and by the sponsor. Togans would later serve on the Jefferson County Board of Education and become its president.

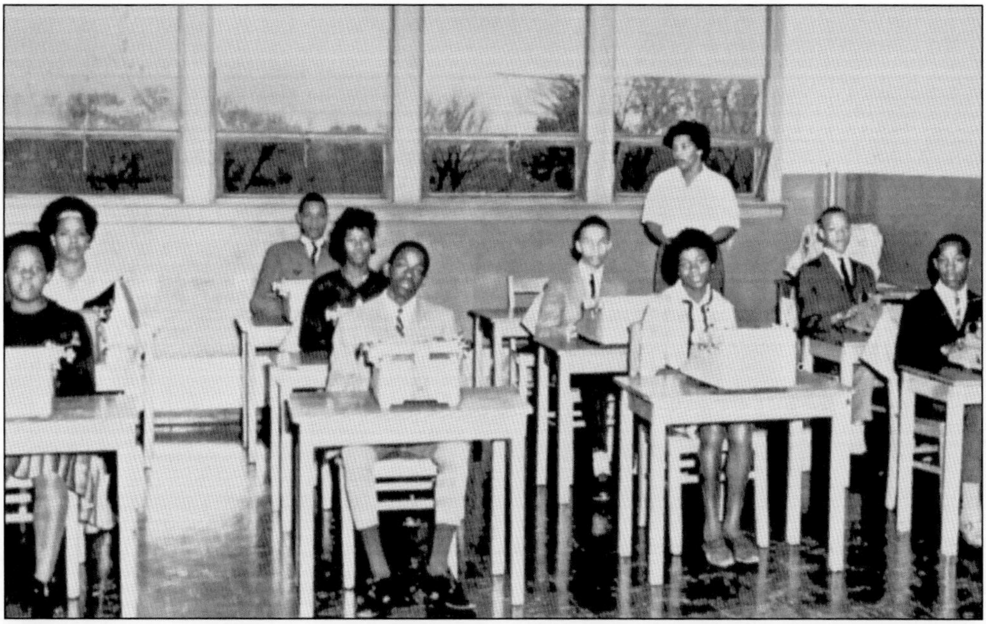

High school clubs are where young adults can practice their skills for their future, such as the Future Business Leaders of American. Pictured from left to right are the members in 1965: (first row) D. Berry, R. Yates, L. Harris, and R. Jones; (second row) R. Luckett, D. Roy, E. Dandridge Jr., and C. Lindsey; (third row) R. Lindsey and Mrs. Walker, advisor.

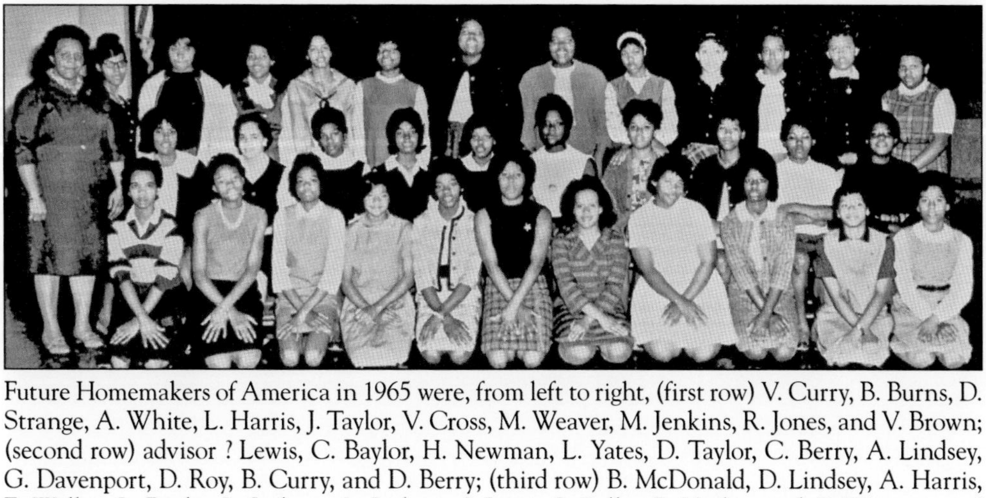

Future Homemakers of America in 1965 were, from left to right, (first row) V. Curry, B. Burns, D. Strange, A. White, L. Harris, J. Taylor, V. Cross, M. Weaver, M. Jenkins, R. Jones, and V. Brown; (second row) advisor ? Lewis, C. Baylor, H. Newman, L. Yates, D. Taylor, C. Berry, A. Lindsey, G. Davenport, D. Roy, B. Curry, and D. Berry; (third row) B. McDonald, D. Lindsey, A. Harris, E. Walker, L. Reeler, L. Jackson, L. Jackson, J. Jones, S. Puller, B. Underwood, P. Winston, and L. Jones.

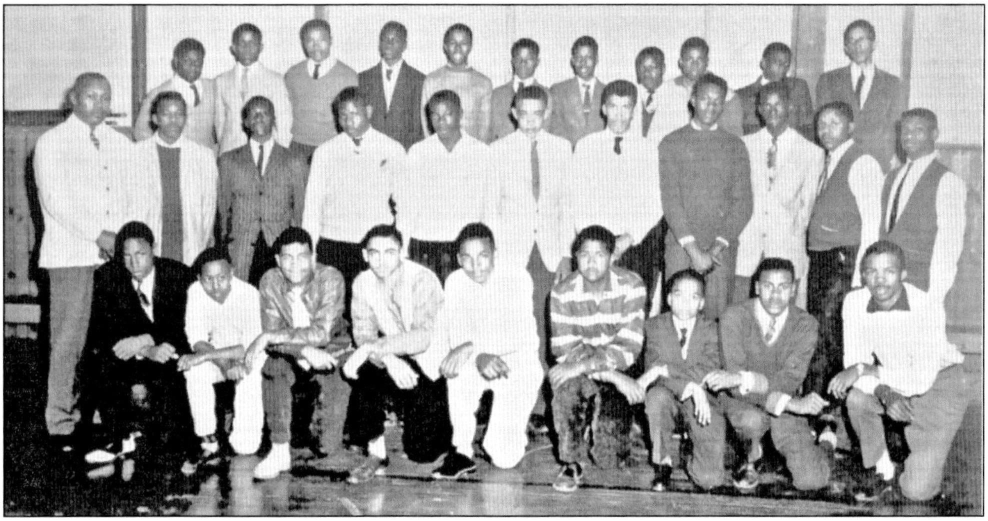

FFA members in 1958 were, from left to right, (first row) Harry Rideoutt, Leroy Thomas, Raymond Galloway, Paul Sims, Ralph Clinton, James Hopewell, Wilson Johnson, John Newman, and Norvel Willis; (second row) Q. D. Fleming (advisor), Clarence Holmes, Samuel Taylor, Hamilton Grey, Clarence Branson, Albert Brown, Richard Stevenson, Edgar Kidrick, Harry Jenkins, Harry Brown, and Stephen Greene; (third row) Maurice Winston, Charles Brown, Charles Newman, Thomas Payton, George Mitchell, Ashton Pinkcett, Phillip Braxton, Lawrence Johnson, Harry Carter, James Carr, and Theodore Togans.

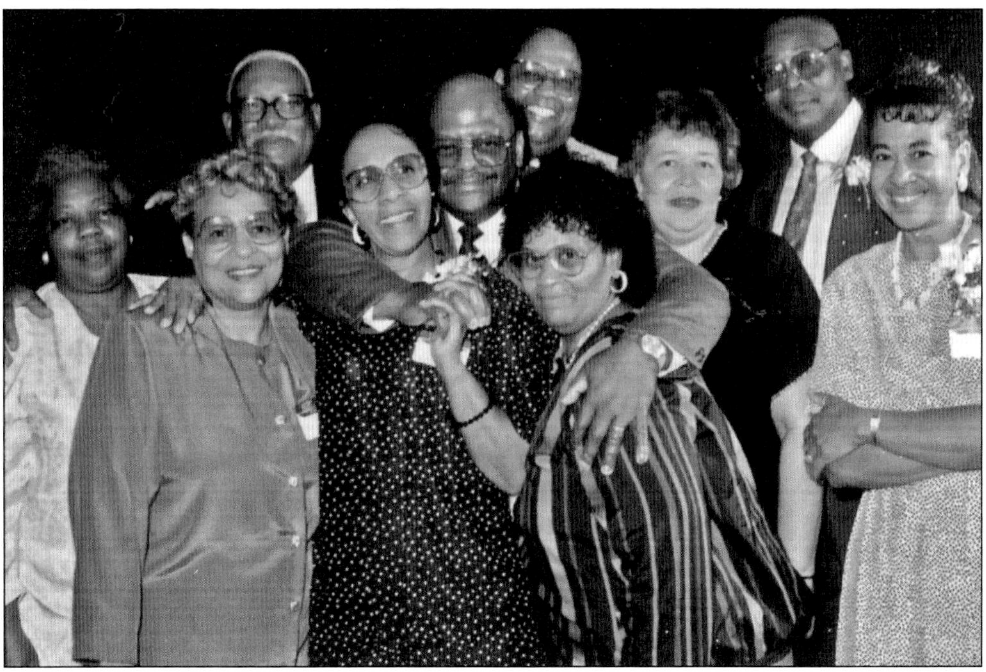

Pictured here are happy Page-Jackson High School alumni at a reunion in Charles Town, West Virginia. In the center is Ethel McDaniel. From left to right are (first row) Currina Jackson, Edith McDaniel Clay, Ronald Blackwell, Willeter Brown, and Dorothy Young Taylor; (second row) Willa Mae Pinckney Doleman, Thomas Doleman, Robert Brown, and James L. Taylor. The alumni of Page-Jackson High School hold reunions annually.

Nine

Daily Life

Jefferson County African Americans have generally lived in the same neighborhoods as their parents and grandparents generations beforehand. These neighborhoods were nicknamed "Dog Town," "Angel Hill," and "Big End," to name a few. In many instances, church attendance was also based on the section of town where one lived. For example, many from "Dog Town" attended the Colored Methodist Church, now Mount Zion United Methodist Church. Most of the predominantly African American churches in Jefferson County were organized and built after the Civil War and in the early 1900s. It was during the 1900s that many black businesses were established and there were racially separate businesses, churches, and schools; many remain today. South West Street was the black business corridor in Charles Town and Jefferson County. In later years, after the migration of many black families to find employment, some of the churches and some neighborhoods began having "homecomings" and reunions. Black men constructed many of the stone fences, picked the fruit, and worked the farms and quarries. Later machines would take the place of many laborers. Black women were housewives, domestic workers, teachers, and self-employed beauticians.

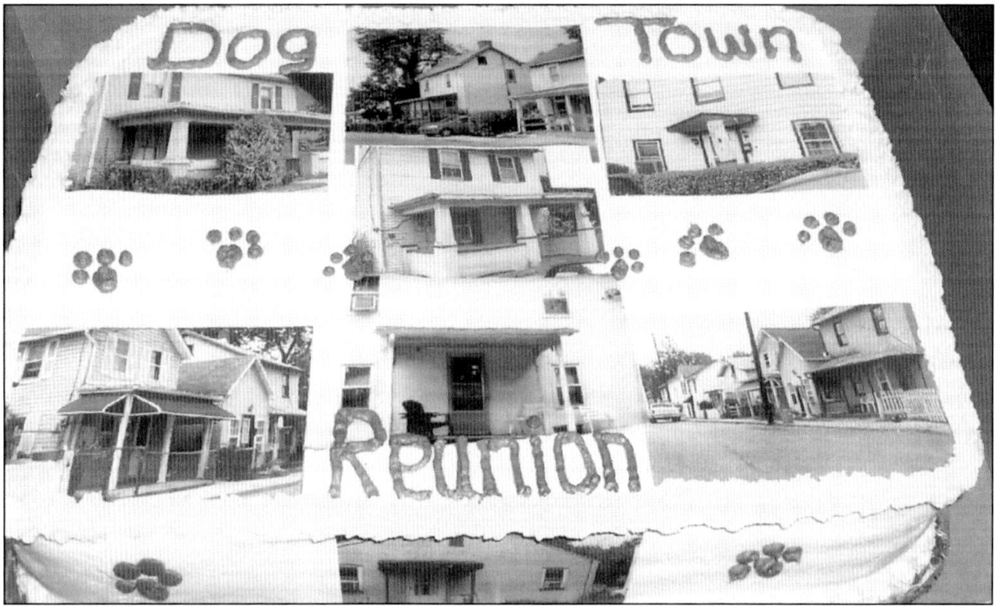

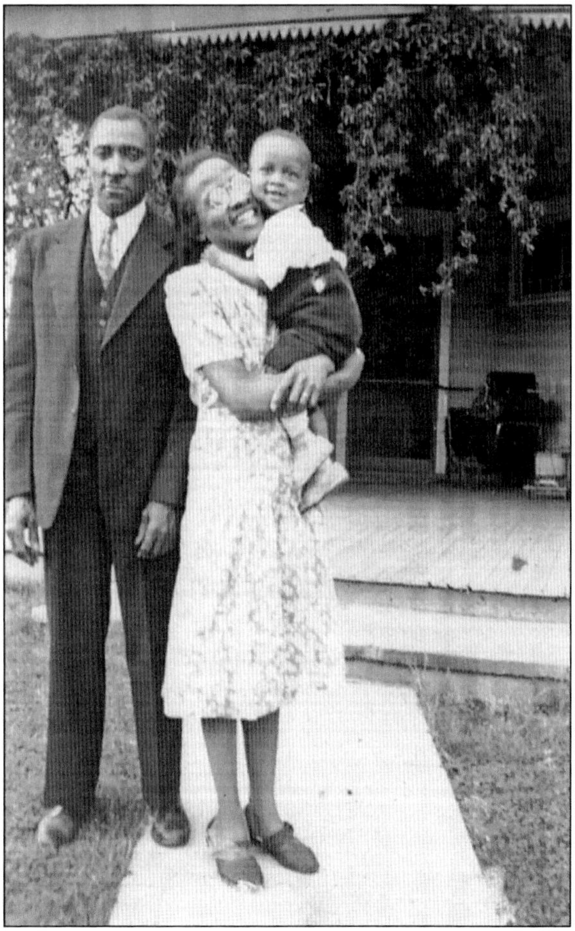

Pictured here is a cake that contains photographs on it of Dog Town in Charles Town, West Virginia. In Jefferson County, there were 24 African American communities that were nurturing and friendly to African Americans and embraced them with open arms. In these communities, children felt 100-percent loved and accepted. When they ventured outside of these areas, then they had to deal with racism and segregation.

Pictured are Thomas Claiborne Johnson (left) and Dorothy Johnson, who is holding their son Randolph Johnson. The photograph was taken in 1939 when they lived in Harpers Ferry, West Virginia.

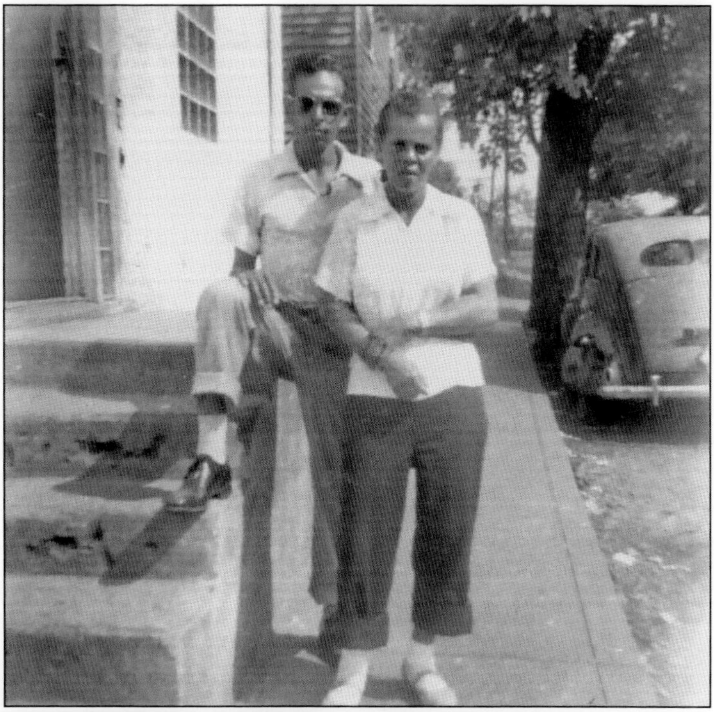

Taken in the late 1940s or early 1950s, this photograph shows Mary Stanton (right) with an unidentified friend. They are standing in front of Taylor's Tavern on South West Street in Charles Town. South West Street was considered to be an African American community. In total, there are 24 neighborhoods in Jefferson County. Taylor's Tavern was a business establishment run by an African American.

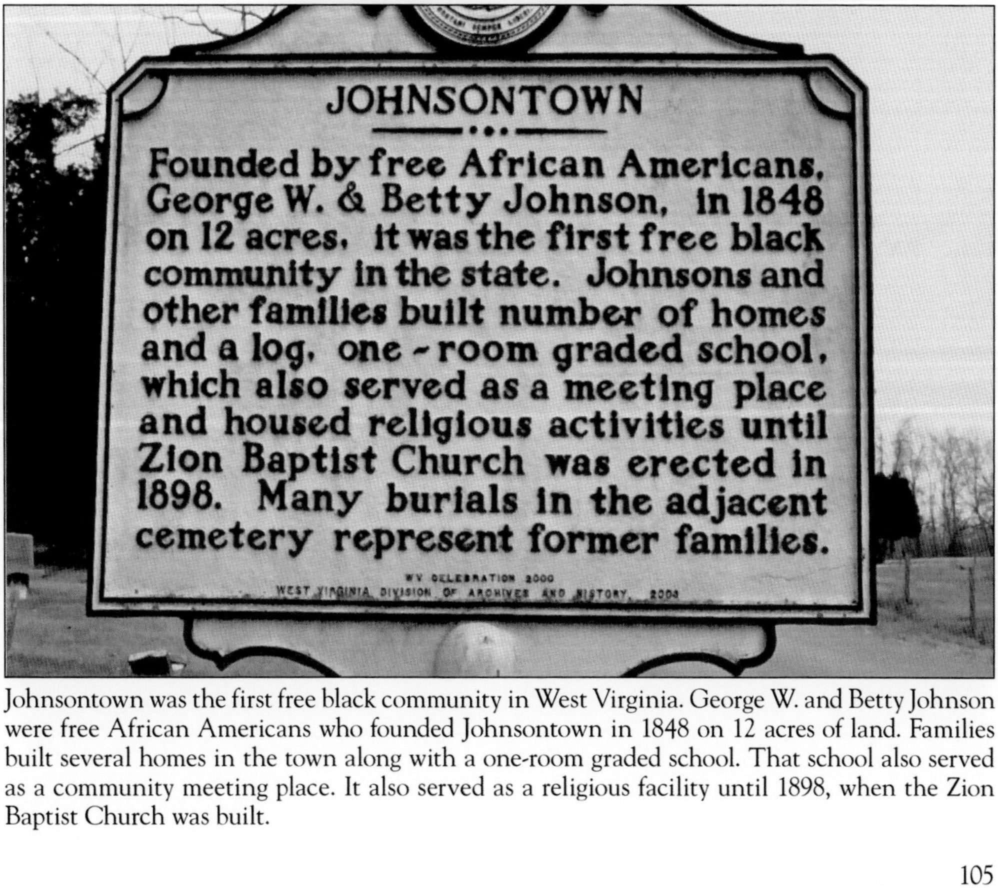

Johnsontown was the first free black community in West Virginia. George W. and Betty Johnson were free African Americans who founded Johnsontown in 1848 on 12 acres of land. Families built several homes in the town along with a one-room graded school. That school also served as a community meeting place. It also served as a religious facility until 1898, when the Zion Baptist Church was built.

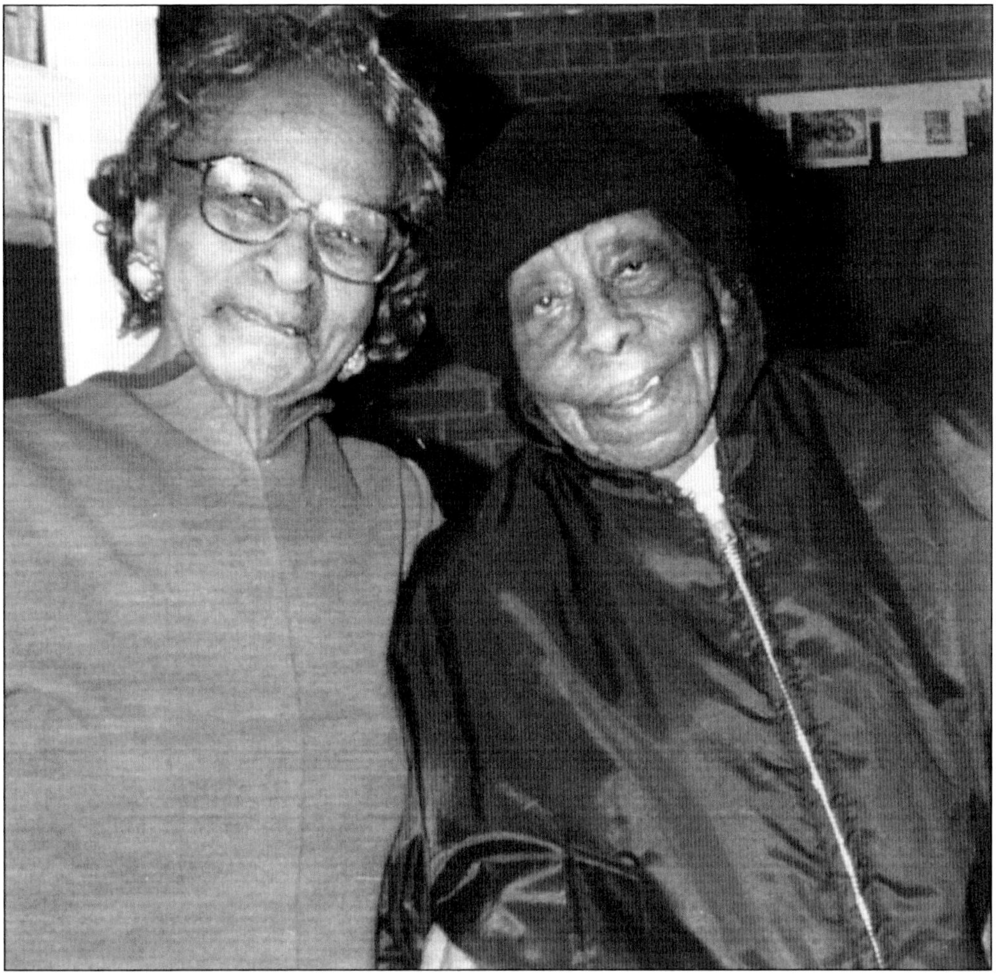

Pictured here are Dorothy Johnson (left) and Fanny Curry. Both are in their eighties. They have been close friends for many years, and both live on West Third Avenue in Ranson, West Virginia. Johnson was a member of Wainwright Baptist Church, and Curry was a member of King Apostle Holiness Church, both senior members in their respective churches.

From left to right are Fannie Pendleton Stanton, Anna Pearl Posey Williams, and Mary Walker. The photograph was taken at Taylor's Tavern "Fishermen's Hall" in the 1950s. Anna Pearl Posey was a 1950 graduate of Page-Jackson High School. Taylor's Tavern was located on South West Street.

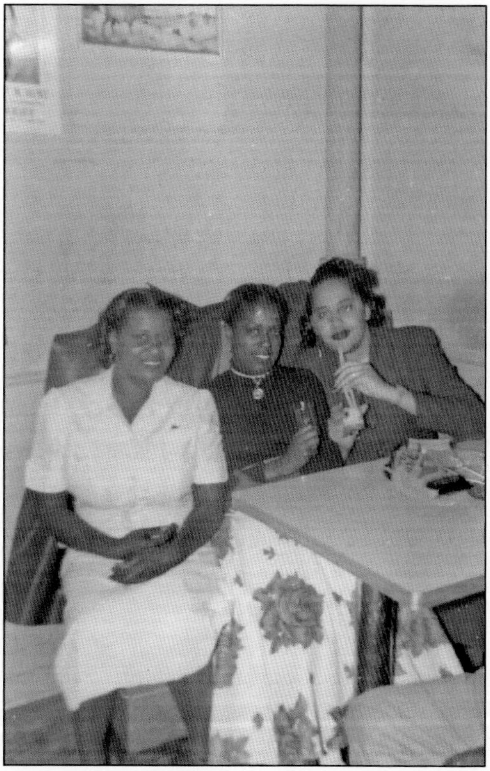

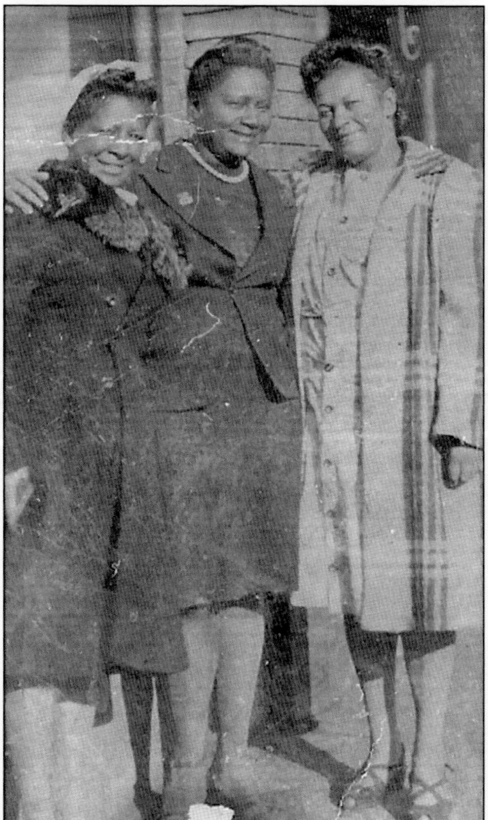

Pictured from left to right are Lula Hester, unidentified, and Nora Bailey on South West Street in Charles Town. The photograph dates from the 1940s. South West Street is in Charles Town and was not just a street but an African American community. In all of Jefferson County, there were 24 such African American neighborhoods.

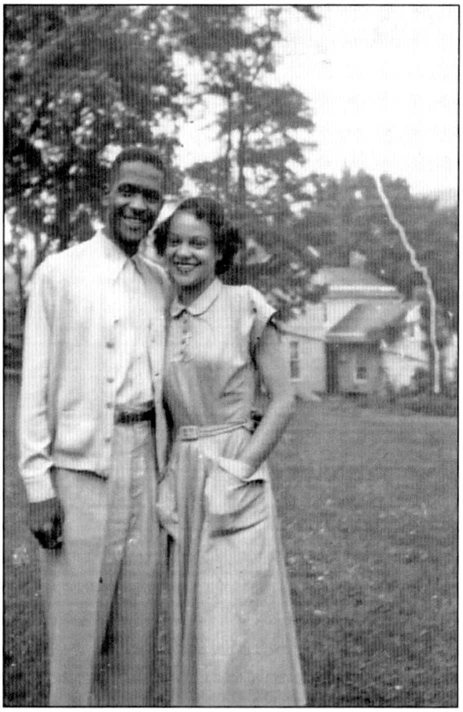

Pictured here are John and Ira Willis Pendleton. Ira taught at Eastside School in the Shepherdstown area, and John taught in the Virginia school system. They were both graduates of Storer College in Harpers Ferry, West Virginia. John also became an avid photographer of prominent blacks throughout Jefferson County. Both were active supporters of the NAACP.

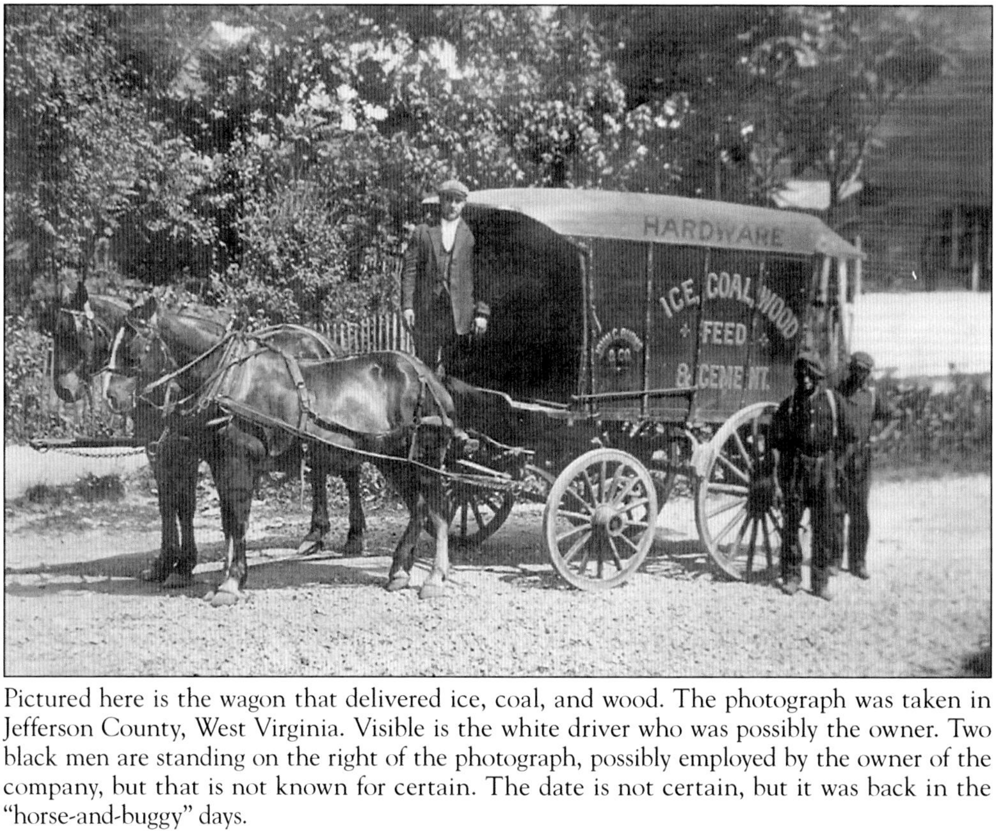

Pictured here is the wagon that delivered ice, coal, and wood. The photograph was taken in Jefferson County, West Virginia. Visible is the white driver who was possibly the owner. Two black men are standing on the right of the photograph, possibly employed by the owner of the company, but that is not known for certain. The date is not certain, but it was back in the "horse-and-buggy" days.

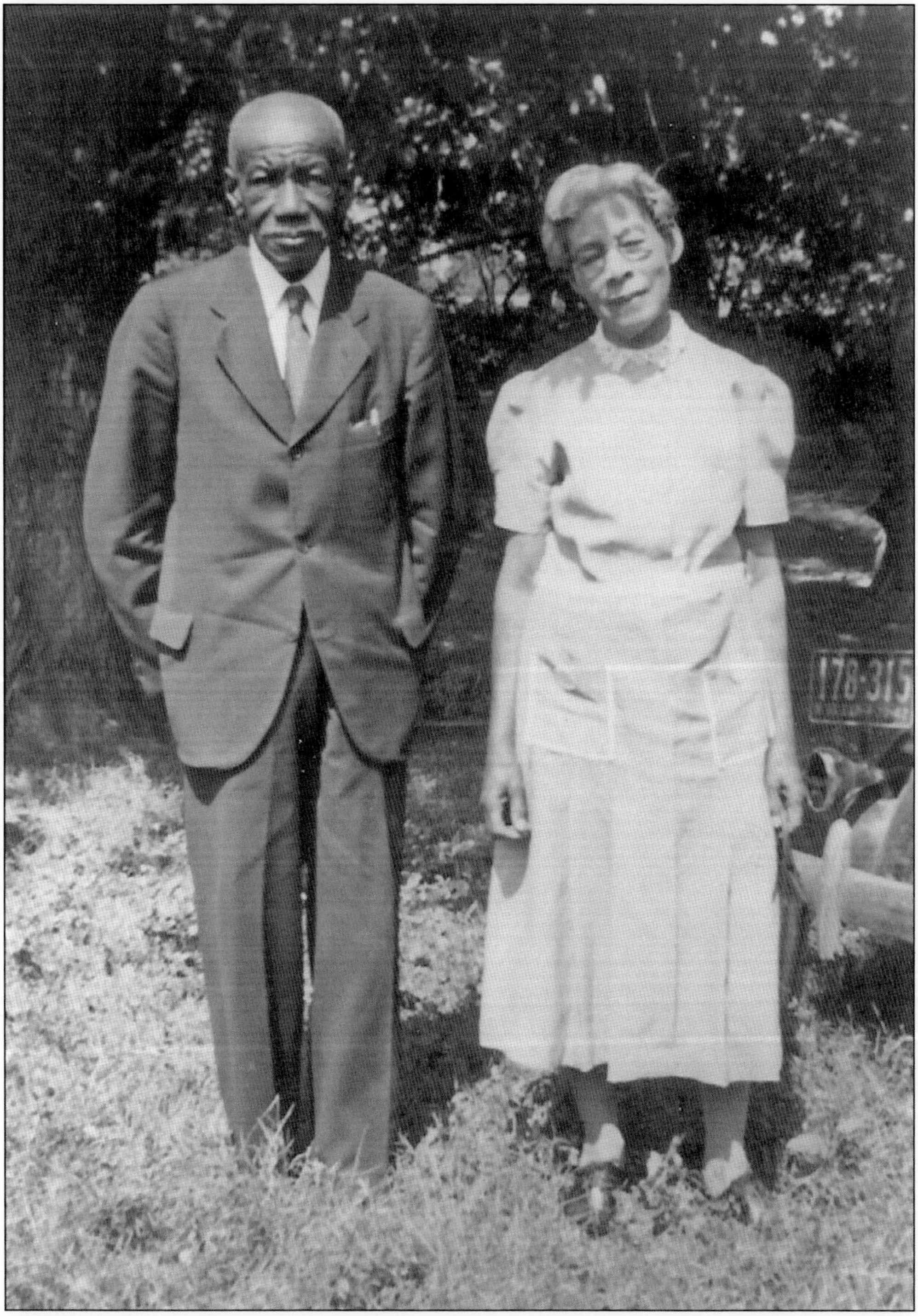

Edward and Fannie Braxton are pictured here. Edward, an educator in Jefferson County, taught at First Eagle Avenue School. The lot on which the original school sat had been purchased for $500 from George and Emily Washington. The original school was replaced in 1929 when a new facility named Charles Town District Colored Graded School was constructed on Eagle Avenue.

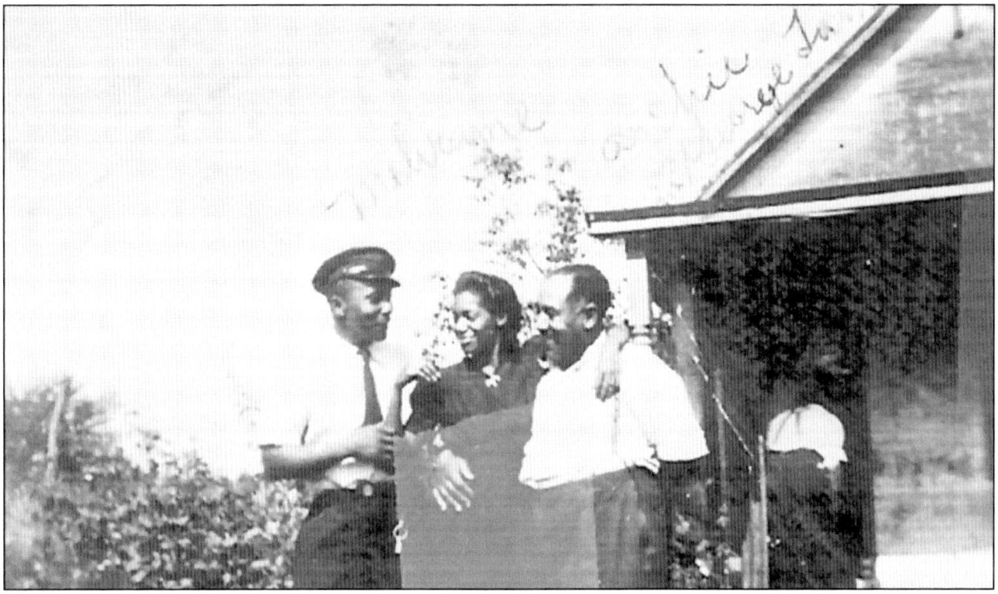

In this photograph can be seen George Turner (wearing the cap) along with his friends. Turner was owner of the Turner Taxi Service located in Jefferson County, West Virginia. Two other taxi companies are known to have been owned by African Americans in Charles Town and Harpers Ferry. One was owned by Russell Roper and one by Max Evan.

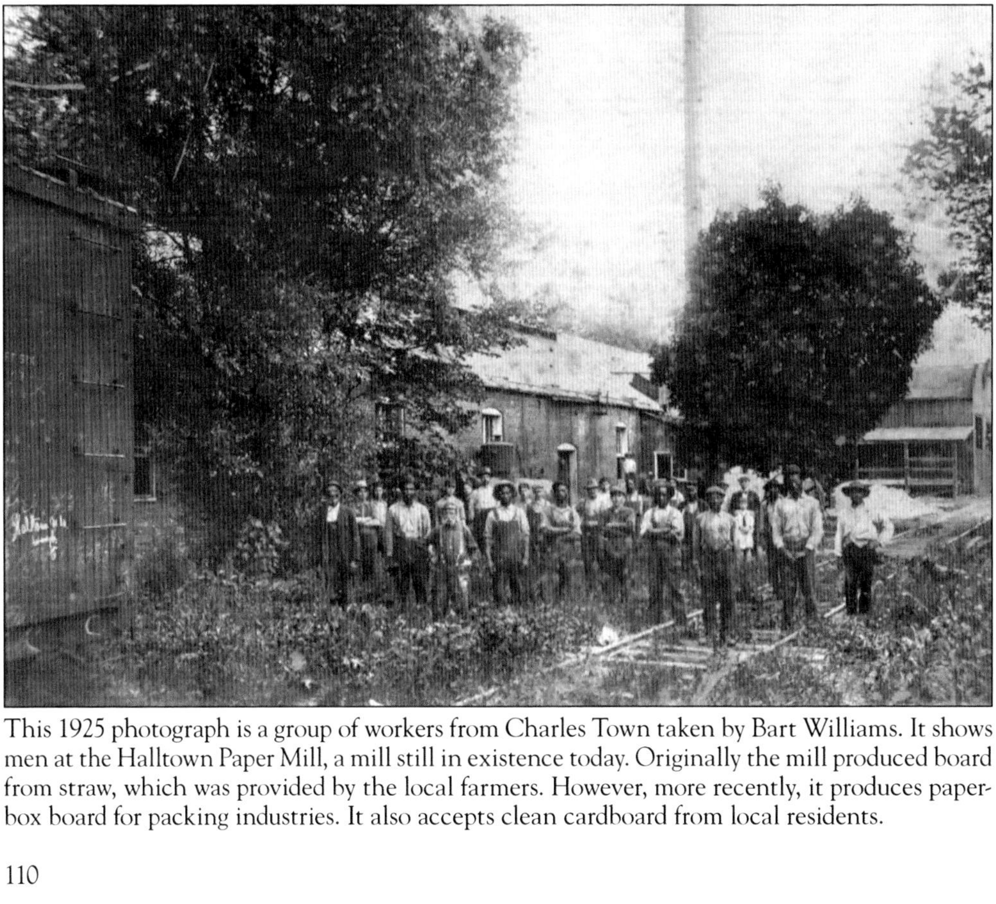

This 1925 photograph is a group of workers from Charles Town taken by Bart Williams. It shows men at the Halltown Paper Mill, a mill still in existence today. Originally the mill produced board from straw, which was provided by the local farmers. However, more recently, it produces paperbox board for packing industries. It also accepts clean cardboard from local residents.

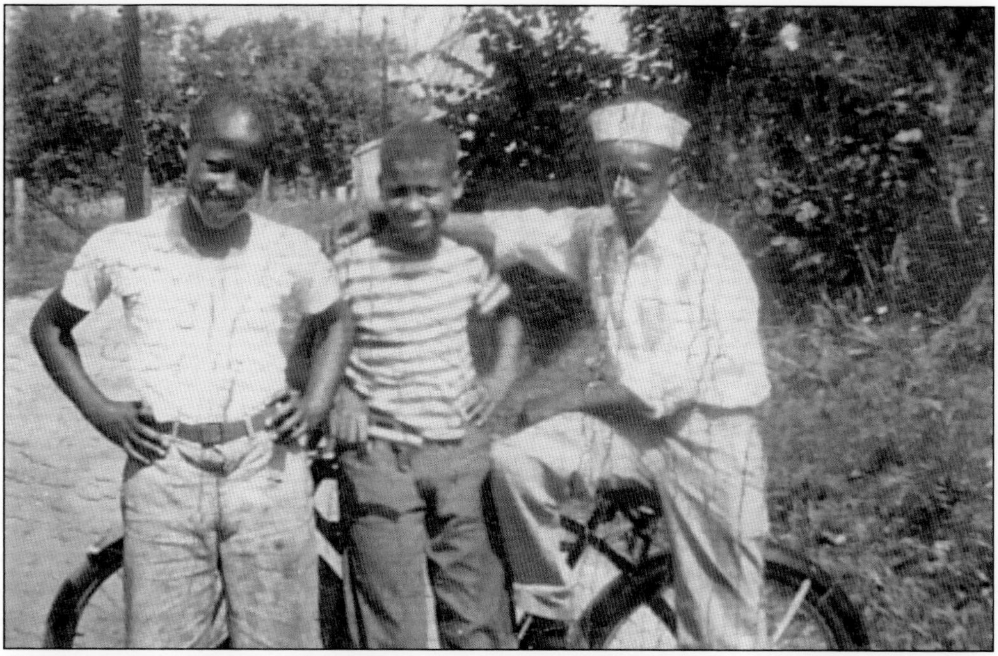

Three young men appear to be enjoying their summer vacation in the early 1940s. From left to right are Robert S. Brown, James Alvin Tolbert, and William Clay. The photograph was taken on Wysong Lane in Charles Town, West Virginia. The popular mode of transportation for young people in those days was bicycles, which these young men have.

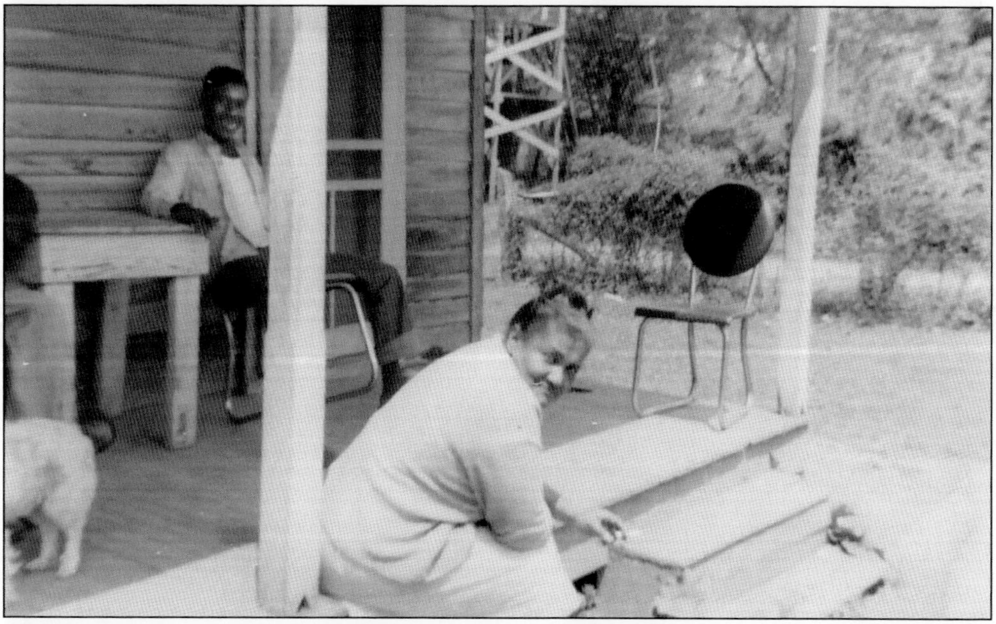

This photograph was taken in Big End, which was a part of Charles Town. It was located on the South George Street extension. Big End was one of the communities in Charles Town. There were no official boundary lines, but residents knew where they were. Examples of communities in Charles Town include Dog Town, Gibson Town, Hominy Town, Potato Hill, South West Street, and Werick Street.

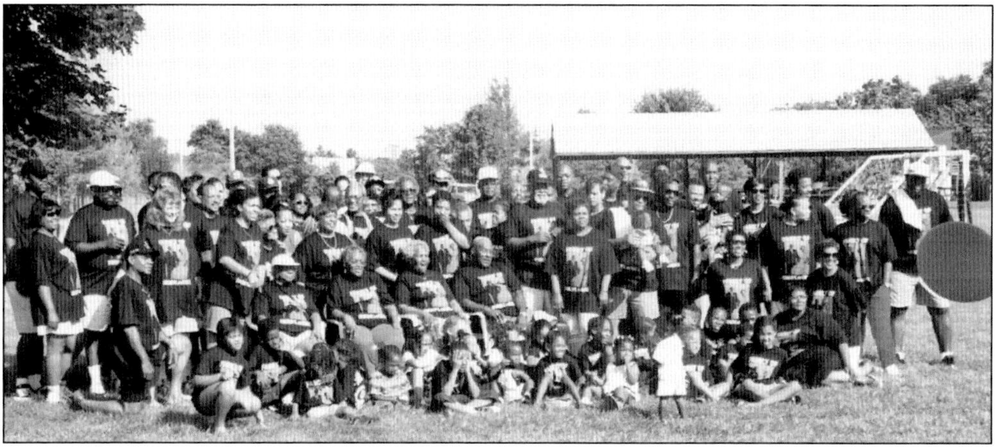

This photograph shows the reunion of the extended Taylor family of Charles Town in 1996. Reunions like this are held throughout Jefferson County. Not only are there family reunions, there are also church homecomings, community reunions, and school reunions, such as those for Page-Jackson High School and Storer College.

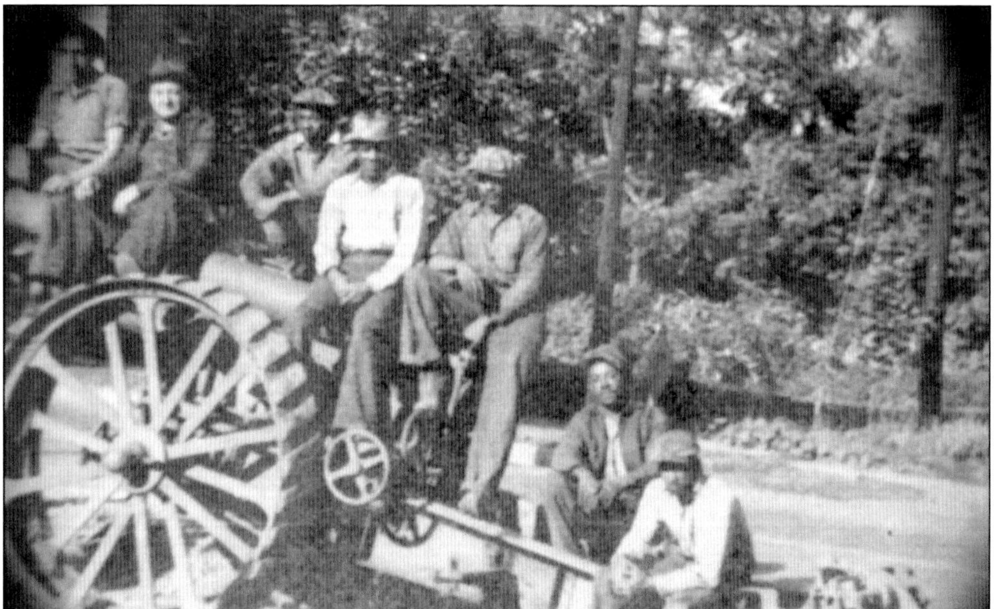

This photograph dates from sometime between 1920 and 1940. The dates are estimated based on the clothing styles and the age of the machinery, for lack of a better method. Workers are shown resting. Whether they are just beginning their day or just ending their day is not known. In 1934, the average weekly earnings amounted to $22.97.

African Americans are shown while working on the new county building and the new post office in Charles Town. The photograph was taken December 1, 1922. This is where the old jail stood on the corner of Washington and George Streets, the jail that housed the John Brown Raiders, including John Brown himself.

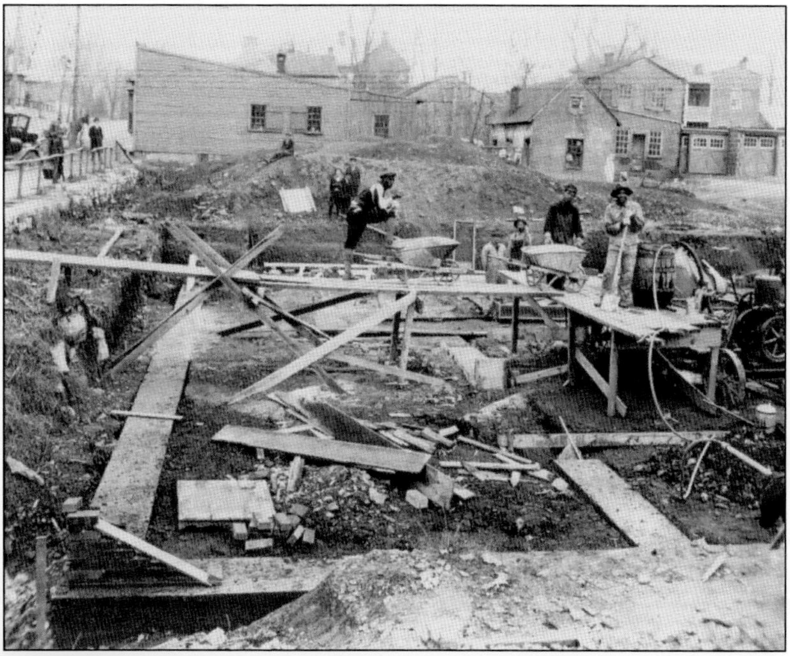

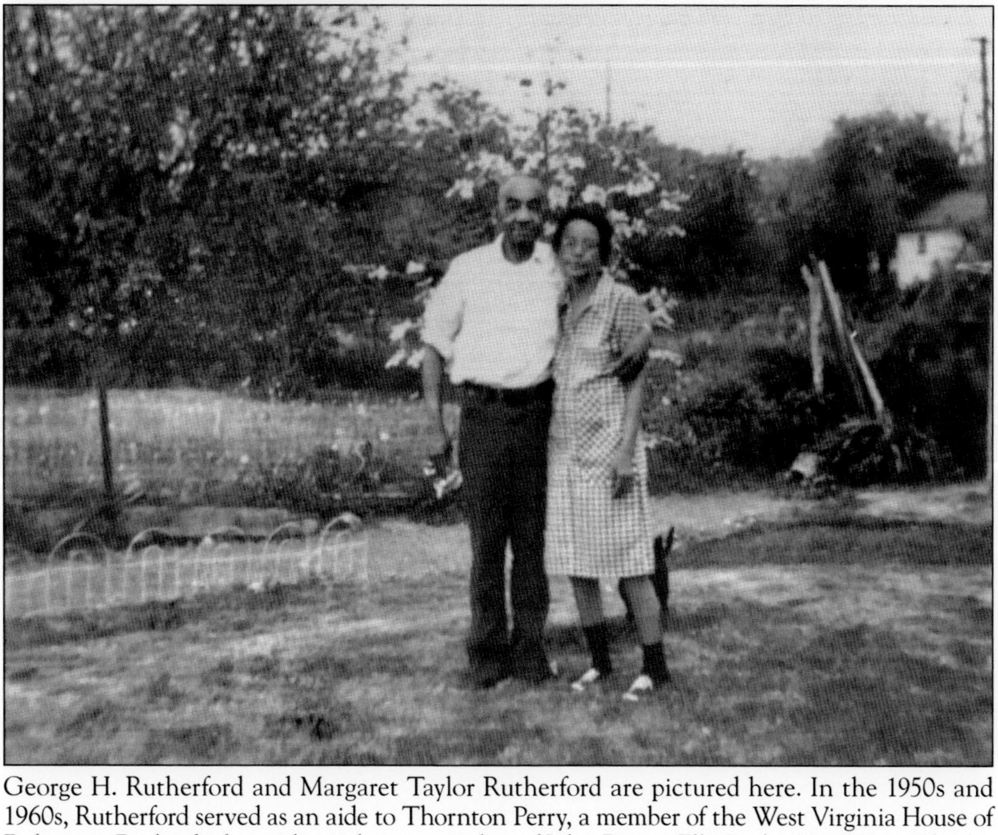

George H. Rutherford and Margaret Taylor Rutherford are pictured here. In the 1950s and 1960s, Rutherford served as an aide to Thornton Perry, a member of the West Virginia House of Delegates. Rutherford was also a charter member of John Brown Elks Lodge No. 841 in Charles Town, which was chartered in 1928.

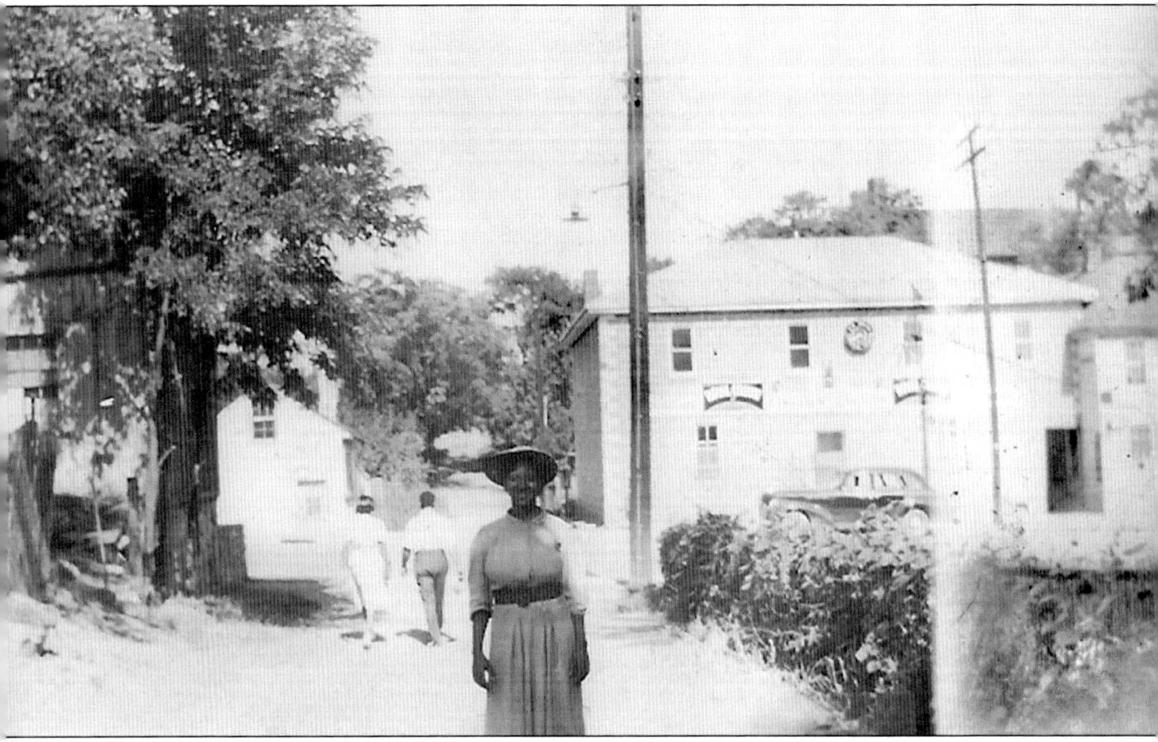

In the early 1950s, Eleanor Waters is pictured here as she is preparing to go to church at the Wainwright Baptist Church in Charles Town. In the background on the right is the building that housed John Smith's Tavern in Charles Town. Smith's Tavern was a prominent African American business at that time and was located on South West Street.

Madeline Lawson McIver stands with her father, Venning Lawson, on South West Street in Charles Town, West Virginia. The Gold Kettle was a black business in Charles Town that was renowned for its courteous service.

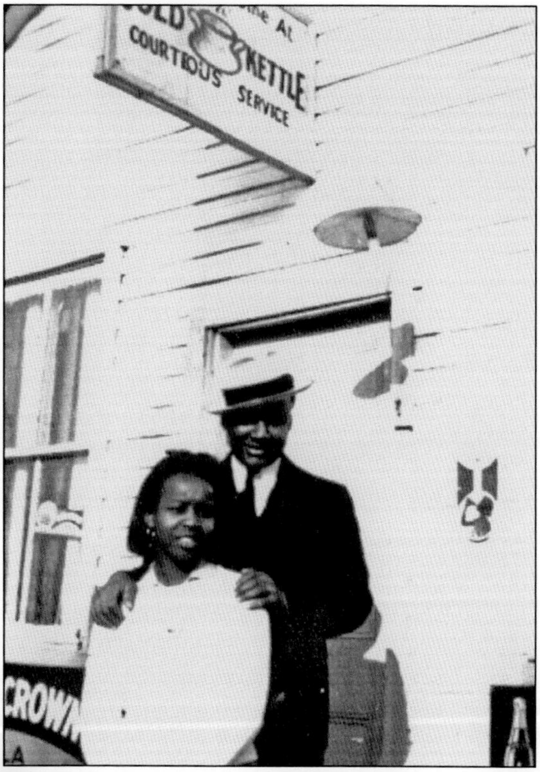

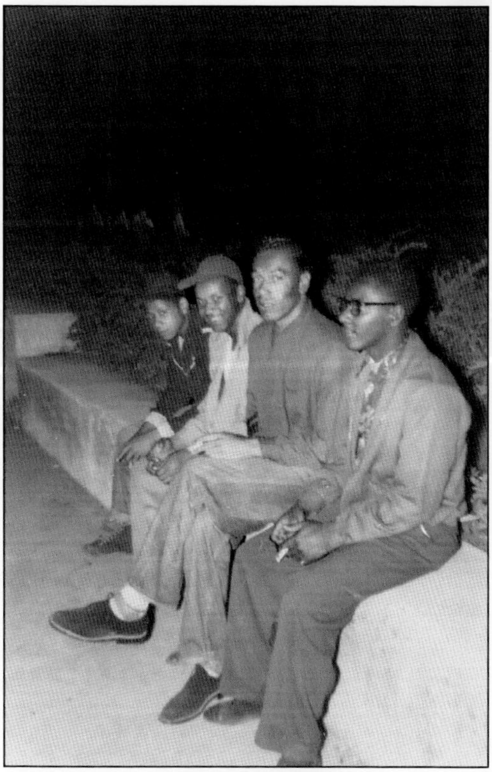

This photograph was taken near the old Charles Town Presbyterian Church graveyard. From left to right are Paul Turner, William Turner, Garfield Williams, and Arthur Gales, sitting on a wall on South West Street. This area was a Saturday night hangout when the temperatures were fairly warm.

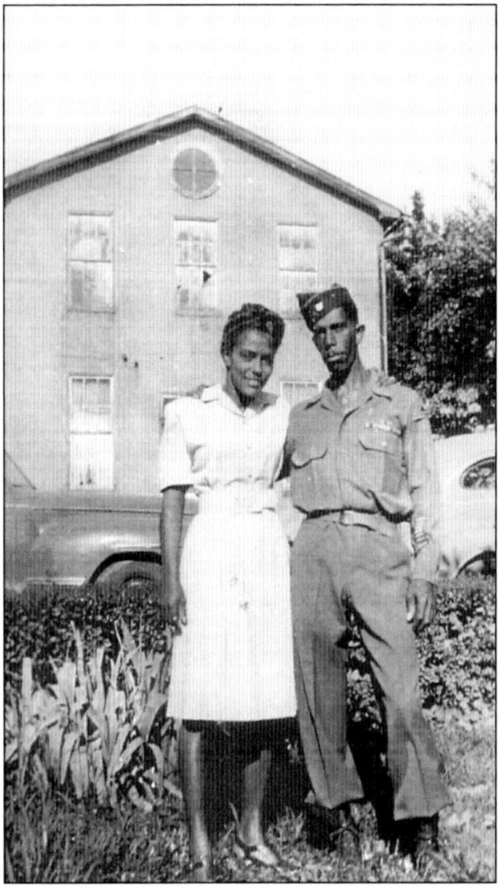

On the left is Genevieve Bradford Baylor, and on the right is her brother, World War II veteran Jesse "Bus" Bradford. They are standing in front of Fishermen's Hall on South West Street in Charles Town. South West Street was one of eight African American communities in Charles Town.

Pictured in this late 1950s or early 1960s photograph are Sandra Smith and Cora Page on South Lawrence Street in Charles Town. St. Philip's Church is in the background. In addition to being an Episcopal church, it was also a parochial and industrial school that was begun in 1900 by Reverend J. H. Deaver and continued until the years of the Great Depression.

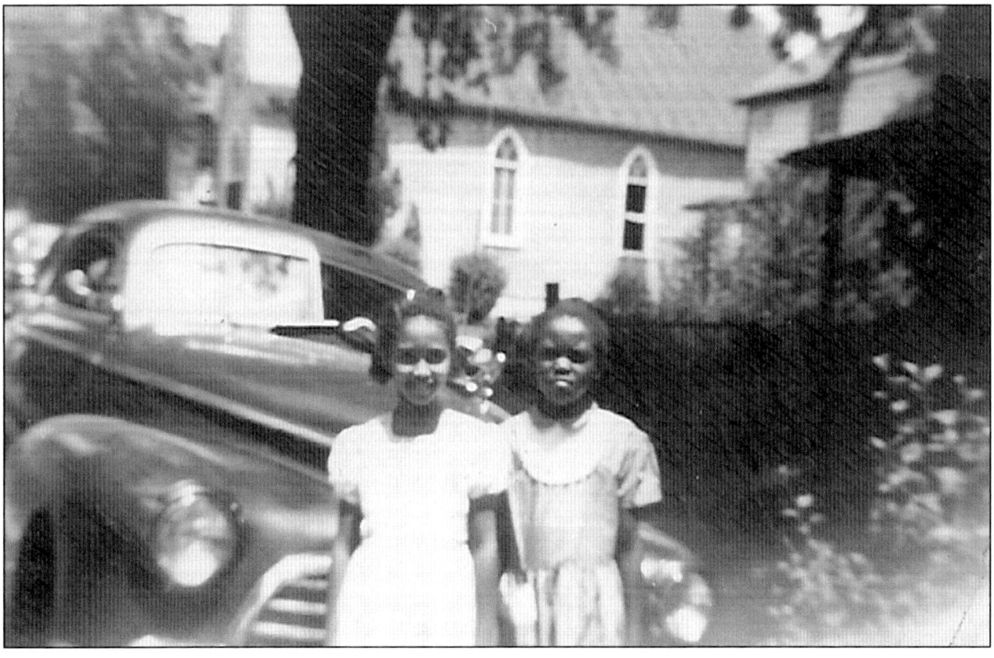

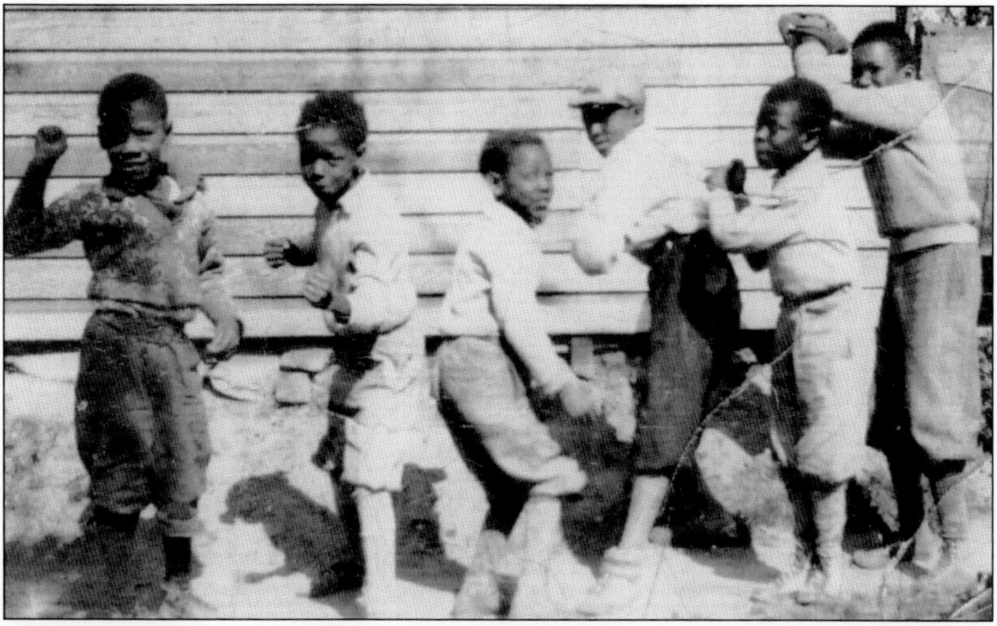

This picture from the 1920s shows young men from Shepherdstown in various boxing poses. From left to right are Wallace Robinson, Gordie Clark, Warren Clark, Burton Brown, Adrian Robinson, and Henry Washington. Most of these young men probably had made the boxers of the day their heroes. Jack Johnson had earned the heavyweight championship from Tommy Burns in 1908. Johnson might have been one of their role models.

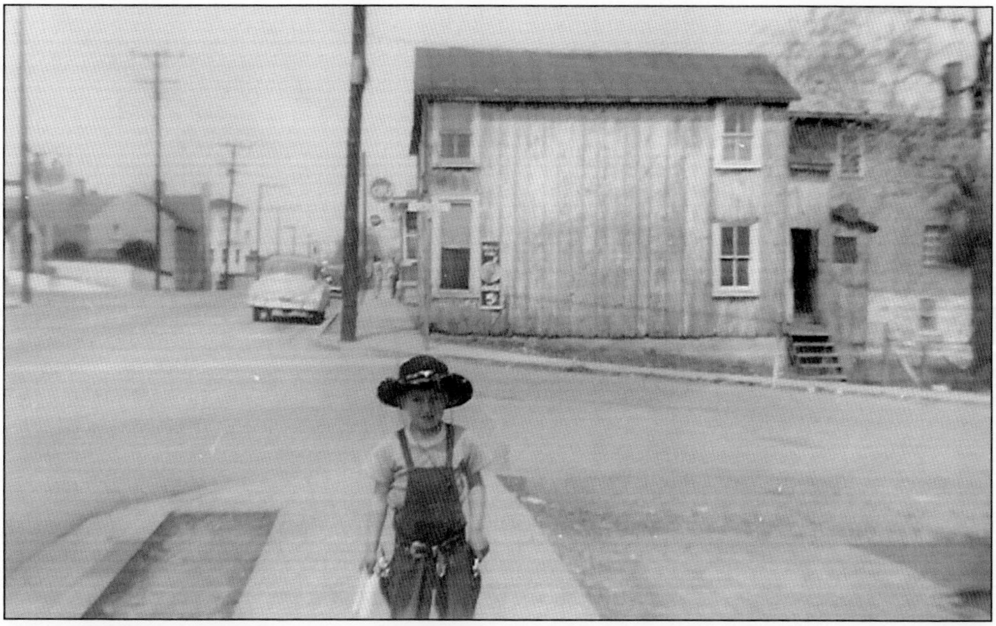

At South West and West Congress Streets, the apartment above the building was once occupied by Pete Lee, who ran Pete Lee's Billiards; the lower portion, Bowie's Barbershop and Bradford's Pool Room. Many businesses were located on South West Street. Other African American communities in Charles Town include Big End, Dog Town, Gibson Town, Hominy Town, Mill Lane, Potato Hill, and Werick Row.

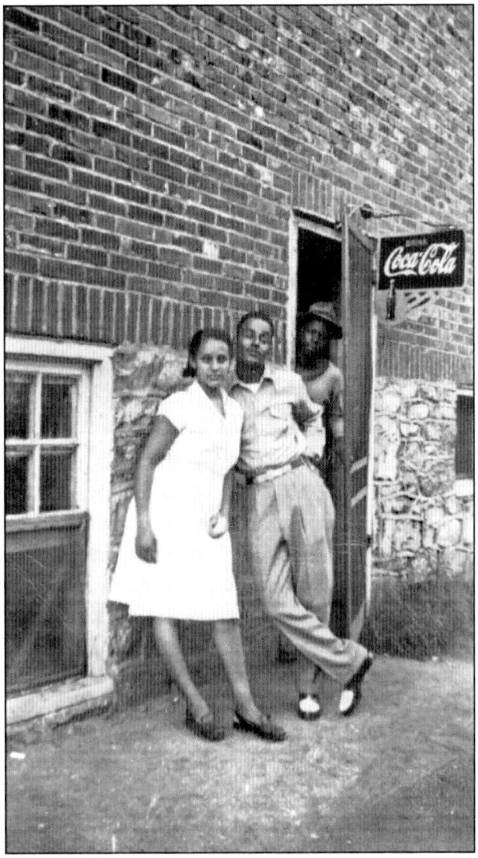

Shirley Rideoutt and Calvin Walker are pictured in front of Payne's Tap Room on South West Street, a favorite hangout for young adults. Payne's Hotel was located above the Tap Room. Payne's Hotel was owned by William and Lavinia Payne. William Payne was a veteran and a charter member of Green-Copeland American Legion Post No. 63, which was chartered September 17, 1929, in Charles Town, West Virginia.

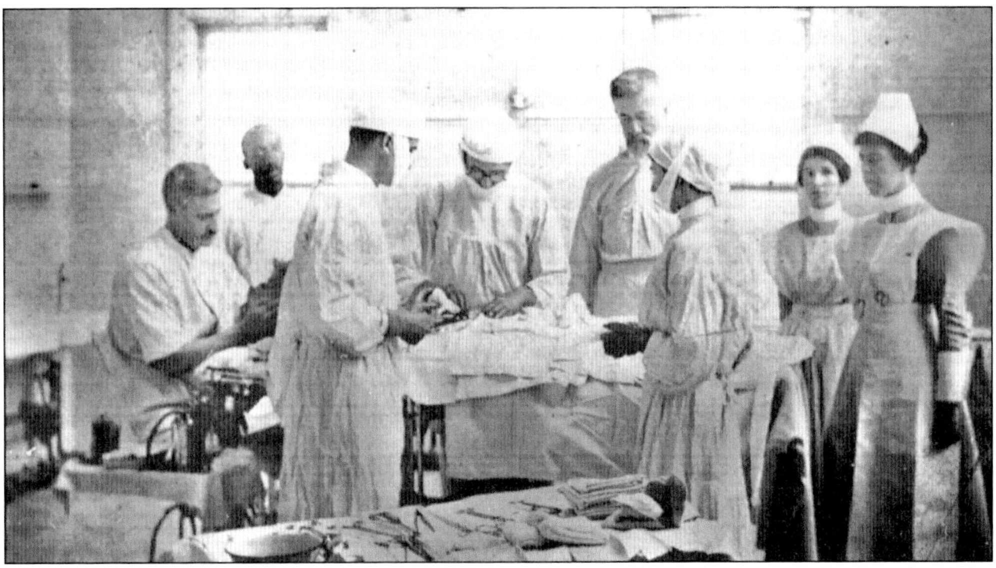

This photograph from 1912 was taken at the Old Charles Town Hospital. On the far side of the operating table, the African American man second from the left is John W. Rutherford, who was a slave as a child of nine years old. He was the great-grandfather of George C. Rutherford, the treasurer of the Jefferson County Black History Preservation Society.

Ten

Religious Life

In Jefferson County, as in most of the South, blacks were not allowed to assemble and worship. However, they were allowed to sit in the back or the balcony of the whites' churches. Records show that as early as the 1840s, blacks were allowed to attend, but not participate in, the white services. Immediately after the freeing of the slaves, black churches began to be established. Two of the earliest churches were the Mount Zion Methodist Episcopal Church (1867) in Charles Town and St. Andrews Episcopal (1859) in Shepherdstown. The black religious leaders focused on social issues. For example, St. Philip's Episcopal Church established a school, and during the influenza epidemic it was used as a hospital.

In the early 1960s, the majority of the black religious leaders were deeply involved in the local civil rights movement. The majority of the leaders were also leaders in the newly formed Jefferson County NAACP. The black church has been the backbone of the black community since the days of slavery.

Wainwright Baptist Church was the oldest black Baptist church in Jefferson County, established in 1868 as part of the Freedmen's Bureau by Rev. Nathan Brackett.

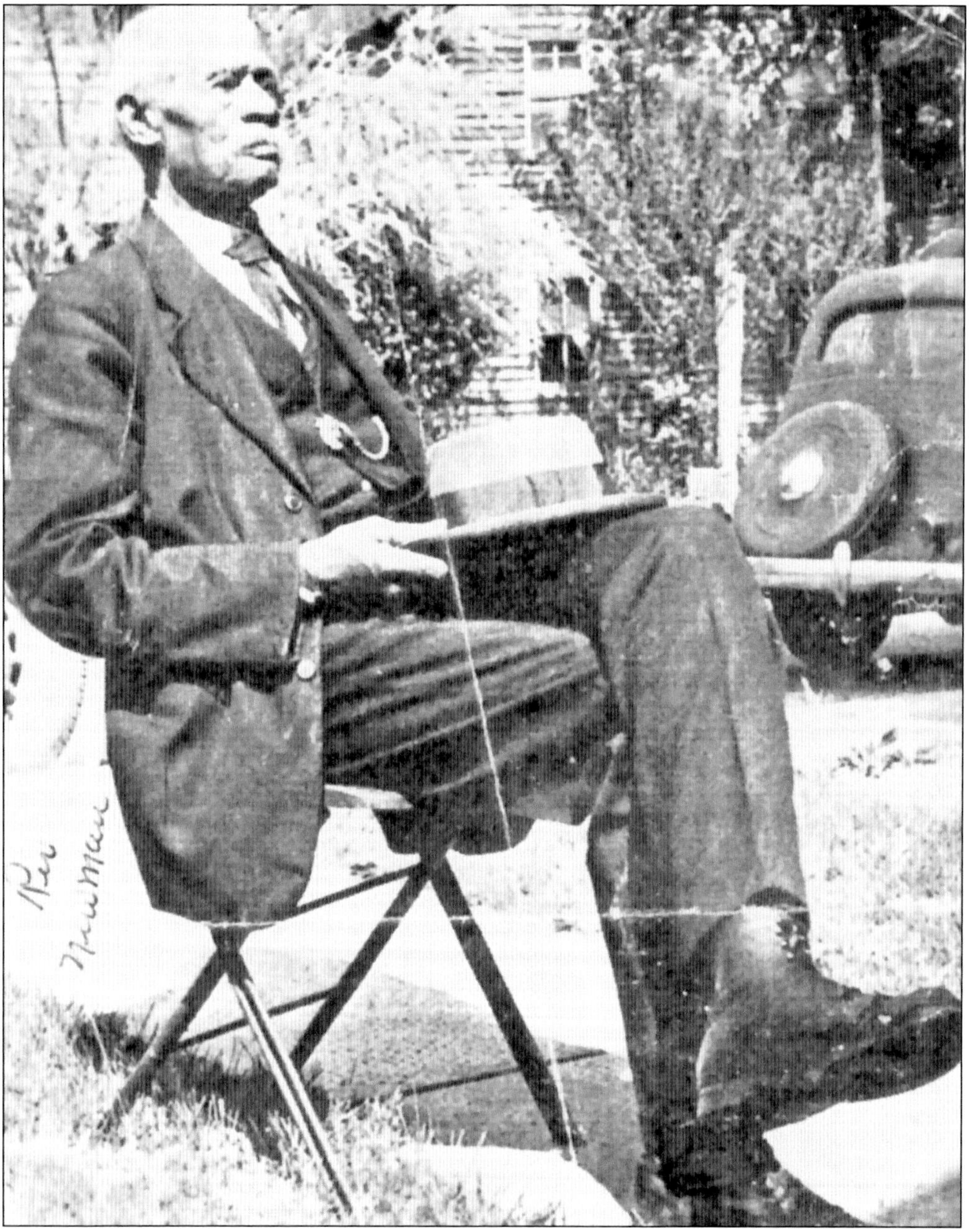

Rev. J. C. Newman was the pastor of the Wainwright Baptist Church in Charles Town, West Virginia. The church had been founded in 1868 and is still very active today. In addition to religious activities and services, the church hall is also used for community events.

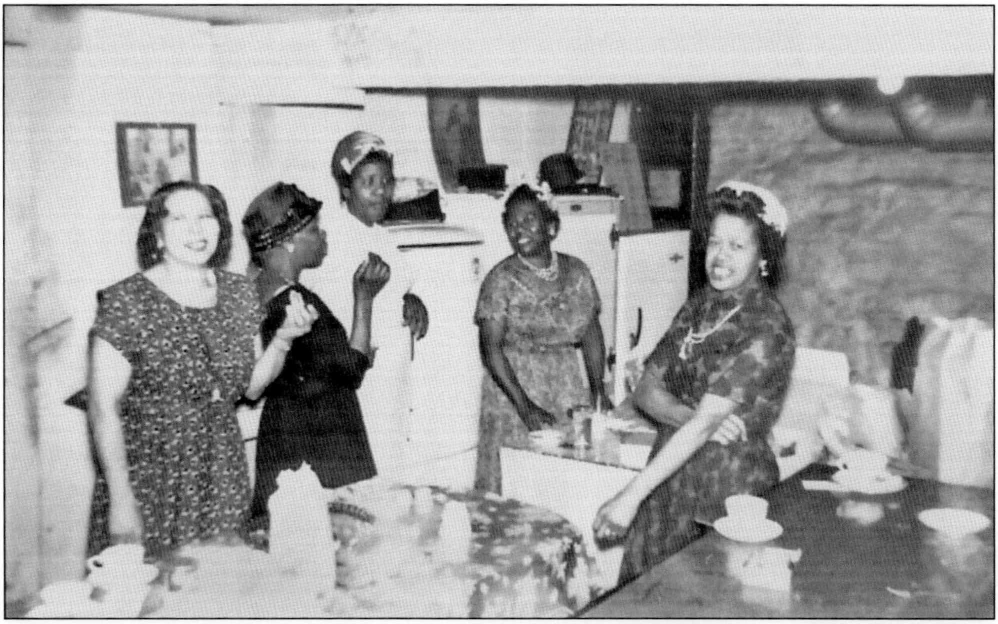

Pictured here are ladies enjoying a church function. From left to right are Mary Butler, Eva Sprigg, unidentified, Elizabeth Luckett Mitchell, and Mildred Mitchell Jackson. They are pictured in the basement of Mount Zion United Methodist Church in Charles Town.

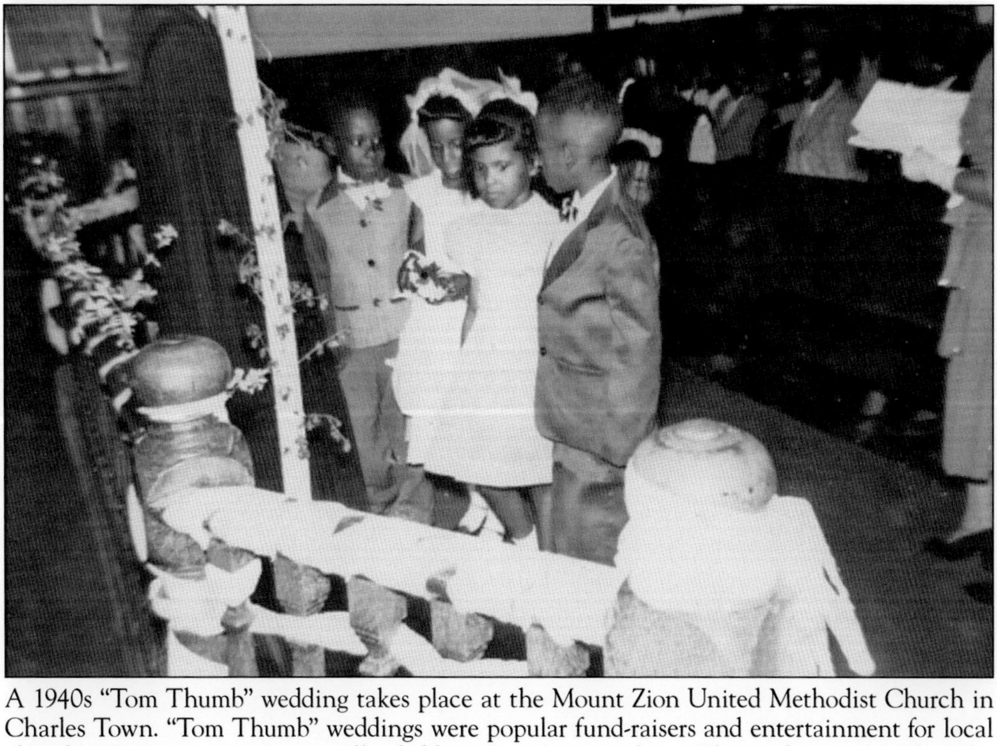

A 1940s "Tom Thumb" wedding takes place at the Mount Zion United Methodist Church in Charles Town. "Tom Thumb" weddings were popular fund-raisers and entertainment for local churches. Participants were usually children 5 or 6 years of age. The tradition started in the 1800s after the marriage in 1863 of Charles Stratton and Lavinia Warren, little people who had appeared at P. T. Barnum's American Museum in New York in the 1800s.

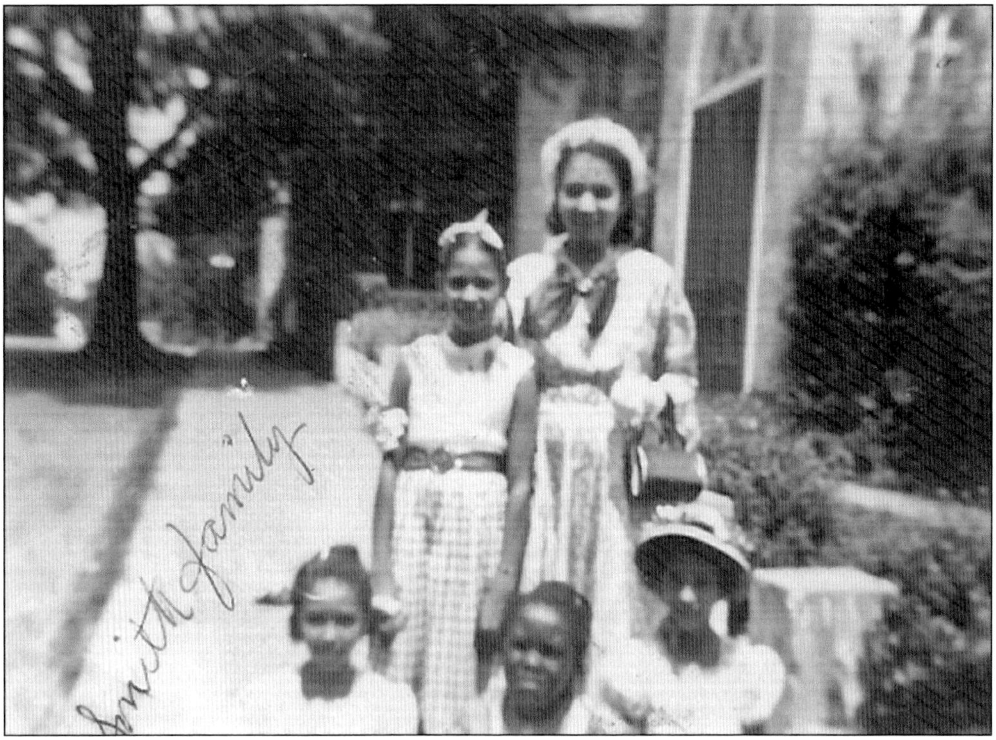

The family of Fr. Eugene Smith of St. Philip's Episcopal Church is pictured in Charles Town, West Virginia. The date of the photograph is unknown. From left to right are (first row) Sandra Smith, Cora Paige, and Allison Smith; (second row) Barbara Smith and Mrs. Smith. The church is located on South Lawrence Street.

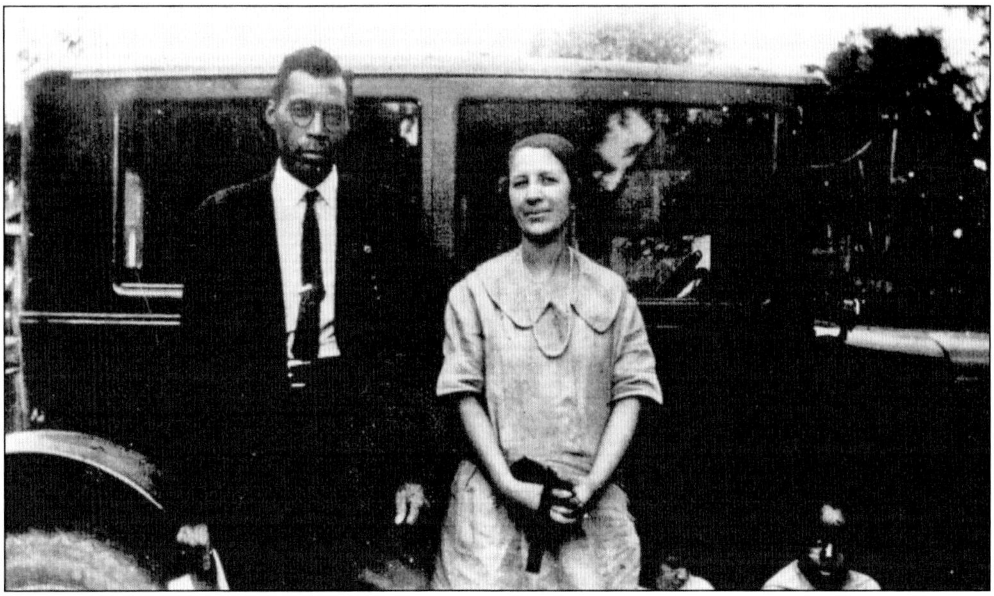

This 1920s photograph shows Rev. William Craven with his wife, Cerelle Page Craven. Reverend Craven was pastor at Wainwright Baptist Church. Cerelle Page Craven was a teacher at the first Eagle Avenue School. The land on which the school sat had been purchased for $500 in 1894.

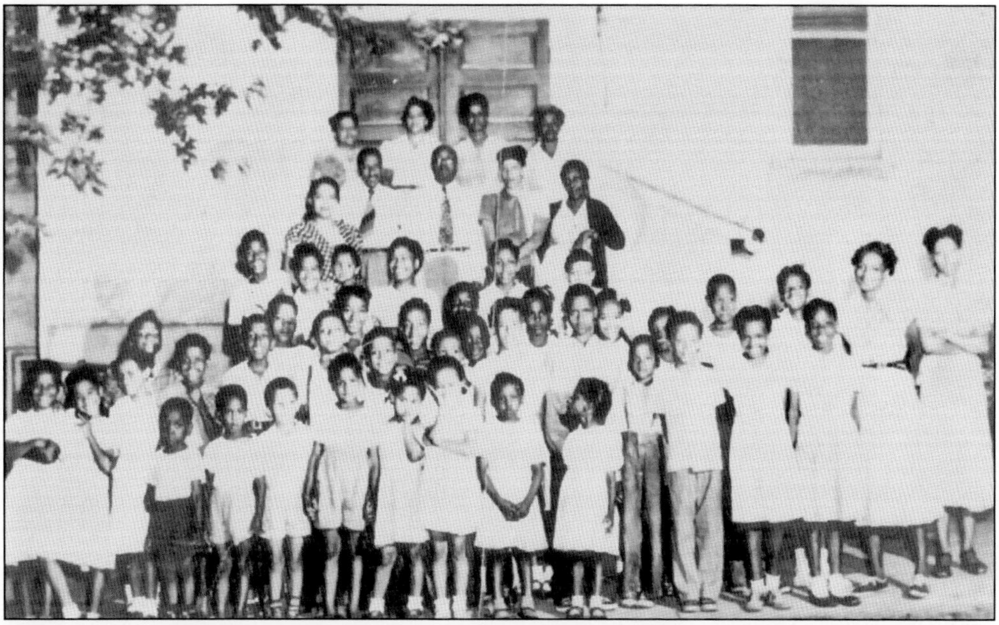

Pictured is the Vacation Bible School at Wainwright Baptist Church in the early 1950s. Most churches offered Vacation Bible Schools each summer for a week, where the children would come for socialization and religious education in a fun manner. Usually the students completed projects throughout the week related to a biblical theme. The church was founded in 1868. Among others who served as pastor was Rev. J. C. Newman.

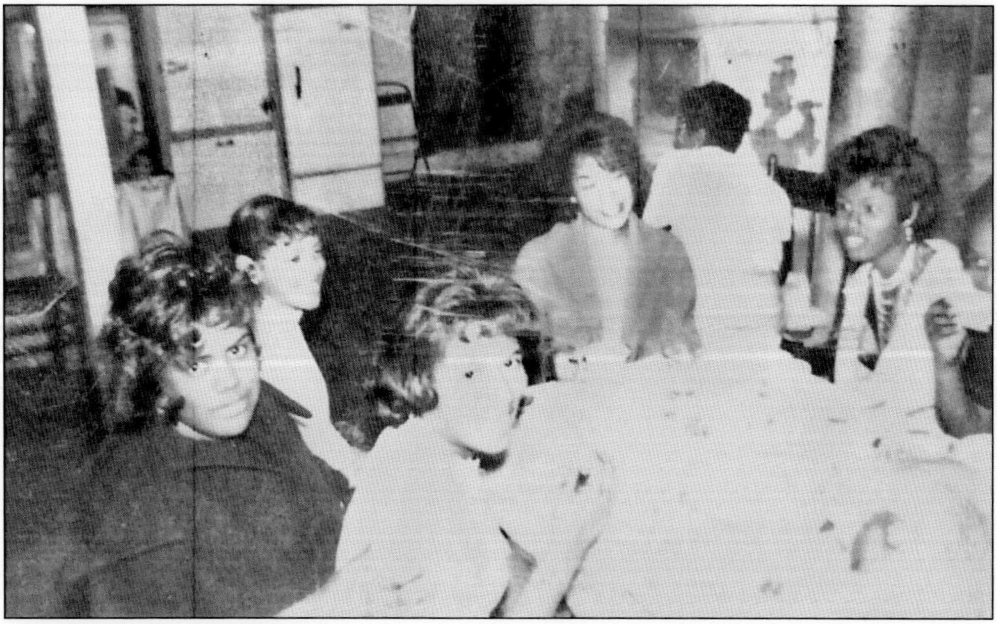

Pictured here is a Girls' Club get-together in the basement of the Mount Zion United Methodist Church in Charles Town. The club had regular "teas" in the early 1950s. Clockwise around the circle starting at front left are Vivian Braxton, Charlene Baylor, Janice Baylor, Gloria Russ, Gwenny Bradford (facing the other direction wearing white blouse), Fonda Braxton, and unidentified. Mount Zion United Methodist Church was founded in 1867.

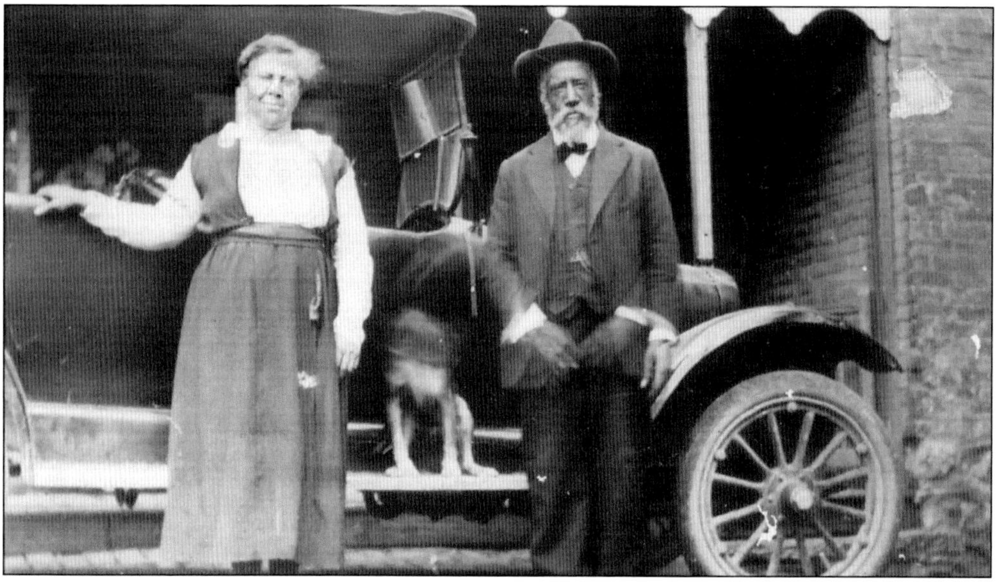

This c. 1920 photograph shows Br. Peter Hall and his wife, Essie Brookings Hall, in front of their residence on Water Street. In Charles Town in 1936, the only African American Pentecostal Holiness congregation was the House of Prayer. The congregation met in members' homes for three years. In 1939, the estate of Brother Hall provided part of the funds necessary to purchase a building, located on the corner of Water and Congress Streets.

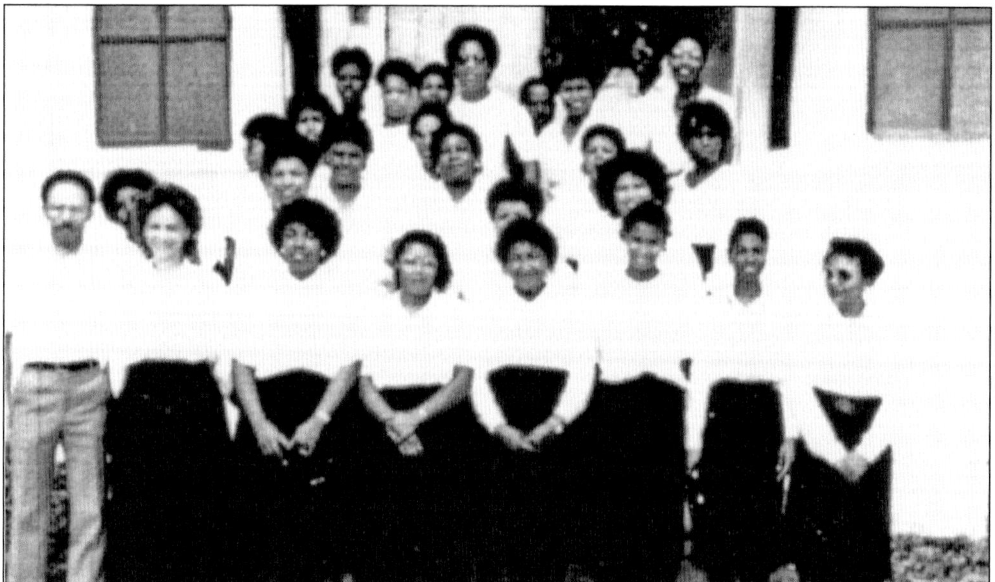

The Mount Zion United Methodist Church Choir is pictured. From left to right are (first row) Ernest Dandridge, Carolyn Bradford, Valorie McDaniel, Elizabeth Daniel, Gustine Strother, Jennifer Mitchell, Lisa Downing, and Annette Stanton; (second row) Ruth McDaniel, Joanna Hendricks, Charlene Baylor, Stella Robinson, Gwenny Bradford, and Vivian Braxton; (third row) Ramona Jones, Edith Clay (behind Stella Robinson), Bernice Page, and Theresa McDaniel; (fourth row) Fonda Braxton, Jody Page, Esther Page, Danene Jackson, and Ora Dixon; (fifth row) Vanette Jackson, Janet Robinson, James Brown, and Michael Dixon.

Founded in 1883 by trustees John H. Fox, George W. Johnson, Lewis Somner, and Harrison Morgan, St. Paul's Baptist Church began in Kearneysville on a lot that cost $172, purchased from George Watson. The first pastor was Rev. Rawson. Other leaders have included Rev. J. R. Ruffins, Rev. Enoch Churchill, Rev. L. A. Laws, Rev. R. L. Nickens, Rev. George Carter, Rev. Rodye H. Butler, Rev. L. C. Jackson, Rev. James Coleman, and Rev. Robert Moton.

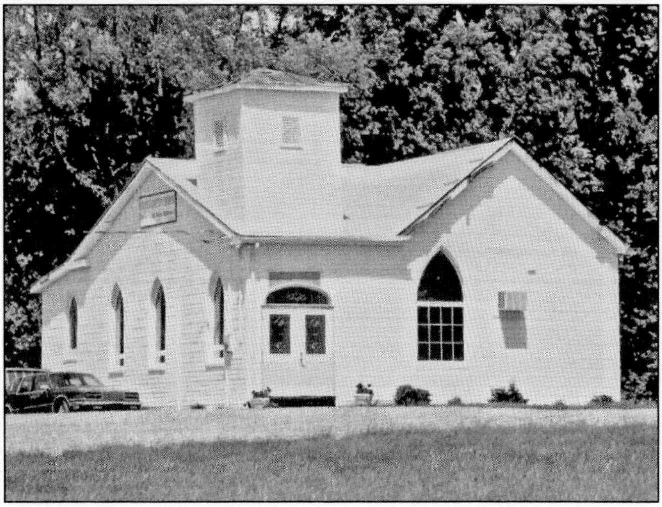

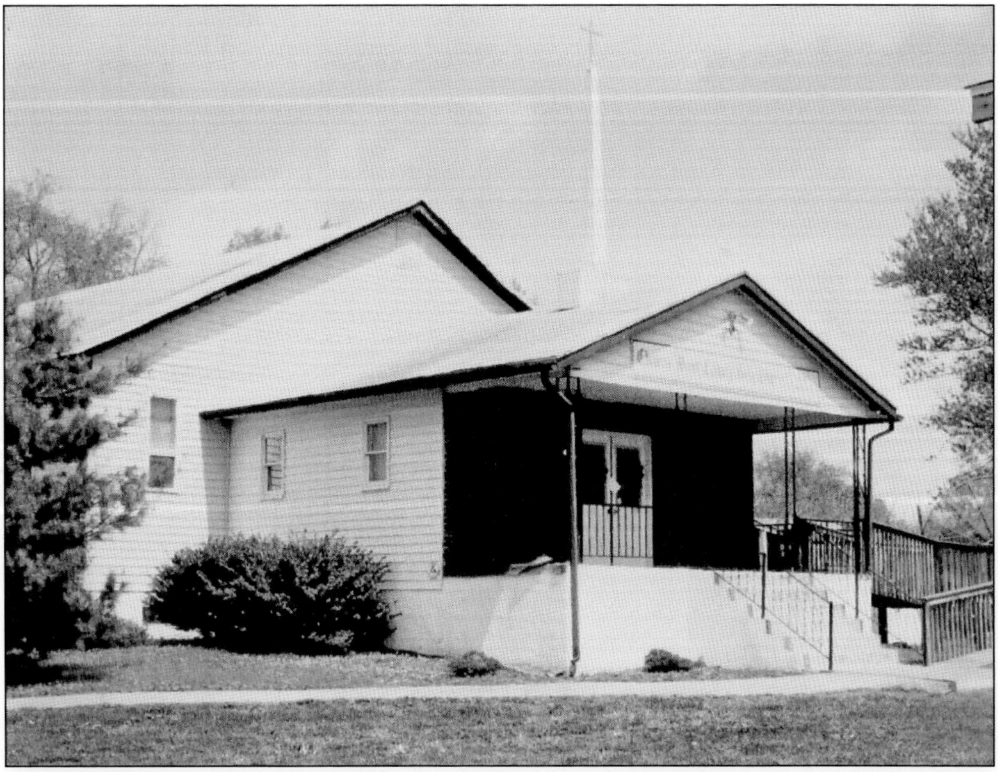

Ebenezer–Mount Calvary Holy Church of America in Summit Point (Mount Pleasant) was founded in 1878—it was known as Ebenezer Methodist-Episcopal Church. After the Civil War, Mount Pleasant was established for the freed slaves so they could develop their own businesses, churches, and schools. Glen and Elizabeth Dixon gave the land on which the original building was constructed. The original edifice burned and was later rebuilt.

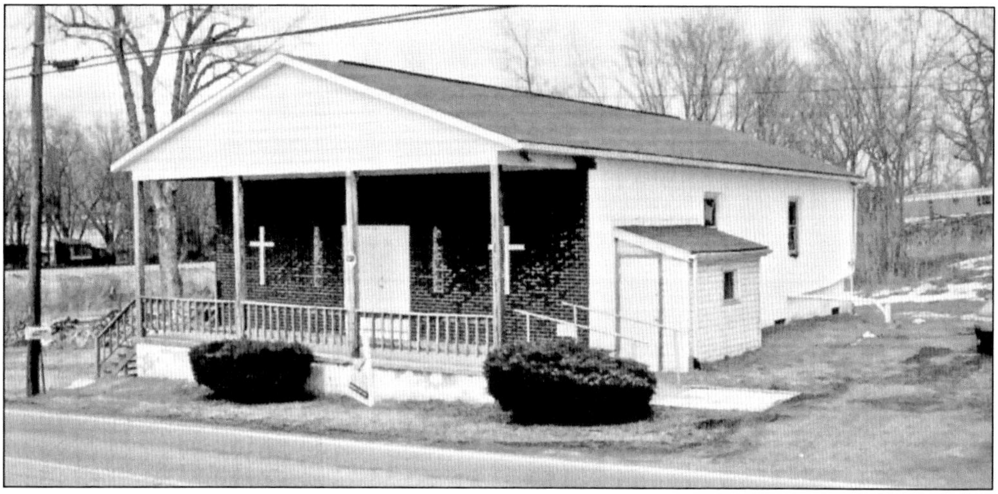

Mount Zion African Methodist Episcopal Church was established in 1870. That building burned in 1966, destroying all records. They rebuilt in Duffields on a parcel of land on Flowing Springs Road. The original building was located one-half mile north of the B&O railroad tracks, on Route 230. After the Reedson fire, one lone artifact was saved—a small communion wafer tray, which was resilvered and returned to service.

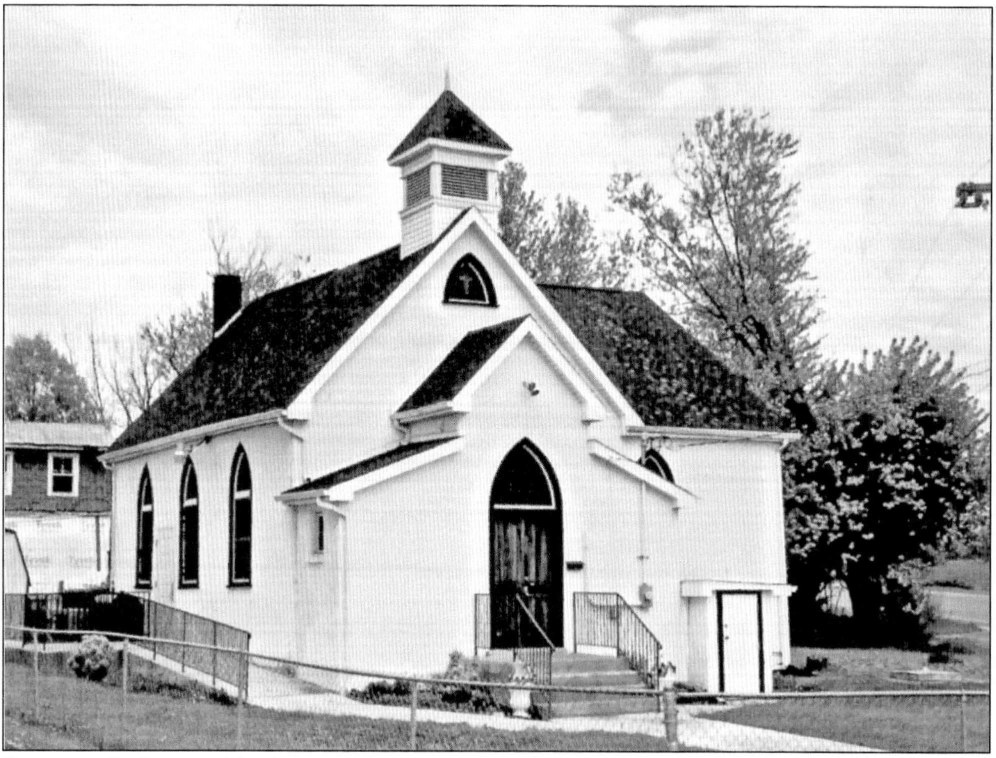

Rippon is the home of the Sylvannah Baptist Church. Established in 1908, it was originally called the New School Baptist Church. The first pastor was Rev. W. B. Duson, who originally led the congregation to worship in a schoolhouse. In 1914, an addition was built to enlarge the original church under the leadership of Rev. Eugene Baylor. In 1946, the church acquired property for a church cemetery.

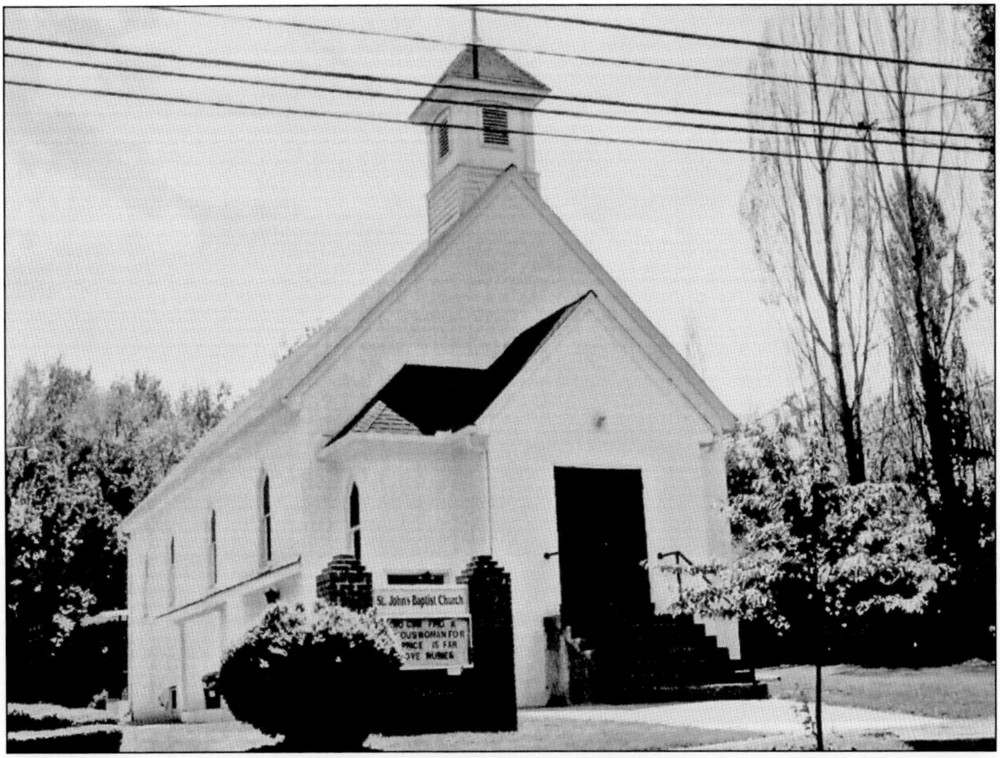

St. John Baptist Church was established 1868 in Shepherdstown. It was in 1869 that Dr. Nathan C. Brackett and Rev. Alexander H. Morrell had a mission to assist the African Americans in acquiring a place of worship. The original building was a two-room house, called St. John Baptist Church. Rev. D. L. Dandridge was the first pastor. In 1896, Reverend Dandridge passed away. In 1897, Reverend Foxx assumed leadership.

Zion Baptist Church in Charles Town was founded in 1881. Originally the freed slaves had worshipped with a white congregation, the First Baptist Church. The new church was led by Rev. Jesse Saunders. William Hull, a white businessman, agreed to help the congregation with financial support. They worshipped there until 1919, when a fire destroyed the building. A new church was completed in 1921 and is still being used today.

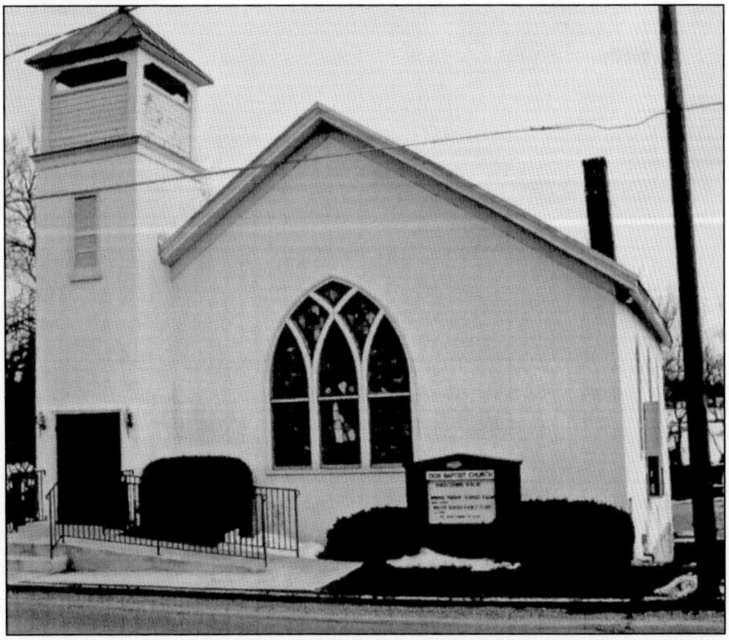